The Rise and Fall of the Black Hole Paradigm

ABHAS MITRA is a member of the International Astronomical Union, and a former full member of the American Astronomical Society. He headed the Theoretical Astrophysics Section of the Bhabha Atomic Research Centre, Mumbai from 2005 to 2015. In 1989, he won the First Prize at the Young Physicists Colloquium organized by the Indian Physical Society. He has authored, mostly single-handedly, more than 100 research papers and articles on a wide array of topics ranging from High Energy Astrophysics to General Relativity to Cosmology. He has delivered nine TEDx talks and has been invited as chief guest or speaker to many Techno Management festivals of several Indian Institutes of Technology, National Institutes of Technology and Birla Institutes of Technology.

Times of India (Kolkata) described him as one of the 'Trailblazers' in its year-end annual survey in 2015 and that same year the lifestyle magazine *The Label* declared him the sixth among the most-talked-about Indian men.

PRAISE FOR THE BOOK

'I concluded – black holes don't exist. In fact, I like the term I found in the introduction to [this] book, "eternally collapsing objects" or ECO'

Richard A. Muller, Emeritus Professor of Physics, University of California at Berkeley

'I continue to be impressed by how much [Dr Mitra has] learned and how much work [he has] done. I admire [his] courageous stand in seeking the truth'

Fred Cooperstock, former Professor, University of Victoria

'Dr Mitra has shown with calculations that black holes are not what cosmologists and physicists think them to be'

K.D. Krori, cosmologist and former Professor, Cotton University

'[This book] is a critical discourse on all aspects of black holes, delivered with the highest standards of scientific critique'

N. D. Haridass, former Professor, Tata Institute of Fundamental Research, Fellow of the National Academy of Sciences

'I hope that this book will provide a good framework to a wider class of readers, motivating further studies on the subject'

Daya Shankar Kulashrestha, former Head, Department of Physics and Astrophysics, University of Delhi

'This book is a revolution in itself. The author has fantastically written the "truth" in an articulate manner ... The reader just keeps on flipping the pages in an excitement to know more'

Rishabh Naakra, founder of the astrophysics blog 'The Secrets of the Universe'

'Impactful and truly helpful. The book is truly unique in its approach – and kudos to Dr Mitra for coming forth with such a daring work'

Pushkar Ganesh Vaidya, Head Scientist, Indian Astrobiology Research Foundation and Centre for United Nations

'The black hole paradigm has always been controversial as, apart from Albert Einstein, almost two dozen general relativists who have argued that true mathematical black holes should not occur even within the context of classical general relativity ... A must-read for not only students of physics but also for all professional astrophysicists and general relativists'

Dr Kanika Das, Professor, Department of Mathematics, Gauhati University

The Rise and Fall of the Black Hole Paradigm

Abhas Mitra

PAN

First published in India 2021 by Macmillan
First published in paperback 2024 by Pan
an imprint of Pan Macmillan Publishing India Private Limited
707 Kailash Building
26 K. G. Marg, New Delhi 110001
www.panmacmillan.co.in

Pan Macmillan, The Smithson, 6 Briset Street, Farringdon, London EC1M 5NR
Basingstoke and Oxford
Associated companies throughout the world
www.panmacmillan.com

ISBN 978-93-6113-227-8

3 5 7 9 8 6 4 2

Typeset in Joanna MT Std by Manmohan Kumar
Printed and bound in India by Repro India Ltd

Contents

Foreword

One of the landmarks in the history of science was the introduction of the general theory of relativity by Albert Einstein in 1915. This revolutionary theory identifies gravitation with the curvature of space-time. In the following year 1916, as general relativists solved for the space-time geometry around a 'point mass', the idea of 'black holes' came into being. Following the grand success of general relativity, since the 1970s, black holes have become the accepted model for many objects of stellar mass and also for the super massive cores of galaxies.

The quintessential feature of a black hole is its vacuum boundary known as the event horizon. This imaginary boundary separates the space-time around the point mass into an interior and an exterior regime. Matter that would enter the interior would be crushed to a singular point, never to communicate with the exterior except via the gravitational force that it could still exert on external matter. Nonetheless, for many years, many leading physicists believed that matter might never be so compacted as to produce a black hole. Einstein even published work that argued against the possibility of the formation of any true black hole. Things changed in the 1960s *when coordinate transformations* were found that permitted a *continuation of the Schwarzschild solution into the interior of a black hole.* The event horizon has since been considered a 'coordinate singularity', analogous to a pole on a sphere at which meridians converge to a point. It is claimed that there is nothing unusual about the geometry at the event horizon because the space-time curvature is finite (under the assumption that black holes have non-zero finite masses).

This book will, however, show that despite the wide acceptance of the concept of black holes, the black hole paradigm suffers from fundamental problems. It would seem to have necessitated some thought among theorists when it was realized that the gravitational force on a particle at the event horizon would become infinite at a place where there was neither curvature singularity nor mass concentration. Ubiquitous strong magnetic fields near an expected event horizon of a black hole should also have provoked some serious reconsideration of the black hole models by the observers because magnetic fields are forbidden attributes of black holes.

This unsatisfactory state persisted for decades until Dr Abhas Mitra and I started studying both the theory and observations of black hole candidates. Further, we and Rudolph Schild and (the late) Darryl Leiter have found evidence that favours a magnetic compact object model that is not a black hole. The things thought to be black holes are instead examples of Mitra's eternally collapsing objects (ECO), which when strongly magnetic are also known as magnetospheric eternally collapsing objects (MECO). While our findings have been published in peer-reviewed, top-of-the-line journals, it has not been easy. Some journal editors apparently believe that it is their responsibility to be gatekeepers that shield prevailing theories from criticism or competition. While it is clear that the black hole paradigm is dying, it has not yet departed.

It is an honour and a pleasure to write this foreword to a book that provides the history and descriptive details of our state of knowledge of the astronomical objects now known as black hole candidates. Contrary to what one usually finds in the popular press, the reader will find that many esteemed and accomplished physicists have raised serious objections to the black hole theory and offered warnings that have gone unheeded. The caution and scepticism that once pervaded physics seems to be lacking in recent years, but this will change. This book gives an account of a paradigm shift that is currently in progress. Readers will find a wealth of other information and ideas along the way. They will learn of the life cycles of stars, the foundations of gravity theory and some of the ways we can observe these exotic objects that in the future will become known as MECO.

Stanley L. Robertson
Emeritus Professor of Physics
Southwestern Oklahoma State University

Preface

The concept of black holes has occupied a central role in astronomy and astrophysics since the 1950s though it arose from Einstein's general theory of relativity way back in 1916. And seventy-four years later, the notion of black holes plays a crucial role in cosmology and elementary particle physics too. On top of it, the detection of gravitational waves by the Laser Interferometer Gravitational Wave Observatory (LIGO) since 2016 is supposed to have given firm evidence for the existence of event horizons, the mathematical boundary of true black holes. Further, on 10 April 2019, the Event Horizon Telescope released the 'image' of the black hole candidate in a nearby galaxy Messier 87. Given this backdrop, it would be of profound importance for astronomy, astrophysics and physics in general if it is realized that despite such claims, the observations never detected any event horizon and therefore, no true black holes.

Most present-day astrophysicists argue that if a massive star would contract up to its event horizon, then in a flash, it would also collapse to a 'point mass', a mathematical object having zero volume, zero dimensions, and which would be the 'singularity' of the resultant black hole. However, it may sound ironical that Einstein and many of the founding fathers of general relativity refused to believe in black holes because of their apparently unphysical features. They argued that *massive stars could not contract all the way up to their event horizons.* Even as late as 1962, when the black hole paradigm was fully established, Paul Dirac, one of the finest theoretical physicists ever and a Nobel laureate, held the same view.

This year Roger Penrose won the Nobel Prize in Physics for supposedly showing in 1965 that massive stars should develop 'trapped surfaces' and must collapse into point masses. But this book will discuss that such 'trapped surfaces' do not form. And in 1972, Steven Weinberg (1933–), who won the Nobel Prize in Physics in 1979 and is widely considered to be one of the best theoretical physicists of modern times, too expressed a similar view. Indeed, by citing innumerable research papers, this book will indicate that the hallowed black hole paradigm may have already fallen.

The peer-reviewed research papers by my colleagues Stanley Robertson and (late) Darryl Leiter and I have shown that while the mathematical black hole solution is indeed correct, it actually corresponds to the lowest energy state of the collapsing massive stars: $E=Mc^2=0$ or $M=0$. In other words, the mathematical black hole solution actually corresponds to only mass-less black holes. On the other hand, since the *so-called black holes are extremely massive, they must be only black hole pretenders or mimickers.*

Ideal astrophysical black holes have no intrinsic magnetic field, and the magnetic field arising from disks of swirling gas surrounding them is relatively weak. On the other hand, Robertson, Leiter and I showed that *astrophysical black holes are likely to be some sort of ultra-compact form of the Sun and possess strong intrinsic magnetic fields*. And we dubbed such objects as eternally collapsing objects (ECOs). By now, there is almost direct evidence that indeed there are strong magnetic fields around most of the astrophysical black holes, which is best explained by considering that the so-called black holes are ultra-magnetized ECOs.

The 'ring down' features seen in the gravitational waves detected by LIGO were initially believed to be a unique signature of vibrations of the new event horizons formed following the merger of two black holes. But soon, it became clear that the 'ring down' feature actually arises from oscillations of the *photon spheres* or photon rings situated outside the event horizons. Similarly, the image of the massive compact object in the galaxy Messier 87 may correspond to the image of the photon sphere and not any event horizon. And since all black hole mimickers too possess such light rings, *LIGO signals or Event Horizon Telescope images are no evidence for the existence of mathematical black holes*.

A crucial difference between true empty black holes and their mimickers is that *unlike the former, the latter is full of matter and possesses a physical boundary*. If the merger of two black holes or neutron stars produces a bigger black hole, then the gravitational waves formed during the final stages of this process cannot be reflected by the resultant event horizon. On the other hand, if the merged product is a horizon-less compact object, gravitational waves trapped between it and its photon sphere may slowly leak out. Accordingly, in such a case, the final gravitational wave signal may contain signs of repeated reflections or echoes. And there has been tentative evidence that such echoes follow some of the LIGO signals. If true, this will be a confirmation that the astrophysical black holes are not true black holes.

One of the pillars of the black hole paradigm is that an observer falling in a black hole would never be able to detect its boundary – the event horizon. But in 1982, it was found that this assertion is wrong and the event horizon is very much detectable.

The book is written in an accessible manner so that readers can appreciate the physics and history of the subject even without bothering about the equations. In general, relevant peer-reviewed research papers or actual astrophysical observations support all arguments made in the book. There are many quotes with emphases at many places. All such emphases are mine. The purpose of this book is to clearly show that the so-called astrophysical black holes are only black hole mimickers possessing strong intrinsic magnetic fields quite unlike the mathematical true black holes which have always been dominant in academic or popular discourses on the subject.

CHAPTER 1

Introduction

The important thing is not to stop questioning – Albert Einstein

KEY POINTS: A Schwarzschild black hole is just a point mass and the surrounding empty sphere of intense gravitation. Starting with Einstein, most founding fathers of general relativity refused to accept the idea of black holes because of their unphysical properties. Such objections continue even today, and, thus, contrary to popular perception, the black hole paradigm has always remained controversial. Indeed contrary to many sensational claims, there has been no detection of an event horizon, the ultimate signature of a black hole, ever. On the other hand, if the tentative claims of detection of echoes from few LIGO gravitational wave events would be confirmed, we would have solid evidence that the compact objects responsible for gravitational waves are horizon-less compact objects and not true black holes. The first confirmed black hole is supposed to have been detected in the X-ray binary Cygnus X-1, because the compact object therein is much more massive than any neutron star. But if the claim of detection of a strong magnetic field in Cygnus X-1 is genuine, it is likely to contain a magnetized horizon-less compact object rather than a true black hole. Such an idea gets corroborated because now we have direct evidence that there are unexpectedly strong magnetic fields around many astrophysical black holes. Further there are reports that some astrophysical black holes eject 'balls of fire', which suggests that the so-called black holes maybe magnetized balls of fire, something like an extremely compactified Sun.

The term 'black hole' is familiar to not only physicists and astronomers but also perhaps to lay persons. Even those who follow only social media and not any science news site regularly come across various news and illustrations about black holes. Science fiction films do feature black holes, and in particular, one of the stars in the 2014 blockbuster *Interstellar* was Gargantuan, a massive and rapidly spinning black hole. *In the movie, Gargantuan spread its mystique as the tool for travel through space and time in an attempt to save the people on Earth.*

But are black holes as fanciful as shown in popular representations? Have true black holes really been discovered by astronomers? In order to explore such issues with hard science rather than the usual hype and whitewash, let us expound first the basic idea of mathematical black holes.

Einstein's revolutionary theory of gravity, known as general relativity, was formulated in 1915, and mathematical physicists used general relativity to solve the simplest physical problem:

The structure of the gravitational field due to a single neutral mass point.

To be more precise, the problem they attempted to solve for is the empty or vacuum space-time around a single neutral point mass having an undefined mass M. It was found that the gravitational field within a spherical region having a radius of $R_s = 2\ M$* is so strong that nothing, not even light, can escape from within this sphere.

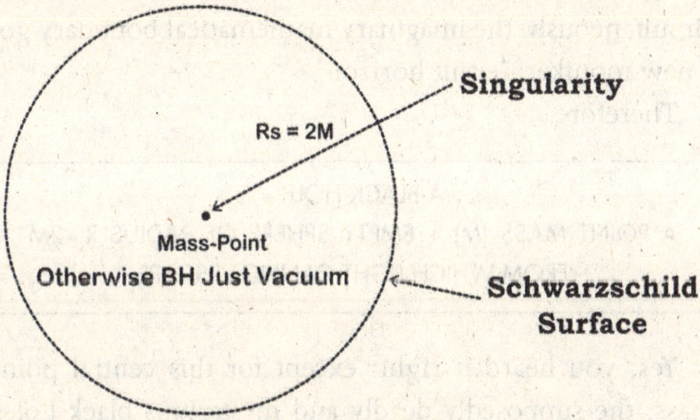

Fig. 1 Sketch of a mathematical black hole

This sphere of extreme gravitational pull is extremely compact and has a radius of a mere $R_s \approx 3$ km for a point having a mass of one solar mass.** The radius of a black hole increases in proportion to its mass, that is, a black hole 10 times more massive has a radius of 30 km, and a black hole a billion times more massive has a radius of 30 billion km.

Black holes are 'black' or invisible as no light can escape them. The radius of a black hole R_s is known as

* $R_s = 2GM/c^2$, where G is the Newtonian constant of gravitation, and c is the speed of light in vacuum. But for mathematical simplicity, one works in a unit G=c=1, though G and c remain in the background.

** The sign ≈ implies approximately equal to.

Schwarzschild radius in honour of Karl Schwarzschild, who is (mistakenly) credited with the mathematical solution that suggests existence of black holes. The mathematical boundary of this sphere of strong influence was originally known as 'Schwarzschild surface'. Thus originally black holes were known as 'Schwarzschild singularity' but got rechristened as 'black hole' as late as in 1967! Simultaneously, the imaginary mathematical boundary got a new moniker: 'event horizon'.

Therefore,

> A BLACK HOLE =
> A POINT MASS (M) + EMPTY SPHERE OF RADIUS R_s=2M
> FROM WHICH LIGHT CANNOT ESCAPE

Yes, you heard it right: except for this central point mass, the supposedly deadly and mysterious black holes are vacuum without any matter or energy!

Note, the concept of a 'point mass', an object (sphere) having zero volume, is a mathematical one, and it may not exist in real world! However, once one *assumes* the existence of such a 'point mass', by definition, its density becomes infinite. Thus it is this *very assumption about the existence of a mathematical 'point mass' that leads to a singular situation involving infinite gravity and infinite density*.

Modern physics and astronomy is based on this idea that sufficiently massive stars must eventually turn into black holes as they inexorably get crushed to a geometrical point under their own weight. This conclusion is based on the tacit assumption that *those massive stars cannot radiate away their entire mass–energy towards the end of their lives*. In other words, most astronomers believe that black holes (née point masses) could be *arbitrarily massive* unlike other compact objects like white dwarfs and neutron stars.

Accordingly, most astrophysicists believe that the ultra-massive compact stars found in the universe are true mathematical black holes. In this book, we shall refer to this most powerful and all pervasive scientific idea/faith as the *black hole paradigm*.

Since a singularity cannot evolve unlike other compact stars like white dwarfs and neutron stars, black holes represent the ultimate graveyards of most massive stars, and left to themselves, they are lifeless.

As an astrophysics researcher, I too believed that the fascinating massive compact objects of the cosmos, whose masses range from tens to billions of solar masses, are indeed true black holes predicted by general relativity. I believed so because other known famous compact stars, namely, neutron stars cannot be more massive than three solar masses. Also,, even twenty years ago, there were no meaningful alternatives to black holes. Thus like everybody else, I too believed in the black hole paradigm despite being aware that Einstein never accepted the idea of black holes, and in his research paper of 1939, he even claimed that[1], 'The basic result of study is the distinct understanding that there are no "Schwarzschild singularities" in the real world. The Schwarzschild singularity is absent, because the matter cannot be concentrated in an arbitrary way; otherwise particles composing the clump will reach the speed of light.'

Einstein's idea that at very high concentrations, stellar matter may move in circular orbits with the speed of light and can prevent formation of black holes, may not be realizable for actual gravitational collapse. Further, in the same year (1939), Julius Robert Oppenheimer (1904–67), a famous theoretical physicist, and his student Hartland Snyder apparently showed that the collapse of massive stars should result in the formation of black holes.[2]

Therefore, like most astrophysicists and physicists, I too believed that Einstein's foregoing comments should be respectfully ignored because they were not based on actual analysis of the gravitational collapse of massive stars. But what I was not aware of was that Oppenheimer and Snyder's study indicated the formation of black holes only after ignoring all real-life physics effects like pressure, heat and radiation. Neither did I know that they admitted that they were *compelled to ignore all physical effects because otherwise there would not be any analytical solution*. It is only much later, when I read their paper between the lines that I noted their stunning comment that black holes may not form if real-life physics effects were to be included in the study of the collapse process: 'Physically, such a singularity would mean that the expression used for the energy-momentum, tensor does not take account of some essential physical fact which would really smooth the singularity out.'[3]

They further added that a real star, which has no initial singularity, could never develop into a black hole or any other singularity. 'Further, a star in its early stage of development would not possess a singular density or pressure; *it is impossible for a singularity to develop in a finite time*.'[4]

During 1995–2000, one of the topics of my astrophysics research was the physics of the central engine of cosmic gamma-ray bursts (GRBs), mysterious bursts of gamma

Fig. 2 A mental illustration of a cosmic gamma-ray burst

rays, a radiation which could be several million times more powerful than the visible light.

In fact, I was quite happy that my first paper on this topic was cited by none other than Martin Rees (1942–), one of the most distinguished British theoretical astrophysicists ever. Meanwhile, since 1967, there has been a great debate in astrophysics on the question of the location of the source of the GRB events.

The majority of astrophysicists thought that GRBs originate within our own galaxy, while the other camp thought that they were located in faraway galaxies. In the former cases, the energy output would be modest or at least manageable by astrophysical standards. But in the latter case, the energy emission associated with GRBs could be even billion times larger as the distance of faraway galaxies could be hundreds of thousand times larger than the extent of our galaxy, the Milky Way.

In fact, I belonged to the former camp and even had a model to explain the origin of GRBs supposedly occurring within our galaxy. But problems started creeping in by April 1997, when I attended the Fourth Compton Symposium on Gamma Ray Astronomy and Astrophysics (27–30 April 1997) in Williamsburg, Virginia. At this conference, convincing evidence was presented that the recently detected GRB 970228 (the event detected on 28 February 1997) had originated in a galaxy that is 8.1 billion light years away, that means, it is so far away that light from this galaxy requires 8.1 billion years to reach our galaxy. This indicated that GRBs could be the most powerful explosions in the cosmos. Since there were already (right) conjectures that GRBs could be of cosmological origin, there were models that proposed that GRBs could be associated with the birth of black holes. But such models were not convincing at all. Till date (2020), it is acknowledged that there is no convincing model for such explosions.

However, I found that there was a fundamental contradiction in such models. *This is so because if gravitational collapse of massive stars would indeed result in formation of black holes from which nothing, not even light could escape, logically, they should not be ascribed to the most powerful energy explosions.* And it is at that time that I started worrying. *Was Einstein's intuition, if not his paper, after all right? Is it possible that instead of true black holes, general relativity allows the formation of only approximate or quasi-black holes from which light and energy can escape?* If so, one might be able to explain the origin of mind-boggling energy output from the cosmic GRBs with relative ease and self-consistency.

Eventually, after correcting some early glitches, my peer-reviewed research papers showed that continued gravitational collapse could never yield exact black holes. Further, although the GR solution of black holes is formally correct, it is fallacious because it corresponds to black holes having no mass at all. My papers also claimed that GRBs could be explained in terms of formations of quasi-black holes. In 1998, I had sent my initial preprints on such research to a highly respectable general relativist P.C. Vaidya (1918–2010) whose research in 1951 had initiated the study of gravitational collapse accompanied by emission of radiation. And he made a quick comment that my treatment of general relativity in these papers was on the right track.

Later I found that, much before me, several noted general relativists had either suggested or shown that true mathematical black holes have M=0. In 1968, Allen Janis, Ezra Newman and Jeffrey Winicour, in a paper in *Physical Review Letters*, suggested that though mathematically black holes appear as spheres (under the assumption that they have finite masses), they might actually be *point singularities.*[5] In the very next year, Luis Bel showed that it is indeed so.[6] If so, the mathematical picture of black hole, illustrated by Fig. 1 would be misleading. Instead of a sphere, a black hole would simply be a point (.), which geometrically is a sphere of zero radius: $R_s=2\ M_{BH}=0$, or $M_{BH}=0$.

Meanwhile, by 2001, two American astrophysicists, namely, Stanley Robertson (Southwestern Oklahoma State University) and the late Darryl Leiter (University of Virginia at the time of his death) had vigorously started research that offered evidence that the so-called astrophysical black holes are not true mathematical black holes, and instead, they are something like ultra-compact forms of the Sun, which comprise highly ionized matter (plasma) and possess magnetic fields. In contrast, *a true black hole is just a region of vacuum except for a central point of infinite density (singularity) and has absolutely no magnetic field*. Incidentally, Darryl Leiter was the last Ph.D. student of Nathan Rosen, Einstein's long-term collaborator, and had been a senior NASA research associate twice.

Later, Rudolph Schild, a noted observational astrophysicist from Harvard Smithsonian Center for Astrophysics, joined Robertson and Leiter in order to offer more direct evidence that the astrophysical black hole candidates are not theoretical black holes. Eventually, in the following decade, a sort of new paradigm got expounded through almost twenty-five research papers published in *Foundations of Physics Letters*, *Astrophysics and Space Science*, *Journal of Cosmology*, *Astrophysical Journal*, *Astrophysical Journal Letters*, *International Journal of Modern Physics (D)*, *Astronomical Journal*, *Monthly Notices Royal Astronomical Society*, *Monthly Notices Royal Astronomical Society Letters*, *New Astronomy* and *Physical Review (D)*.

This may be the only book published so far which has brought out the scientific objections and reservations against the very notion of black holes by most of the founding fathers of general relativity: Albert Einstein himself, Karl

Schwarzschild, David Hilbert, Arthur Eddington, Johannes Droste, Marcel Brillouin, Jacques Hadamard, Cornelius Lanczos, Max von Laue (Nobel laureate), Allvar Gullstrand (Nobel laureate) and Yusuke Hagihara.

And though the black hole paradigm got formulated in the early 1960s, research by many noted as well as not-so-noted general relativists has raised fundamental objections against it ever since. It is interesting to know the name of such researchers: Paul Dirac (Nobel Laureate), Fred Holye, William Fowler (Nobel laureate), William McCrea, Elizabeth Hilton, Allen Janis, Ezra Newman, Jeffrey Winicour, Nathan Rosen, Luis Bel, Jayant Narlikar, William Bonnor, F.I. Cooperstock, G.J.G. Junevicus, A. Karlhede, David Menzel, Ernst Julius Öpik, V. De Sabbata, K.T. Shah, F. Salzman, G. Salzman, G. Cavalleri, G. Spinelli, Leonard S. Abrams, Robert Gautreau, M.S. Borkar, T.M. Karade, S.I. Chermyanin, N.N. Fimin, V.M. Chechetkin, A.A. Logunov, M.A. Mestverishvili, V.V. Kiselev, S. Antoci, D.E. Liebscher, Darryl Leiter, Stanley Robertson and Rudolph Schild, among several others.

This simple statistics show that *contrary to the popular myth, the black hole paradigm has never been universally accepted and has always remained controversial.*

The theory of formation of black holes is based on the hypothesis of formation of 'trapped surfaces' within which even light can only move inwards. Steven Weinberg (1933–), who won the Nobel Prize in Physics in 1979 and is widely considered to be one of the best living theoretical physicist, wrote :'However, it is not known whether a real massive star will actually develop a trapped surface.'[7] And about gravitational collapse, he insisted that 'A realistic discussion... would require that we consider the effects of radiative energy transport, neutrino energy transport, turbulence, nuclear forces, magnetic fields, and above all rotations.'[8]

It is important to note that *there has been no exact solution for black hole formation for such realistic discussions.* Sir Fred Hoyle (1915–2001) was one of the most distinguished and creative as well as controversial physicists of the twentieth century. Many including this author think that though he very much deserved the Nobel Prize, he was denied this honour because of his frequent anti-establishment attitude to mainstream science. One of the steady co-workers of Hoyle was William Fowler (1911–1995), a famous American theoretical astrophysicist who shared the 1983 Nobel Prize in Physics with Subramanium Chandrasekhar. In the 1960s, Hoyle and Fowler showed that:

> In principle, there could be *compact objects of arbitrary large mass* supported against their gravity by purely radiation pressure.
>
> (Usually, stars are supported by their gas pressure as radiation pressure is almost negligible.)

This means the all-pervading idea that compact objects *can be supported against their gravity only by cold quantum pressure is incorrect.* Unfortunately, most physicists as well as general relativists are unaware of radiation pressure supported stars (RPSS).

A series of my papers have shown that the so-called astrophysical black holes are likely to be general relativistic RPSS.

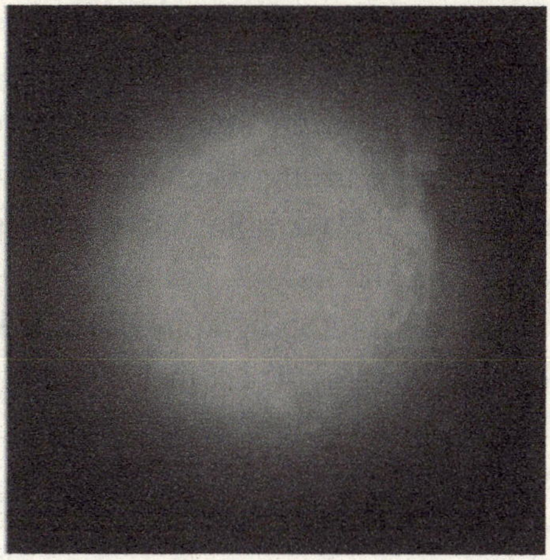

Fig. 3 Unlike a vacuum black hole, an eternally collapsing object (ECO) is a ball of fire, supported against its gravitational pull by outward radiation pressure.

In the absence of an event horizon, such a quasi-black hole keeps on losing bits of mass–energy by eternally leaking some radiation. It turns out that ideally, it keeps on contracting indefinitely and tries to attain the true black hole state marked by zero mass–energy, a state where the negative self-gravitational energy completely offsets all other positive sources of energy such as the mass–energy of protons and neutrons, heat and other internal energies. However, such a well-known classical radiation must not be confused with the mysterious and controversial 'Hawking radiation' supposed to originate due to unknown quantum effects.

Such an eternally contracting quasi-black hole (RPSS) was christened as eternally collapsing object (ECO). Since ECOs are strongly magnetized, having magnetic fields stronger than pulsar (spinning magnetized neutron stars), they were rechristened as magnetospheric eternally collapsing objects (MECOs). *In contrast, uncharged astrophysical black holes have no intrinsic magnetic fields.*

By now, there have been innumerable evidences for existence of unusually strong magnetic fields around the so-called astrophysical black holes and which suggest that they are likely to be MECOs.

Hoyle published his autobiography *Home is Where the Wind Blows: Chapters from a Cosmologist's Life* in 1994, and true to his reputation and notoriety, he used the phrase 'black-hole mania'. He described the black hole paradigm as 'a form of religious fundamentalism'.[9]

Despite being based on an exact solution, the concept of black holes is full of inconsistencies, and it is worthwhile to recall the comments of two well-known Indian relativists, Jayant Narlikar and Thanu Padmanabhan, made in 1988: 'the discussion of physical behaviour of black holes, classical or quantum, is only of academic interest. It is suggested that problems related to the source could be avoided if *the event horizon did not form and that the universe only contained quasi-black holes.*'[10]

But what are quasi-black holes or black hole mimickers?

The following table indicates the fundamental properties of black hole mimickers vis-à-vis black holes:

Black Hole	Black Hole Mimicker
Radius: R= 2M	Larger by a tiny fraction (e) which could be a millionth or a billionth*
Vacuum except for the central point mass	Full of matter like the Sun

* $R = 2M(1+e)$; $e \approx 0$

Has event horizon and singularity (point mass)	No event horizon, no singularity
Riddled with mathematical and physical problems	No mathematical or physical problem
Nothing not even a single photon can escape	One in a billion or trillion photons may escape
No magnetic field, no eruption	Some models may have strong magnetic fields and Sun-like flares

As already hinted, this book will contain discussions based on peer-reviewed research to explain the following:

- Why the exact black hole solutions correspond to the ultimate lowest energy ground states of collapsing stars: $E=Mc^2=0$.
- As per black hole paradigm, the event horizon is a mere pathology of the wrong coordinates used, and an observer diving into a black hole can never detect it. This book will convincingly show why this fundamental premise is wrong and why an event horizon is a physical singularity.
- The so-called observed black holes are thus only approximate black holes or horizon-less compact objects.
- Why continued gravitational collapse of massive stars is bound to trap their heat and radiation to transform them into ultra-compact ball of fires supported by their own radiation pressure (ECOs).
- Why such RPSS should possess their own magnetic fields whose strength, measured locally, can far exceed that of the neutron stars (MECOs).
- The fact that the prediction about strong intrinsic magnetic fields of so-called black holes, first made in 1998, have been vindicated repeatedly.

We briefly recall a report dated 1 November 2012 related to an outburst in a so-called black hole H1743–322: 'Black Hole Ejects Great Balls of Fire'.[11] Similarly, in the past few years, there has been direct evidence for the presence of surprisingly strong magnetic fields around many astrophysical black holes. Here is a report dated 4 June 2014: 'Surprisingly strong magnetic fields can match black holes' pull: Long-neglected magnetic fields have an unexpected presence'.[12]

Though there could be various hypotheses for explaining such observations, arguably, the most natural one is that the so-called black holes are ultra-magnetized balls of fire (MECO), which may spit out magnetized balls of fire.

CHAPTER 2

Astrophysics Tidbits

So many books, so little time – Frank Zappa

KEY POINTS: Stars generate their own energy. While the usual process of energy generation is nuclear fusion of light elements, stars can also generate energy when they undergo gravitational contraction. A key feature of stellar evolution is that under exhaustion of central nuclear fuel, the core undergoes gravitational contraction, heats up and releases energy. Usual stars are hot magnetized balls of fire. The cores of low mass stars eventually collapse into compact configurations called white dwarfs, supported against gravity by quantum repulsion of electrons. Cores of more massive stars contract into much more compact configurations called neutron stars, supported against intense gravity by quantum repulsion of neutrons. Even more massive stars are supposed to undergo continued gravitational collapse and end up as 'black holes'.

> As a massive star contracts, its *negative* gravitational binding energy becomes more and more negative in almost a runaway manner. Hence, in principle, it is possible that the net mass–energy of the star, $E=Mc^2 \to 0$.

This book treats black holes as not only important mathematical objects, apparently predicted by general relativity, but also as key players in astronomy and astrophysics. Accordingly, we shall explore the question whether the black hole paradigm has fallen or not from both theoretical as well as astrophysical perspectives. To this end, it will be prudent to recap some of the pertinent astrophysical topics.

At the outset, I want to remind the readers that, in astrophysical context, I shall be using the term

Trillion = 10^{12} = One thousand billion (12 zeros after 1)

And then, there is a number that is larger than any large number we can conceive of, trillion trillion trillion or anything else. This limitless large number is known as infinity and is indicated by the symbol ∞. If a physical quantity appears to be infinite, *we will be led to a pathological/singular situation*. One mathematically arrives at infinity by dividing a finite number by zero, for instance, $3/0 = \infty$. Since a 'point' has zero volume, its density is infinite.*

We begin taking our baby astrophysics steps by reminding ourselves that what makes our closest star Sun a 'star' is the fact that *it can generate its own light and heat unlike* the Earth, which literally basks in the reflected glory of the Sun!

* Density $= M/V = M/0 = \infty$

Fire in the Stars

Though true black holes are empty objects except for their central singularities, all other stars and compact objects are full of matter. How do stars generate their own light? The answer is 'stars are balls of fire'. For an appreciation of this aphorism, let us understand what 'fire' really is.

Whenever we have some fire, there are runaway oxidizing chemical reactions in certain materials like oil vapour or a piece of paper, which release heat and light. In all these processes, some atomic bonds get broken and electrons are freed. When an electron having negative charge leaves a parent atom, the atom becomes positively charged, and in case the electron gets attached to another atom, it becomes negatively charged. Such charged atoms are known as ions.

Thus, in all fire, in all flame, there are some charged atoms/ions among the abundant neutral atoms. This process of formation of charged matter through displacement of electrons is known as *ionization*. In a flame, ionization of the air atoms occurs because the temperature is high enough to cause the atoms to knock each other and rip off electrons.

Therefore, the atoms of the very hot solar material are highly ionized, much more than what is seen in ordinary fire. Such strongly ionized material is known as *plasma*, sometimes also called the *fourth state of matter* to distinguish it from other known states of matter, namely, gas, liquid and solid.

Though plasma or ionized material is charged at the atomic level, it is charge-less or neutral on a larger scale. Further, any material that is not solid or powdery and has no fixed shape – gas, liquid and plasma – is called *fluid*.

Bosons and Fermions

Stars are made of matter, energy and radiation. Various astrophysical problems like the formation of supposed black holes too involve explosions of radiation and matter. In order to appreciate the structure and formation of stars and compact objects, we need to delve into the basic nature of 'matter' and 'radiation' in terms of the basic constituents, which are various kinds of elementary particles. In the astrophysical context, the nebulous term 'radiation' too implies the flow of elementary particles like 'photons' and neutrinos having near zero (rest) masses. Here, the term 'rest mass' implies mass energy of the particles in their own rest frames.

Mass apart, elementary particles have important physical attributes like charge. Additionally, they also possess intrinsic angular momentum – as if each elementary particle is a tiny spinning top.

In general, particles having nil or integer spins are called *bosons*, while particles having half-integer spins are classified as *fermions*. Protons, neutrons and electrons are fermions, while photons are bosons.

In quantum mechanics, we have the Pauli exclusion principle that posits that two fermions refuse to share the same quantum state, while bosons have no such problem in socializing. A consequence of this is that though bosons offer no resistance when they are packed together tightly, *fermions offer strong resistance. As a result, a dense gas full of fermions, where the particles are pushed together, develops strong repulsive pressure.* For such degenerate matter, the repulsive quantum pressure could be much stronger than the ordinary kinetic gas pressure occurring from the random motion of molecules/particles.

Apart from protons, neutrons, electrons and photons (particles of light), another elementary particle, *neutrino*, is vital in astrophysics. Neutrinos can be categorized as fermions as they have half integer spins. Though they have no charge, they have other quantum properties. While the protons and neutrons are approximately thousand times heavier than electrons, neutrinos could be almost million times lighter than the same. Along with photons, neutrinos are profusely produced in the cores of stars as well as in cosmic explosions.

Compact Stars

There are stars denser than the Sun by a factor of several thousands, that is, one teaspoonful of such stellar material could easily weigh a tonne. Essentially their radius could be as low as 1 per cent of the Sun (the size of the Earth), and yet their masses could be similar to that of the Sun. In view of such small radii, they are called *dwarfs*, and since they appear whiter as compared to the yellow Sun, these compact stars are called *white dwarfs*. This whitish colour indicates that the surface temperature of white dwarfs is higher than that of the Sun. Yet the luminosity of white dwarfs is much lower than that of the Sun because their surface area could be thousand times smaller than that of the Sun. Consequently, white dwarfs are fainter than the Sun. Sirius B, which is 8.6 light years away, is one such well-known compact star. Unlike normal stars, white dwarfs cannot be too massive.

The theoretical upper mass limit of white dwarfs is about 1.44 times the solar mass and is known as the *Chandrasekhar mass limit*.

It is important to realize why white dwarfs have an upper mass limit. As per quantum mechanics, at the microscopic level, even particles behave like waves. The corresponding waves are known as de-Broglie waves in honour of Louis de Broglie (1892–1987) who first postulated about the *wave nature of particles*. Since the density of a white dwarf is at least tens of thousands of times larger than that of the Sun, the electrons are too close to one another and their de-Broglie waves significantly overlap with one another. This is known as a state of quantum degeneracy. Electrons being fermions cannot occupy the same quantum state, and this causes them to repulse one another when pushed too close.

It is this quantum repulsive pressure that stabilizes a white dwarf against its intense self-gravity. The concept of quantum degeneracy pressure of white dwarfs was first given by the British physicist Ralph H. Fowler (1889–1944) in 1926. In 1929, Edmund Stoner (1899–1968) showed that white dwarfs have a mass upper limit of around 1.2 solar mass.[1] This upper limit develops as the quantum pressure associated with *localized* random electron motions saturates when the speed of the electrons attain the speed of light. In the same year, Wilhelm Anderson (1880–1940) too arrived at a similar upper-mass limit of white dwarfs.[2] This issue was studied more rigorously by Subramanian Chandrasekhar (1910–1995) in a series of papers during 1931–35 to fix this upper limit at 1.44 solar mass.[3]

There are other kinds of compact stars, known as *neutron stars*, which are much more compact than white dwarfs. A neutron star could be as massive as the Sun and yet have a radius of only 10 km, approximately, hundred thousand times smaller than that of the Sun. Consequently, the density of a neutron star could be higher than that of the Sun by a mind-boggling factor of one hundred trillion. Neutron stars too cannot be very massive, and the upper mass limit for them is about three times the solar mass. In contrast to a white dwarf, *a neutron star is supported against a much stronger clutch of self-gravity by the equally stronger quantum repulsion of closely packed neutrons.* But for a neutron star more massive than about 3 solar masses, gravity wins over quantum repulsion, and hence it must undergo gravitational contraction.

Obviously, *compactness* of a star increases with higher mass and smaller radius. Hence, the first measure of compactness is given by the ratio M/R. But in the astrophysical context, we measure compactness with the strength of the gravitational potential stars have, which is given by GM/R. It becomes very convenient to *rescale* this compactness into a small *dimensionless* number by dividing it with light-speed-square.* Given this definition, the compactness of the Sun is about three parts of a millionth, while the same for a white dwarf is two orders higher, that is, one part in ten thousand. In comparison, a neutron star can have incredibly large compactness ≈ 0.15, about one hundred thousand times higher than the compactness of the Sun.

Magnetism of Stars

Magnetism is closely related to electricity. In essence, it is a field caused by moving charges. In the case of permanent

* Compactness = $GM/(Rc^2)$

magnets, the moving charges are the electrons within the magnets. In very basic terms, strong permanent magnets have many atoms with electrons spinning in the same direction. In contrast, non-magnets have a more random arrangement of electrons spinning around their nuclei.

As mentioned earlier, most of the stellar material is plasma, which is highly conductive. Though the plasma is charge neutral in the bulk, the vicinity of a moving ion is charged, and hence, plasma is only quasi-neutral. In particular, the local rotational motion of ions generates slight asymmetry and gradients of charges. As a consequence, plasma *always possesses some seed magnetic field*. As stars or compact stars get formed by the compression of initially dilute diffuse plasmas, they develop fairly *strong intrinsic magnetic fields*.

On an average, the strength of the surface magnetic field of the Sun is almost 1 gauss. Our own Earth has a surface magnetic field that is only half a gauss. To understand this unit of magnetism, we may remind that a typical refrigerator magnet has a field ~ 50 gauss. But there are regions in the Sun with magnetic fields much stronger than their ambient values (as high as 4,000 gauss) called *sunspots*.

As the Sun rotates, the plasma in its interior rotates at different speeds on different latitudes. This is known as *differential rotation*, and it helps create the stronger interior magnetic field. Differential rotation causes the magnetic lines of force to wind up into a twisted field of *flux ropes* that become wrapped around the Sun. These fields can become highly concentrated, producing activity when they emerge on the surface. Coronal loops often form above star spots, forming magnetic field lines that stretch out into the corona. These in turn serve to heat the corona to temperatures over a million kelvin.

Solar Flares

By definition, nothing, not even light can escape a black hole. But every now and then, we come across news on explosions and flares from black holes. One of the biggest astrophysics news in 2015 was that two NASA telescopes Swift and NuStar had detected 'flares' from a supermassive black hole in the galaxy Markarian 335.[4] The origin of explosions and flares from astrophysical black holes is hardly understood, and yet in order to have semblance of an understanding, we may revisit flares from our own star, the Sun.

There could be huge explosions on the Sun as hinted in the preceding section. Flares are formed when intense magnetic fields from below the Sun's surface become too tangled and link up with magnetic fields in the outer corona, a region containing very hot ionized gas (plasma) of very low density, in a process called *magnetic reconnection*. Such reconnection results in sudden release of magnetic energy stored in the Sun's corona. Like a rubber band that snaps when it is twisted too far, the tangled magnetic fields release energy when they *snap*.

Solar flares emit huge bursts of electromagnetic radiation, including X-rays, ultraviolet radiation, visible light and radio waves. The energy emitted by a solar flare is more than a million times larger than the energy from a volcanic explosion on the Earth.

A very special kind of powerful solar explosion is the *coronal mass ejection* (CME).

Apart from generating radiation, CMEs spew out solar plasma into the surrounding space by means of extremely

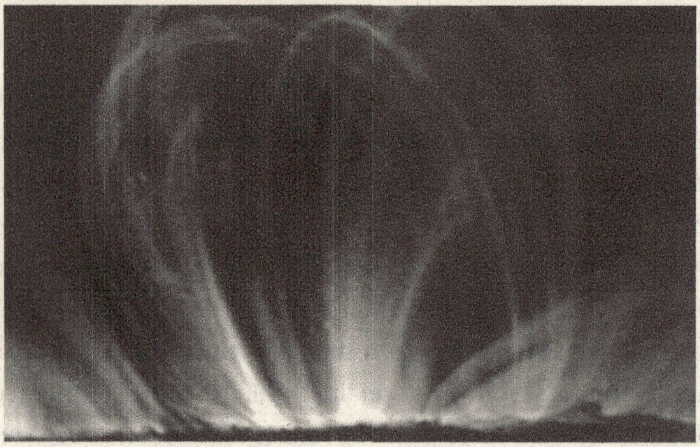

Fig. 4 Artist's impression of a Coronal Mass Ejection event from the Sun.

powerful solar wind. They can be dangerous if they hit the Earth and can seriously disrupt its environment. The burst of charged particles, which arrive only eight minutes after being released in the CME, can alter the Earth's outer atmosphere, disrupting long-distance radio communications. It is likely that giant flares from so-called astrophysical black holes could be CMEs from magnetospheric eternally collapsing objects (MECOs).

Magnetic Field of Compact Stars

Compact stars like white dwarfs and neutron stars have strong magnetic fields. For white dwarfs, the magnetic field could be a million times stronger than the Sun, that is, about a million gauss, and for a new born neutron star, the magnetic field could even be trillion times stronger than that of the Sun, that is, about a trillion of gauss or even much higher.

There are a special variety of neutron stars whose magnetic fields could be even thousand times stronger. Such compact neutron stars with the highest known magnetic fields are called *magnetars.*

For spinning magnetized stars, the rotating magnetic field generates an induced electric field. For extremely magnetized neutron stars, such induced electric fields can rip off charged particles/ions from the star surface even in the absence of any surrounding stellar wind. As the star rotates, the magnetosphere rotates with it, dragging along the charged particles.

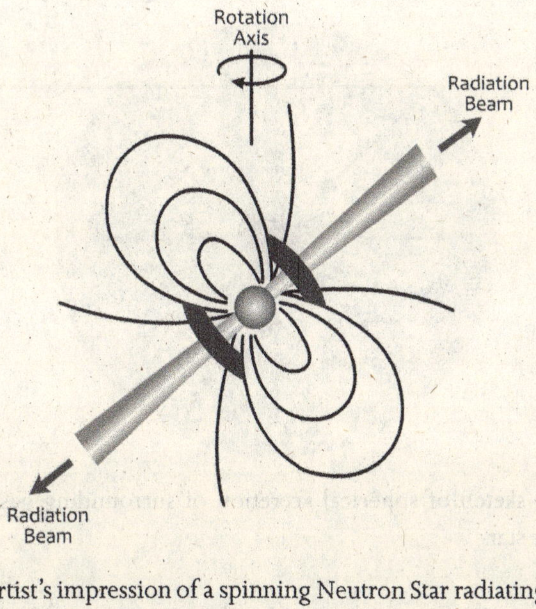

Fig. 5 Artist's impression of a spinning Neutron Star radiating pulsed Radio Beams and acting as a 'Pulsar'. Picture Credit: Department of Physics, McGill University.

The ripped-off charged particles winding along magnetic lines of forces can generate strong radio emissions that get modulated because of the star's rotation. Thus, spinning neutron stars turn into strongly pulsating radio sources and are christened as *pulsars*.

In contrast, when neutron stars are bathed by the wind of a surrounding ordinary star, by virtue of their strong gravity, they keep pulling the wind towards themselves. This process of matter falling or accumulating onto compact objects is known as *accretion*. Even if the loose companion star has no wind, the powerful gravity of a neutron star can strip off matter from the former and accrete the same.

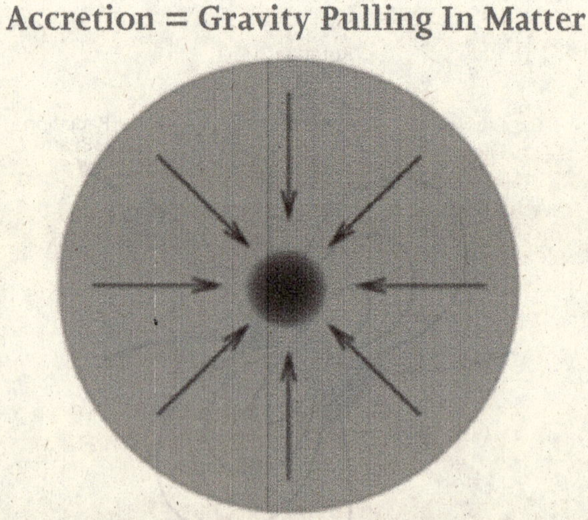

Fig. 6 A sketch of spherical accretion of surrounding gas onto a compact star.

The matter accreting onto the compact object often possesses some angular momentum, that is, the accreting matter is in a state of rotation. And the matter accreting onto astrophysical compact objects often forms *accretion disks* around it.

Fig. 7 Artist's impression of disk accretion of gas pulled from a companion star.

Among all astrophysical objects, astrophysical black holes are the only objects that do not and cannot possess any magnetic field. Why? Because black holes are devoid of any matter except for their central singularities, and astrophysical black holes have no electrical charge either. However, like the neutron stars, astrophysical black holes often have accretion disks around themselves.

The location of the inner disk around un-magnetized black holes is determined by the balance of pull gravity and centrifugal repulsion. For astrophysical black holes, this location is 3 Schwarzschild radii. In contrast, the location of the inner accretion disks around strongly magnetized neutron stars is always far away and due to the immense magnetic push of the neutron stars.

Gravitational Mass

We know that an electron and proton attract one another. And the attractive energy that holds atoms together is always negative. In view of this negative attractive energy:

The mass of an atom is slightly lower than the sum of the masses of the individual nuclei and electrons.

Similarly, in view of the attractive and negative gravitational energy:

The gravitational mass of a star or any object is lower than the original mass of the same.

If a massive star would keep on contracting indefinitely, there is a possibility that the *negative gravitational energy grows so much that its gravitational mass might approach zero.*

Indeed, long ago, while considering an assumed static general relativity equilibrium configuration of dust, a collection of point particles without any random motion, Harrison et al. mentioned that spherical gravitational collapse should come to a decisive end with M = 0. They, in fact, formulated this idea as a theorem:

'THEOREM 23: Provided that matter does not undergo collapse at the microscopic level at any stage of compression, then– regardless of all features of the equation of state –there exists for each fixed number of baryons a "gravitationally collapsed configuration", in *which the mass-energy as sensed externally is zero.*'[5]

In a somewhat more realistic fashion, Zeldovich and Novikov discussed the possibility of having an ultra-compact configuration whose mass tends to be zero: $M \rightarrow 0$. Accordingly, they mentioned the possibility of having a machine that can release the entire initial mass–energy $Q \rightarrow Mc^2$ in order to attain the $E = Mc^2 = 0$ *ground state.*[6]

This suggests that the gravitational mass of a point singularity could be M=0. *If so, there would be no true black hole having finite masses.*

CHAPTER 3

Stars Losing Mass–Energy during Contraction

I cannot teach anybody anything. I can only make them think – Socrates

KEY POINTS: During gravitational contraction, massive self-gravitating clouds and stars must get hotter and radiate photons or neutrinos or both. Thus, even if the central nuclear fuel gets exhausted, a contracting star can keep on generating central energy source. For a star of few solar masses, upon exhaustion of hydrogen at the core, energy generation halts, and the core undergoes gravitational contraction. During such contraction, the hotter core may lead to nuclear fusion of helium into carbon, and eventually the core may collapse into a helium-carbon white dwarf, supported by quantum repulsive pressure of closely packed electrons. But for a low mass star like the Sun, the core does not become hot enough to ignite helium burning, and it collapses into a helium white dwarf. In either case, the heat released by contraction causes the outer envelopes to expand, and depending on the mass, the star may swell into a red giant or hotter blue giant.

For stars having initial masses above 8 solar masses, the gravitational pull during the contraction phase could be so high that the core may get crushed into a much more compact neutron star, supported by the quantum repulsive pressure of neutrons.

The gravitational pull of stars more massive than 20–25 solar masses is so intense that even the repulsive quantum pressure of neutrons cannot halt the core contraction. It is generally believed that cores of such massive stars collapse to form black holes.

Stars more massive than 20 solar masses are generally believed to collapse into black holes at the end of their life cycles. But we note that this *idea of black hole formation usually ignores the fact that net mass of massive stars keeps on decreasing due to emission of radiation.*

Historically, this prediction about the emission of radiation during gravitational contraction was independently made by two renowned physicists of the nineteenth century. The first is the British physicist Lord Kelvin (nee William Thomson, 1824–1907), an eminent physicist with a wide range of interests and enthusiasms. He pioneered the development of thermodynamics, the science of heat and energy. In 1848, he proposed an absolute temperature scale, now called the Kelvin scale. Next, Kelvin formulated the second law of thermodynamics, which states that heat will not flow from a colder to a hotter body.

The next notable personality is the German physicist Hermann von Helmholtz (1821–1894). Not only a famous physicist but also a famous physician and he was the first to formulate the principle for the law of conservation of energy.

Kelvin Helmholtz Mechanism

Kelvin and Helmholtz were the first to apply the law of conservation of energy to a self-gravitating object having negative binding energy. Initially, the negative self-gravitational energy of a star* is negligible, but as the star contracts, it keeps on increasing in magnitude. And in order to *conserve the initial total energy*, an exactly same amount of positive energy** has to be released by the star. Kelvin and Helmholtz showed that while part of this released positive energy goes into heating up the rest is radiated out:

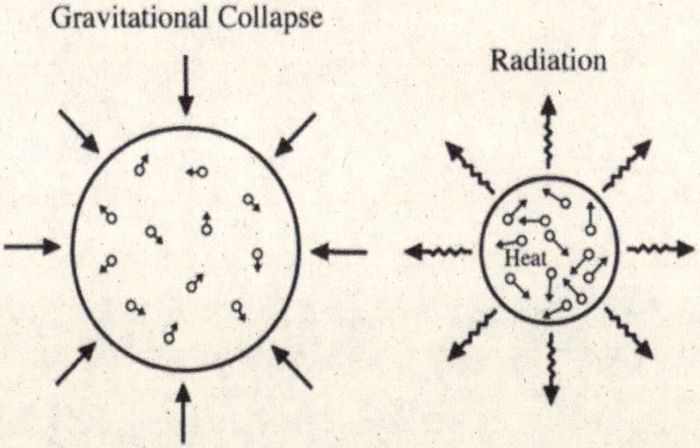

Fig. 8 A sketch of a star heating up and emitting radiation due to gravitational contraction.

* $(-GM^2/R)$
** $(+GM^2/R)$

> During the contraction, *clouds and stars get hotter and hotter, and also keep on radiating out part of the extra thermal energy*. And this process is known as the Kelvin–Helmholtz mechanism.

A general relativistic version of the Kelvin–Helmholtz mechanism was obtained by this writer in 2006.[1]

It is important to bear in mind that the radiation due to the above classical process is real radiation comprising photons and neutrinos. And this must not be confused with feeble 'Hawking radiation' conjectured to be arising from poorly understood feeble quantum mechanical effects.

CHAPTER 4

Black Holes Everywhere

Science is the belief in the ignorance of experts – Richard P. Feynman

KEY POINTS: With the advent of radio telescopes, several quasars got discovered, the most prominent of which was 3C 273. In 1963, it became clear, that this source appears to be more than hundred times brighter than our own Milky Way.

Hoyle and Fowler proposed that quasars harbour supermassive stars supported by radiation pressure alone and radiate at respective Eddington Luminosities. Ginzburg too suggested that supermassive astrophysical clouds might contract to become supermassive stars having *strong intrinsic magnetic fields.*

Indeed, the intense radio emission of quasars required the presence of strong ambient magnetic fields. However, for various reasons, the idea of supermassive radiating stars gave way to the idea of supermassive black holes whose source of luminosity was extrinsic: accretion of surrounding gas onto the black holes.

Relatively much more direct evidence about the existence of astrophysical black holes came in 1975 when it was found that the compact object in the X-ray binary Cygnus X-1 is fifteen times more massive than the Sun. All massive astrophysical compact objects are assumed to be 'black holes' because neutron stars cannot be more massive than 3 solar masses.

Contrary to the claims made, even the Event Horizon Telescope can at the most detect the bloated shadow of the *photon sphere* and not any event horizon. Thus, no external telescope can differentiate between a true black hole and a black hole mimicker, a horizon-less compact object of the same mass and practically the same radius.

One of the brightest radio stars discovered by a radio telescope was 3C 273 (273rd source from the 3rd Cambridge radio source catalogue). But in 1963, from Martin Schmidt's observation, it became clear that 3C273 was no ordinary star within our own galaxy but the farthest object in the universe known at that time.[1] Its distance was approximately 2.4 billion light years, which is overwhelmingly larger than the approximate radius of the Milky Way ~ 50,000 light years. In view of this enormous cosmic distance, the radio and optical luminosity of 3C 273 appeared to be more than hundred times the optical luminosity of the Milky Way galaxy. Further analyses led to the conclusion that most of the luminosity of 3C 273 must be originating from a central compact region, which should be more massive than a billion solar mass. Soon it was found that another radio star 3C 48 too is a super luminous compact source in a distant galaxy. And in view of their compact star-like appearances in the telescopes, they were christened as *quasi-stellar objects* or *quasars*.

Schmidt's milestone discovery, a single page paper, got published in the 16 March 1963 issue of *Nature*.[2] But a month before this, on 9 February, *Nature* had published another short paper by the mercurial British physicist Fred Hoyle (1915–2001) and the great American astrophysicist William Alfred Fowler (1911–1995).[3] These papers as well as another paper[4] suggested that the 'radio stars' could be the nuclei of distant galaxies, which in turn could be hot *supermassive stars* having masses of a million solar masses and supported against gravity by huge *radiation pressure*.

Having heard of stars of such huge masses, one can question whether the idea of Hoyle and Fowler is admissible at all, particularly because we are too familiar with the idea that masses of ultra-compact astrophysical objects are limited by Chandrasekhar mass $M_{ch} \approx 1.44$ solar mass, as explained earlier. Well, it should be noted that,

> Chandrasekhar mass limit is obtained by considering *only cold quantum pressure* exerted by the electrons.

In case a compact object/star is extremely hot and its structure is supported against self-gravity, essentially by *outward radiation pressure rather than cold quantum pressure* or ordinary gas pressure, it can possess arbitrarily high mass.

Eddington Luminosity

The idea here is that, once a hot star attains its critical luminosity called Eddington luminosity, the outward force exerted on plasma (fully ionized stellar fluid/gas) (F_r) by the radiation exactly balances the inward pull by gravitation (F_g):

EDDINGTON LUMINOSITY
OUTWARD FORCE DUE TO RADIATION PRESSURE = INWARD FORCE DUE TO GRAVITY

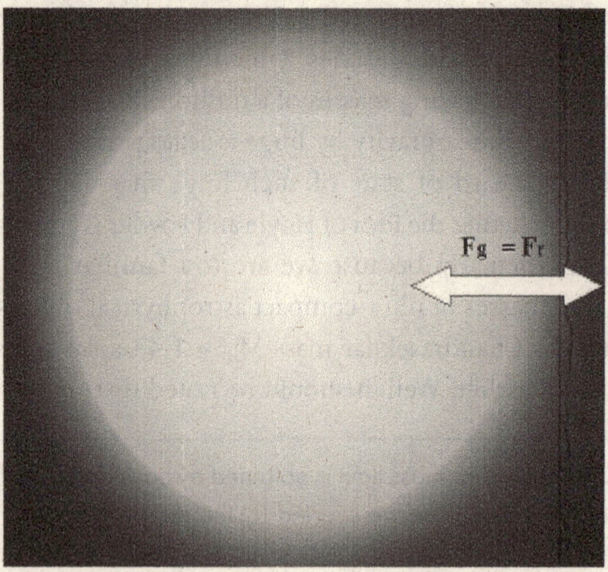

Fig. 9 Mental picture of Eddington Luminosity: Gravitational Pull = Radiation Thrust.

For a star of 1 solar mass made of completely ionized hydrogen, this value is

L_{ed} ~ 35,000 solar luminosity

The foregoing equation implies that the Sun would attain its Eddington luminosity if it would become almost 35,000 times more luminous! Note, the value of L_{ed} increases in proportion to the mass of the star, that is, for a 10 solar mass star, the corresponding value of L_{ed} will be 10 times higher, that is, 3,50,000 solar luminosity.

The idea that the radio stars are actually radio galaxies containing supermassive stars having luminosities approximately more than hundred billion times the solar luminosity was actually discussed even earlier by G.R. Burbidge (1959).[5] The pertinent supermassive stars were considered to have been formed from the gravitational collapse of the most massive primordial gas clouds. Furthermore, in 1964, the famous Russian physicist Vitaly L. Ginzburg (1916–2009) pointed out that such superstars formed by gravitational collapse could be strongly magnetized.[6] He wrote: 'the existence of a gigantic magnetosphere around large collapsing protostars is a possibility which deserves consideration.'

Note that this idea about magnetized compact objects was highly significant as it was before the time when *pulsars* – spinning neutron stars with extremely strong magnetic fields – were discovered in 1967. It is interesting to note that the idea of the black hole alternative, magnetospheric eternally collapsing object (MECO), *is closely related to the foregoing idea of 'gigantic magnetosphere around large collapsing protostars'* of Ginzburg.

However, this proposal that radio galaxies or quasars were powered by supermassive stars or superstars subsequently ran into difficulty. There were shortcomings in the idea that quasars were essentially supermassive stars. Part of the difficulty arose from the fact that supermassive stars were conceived to generate their luminosity by the nuclear burning of hydrogen at their cores. This hypothesis suggested a lifetime of quasars that proved to be shorter than what was required. Further, the supermassive stars were conceived as static Newtonian stars, and they were found to be unstable to perturbations that should push them towards catastrophic gravitational collapse. And, of course, it was believed that such collapse should lead to formations of black holes rather than ultra-relativistic radiation pressure supported stars. Consequently, an idea grew that quasars harboured supermassive black holes rather than supermassive stars.

Black Holes as Quasar Cores

The Eddington luminosity discussed earlier need not refer only to the intrinsic luminosity of stars. On the other hand, in principle, similar luminosity can be generated by extrinsic means too. In the deep gravitational potential well of a black hole or a neutron star, the accreted gas may get so hot that it can shine in the X-rays, and when sufficiently close to the compact object, the X-ray luminosity can attain the Eddington value. In addition, the gas split into ions and electrons (plasma) radiates radio waves in the presence of ambient magnetic fields.

In view of the difficulties associated with the hypothesis of supermassive stars, astrophysicists adopted a new hypothesis:

Quasar luminosity is a result of accretion of surrounding gas on to super massive black holes.[7]

Later quasars were considered part of what came to be known as *active galactic nuclei* (AGN). While quasars are radio-loud, many of these AGNs can be quiet in the radio band but very luminous in the X-ray or optical range. The radio-loud category corresponds to AGNs that have radio emissions produced by both the accretion disk and the jets. Radio-quiet AGNs are simpler in that any jet or jet-related emissions are negligible.

Since galaxies are the basic units of the universe, according to this thesis, black holes *are literally everywhere in the cosmos.*

Apparent Evidence for Black Holes

Until recently, the angular resolutions of most of the radio or any other telescopes were not adequate to peek at the event horizon (actually at photon spheres), the characteristic signature of black holes. Often, telescopes could probe no closer than 10–100 times the radii of supposed black holes. Thus during the 1960s, the idea that AGNs contain either black holes or supermassive stars was a hypothesis arrived at without any real evidence.

And more direct evidence for detection of astrophysical black holes came in 1975 when it got confirmed that the dark compact object in Cygnus X-1, the first X-ray source discovered in the direction of the Cygnus constellation, weighs as much as fifteen suns. Since *neutron stars cannot be more massive than 3 solar masses*, it was concluded that the compact dark star of Cygnus X-1 must be a black hole. By now there may be around forty known X-ray binaries that contain compact objects having masses well above the upper mass limits of white dwarfs or neutron stars. And unlike the compact objects in the AGNs, these are certainly very good blackhole candidates.

Now we must talk about the Event Horizon Telescope, an array of eight ground-based radio telescopes that form an Earth-sized virtual telescope with unprecedented sensitivity and resolution. On 10 April 2019, the Event Horizon Telescope proudly released the maiden image of a 'black hole' having a mass of 6.5 billion solar masses at the heart of the supergiant elliptical galaxy Messier 87 (M 87) situated 55 million light years away.[8]

Thus *prima facie, the 'black hole paradigm' has been firmly established from both theoretical and observational viewpoints.* But such an assertion is absolutely misleading. Since every science lover on this planet has already viewed the fuzzy image of a black hole, we are not pasting the same here. However, in future, it is likely that the Event Horizon Telescope would release a sharp image that at its centre may contain a neat dark circle:

Fig. 10 Ideal central 'dark spot' in the shadow/image of a spherical black hole or its mimicker.

And one may consider such a dark patch as the ultimate image or shadow of a black hole. WRONG! First, a black hole mimicker too would project a similar dark shadow, because almost no light can escape its surface. More importantly, the outer periphery of the dark spot would represent neither the surface of a black hole nor its mimicker but rather the shadow of their photon sphere.[9]

Photon Sphere: Virtual Event Horizon

The physical reason that not even light can ever escape any event horizon is that light orbits get so bent by strong gravity there that even light rays can move only inwards. An almost similar extreme bending can happen at the surface of black hole mimickers. But not many are aware of the existence of a photon sphere, a spherical surface around a black hole or a quasi-black hole where gravity is already so strong that even photons can move in circular orbits. The photon sphere

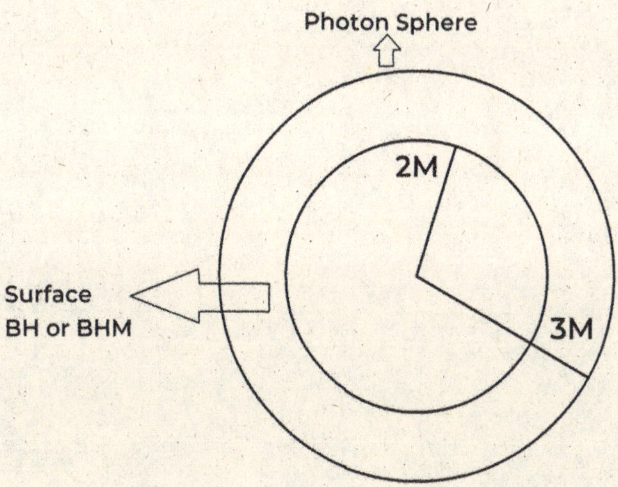

Fig. 11 Both a black hole and its mimicker have practically the same radius (2M), and both are surrounded by their Photon Sphere whose radius is 50 per cent larger (3M).

is 50 per cent larger[10] than the black hole or its mimicker.* Photons moving within the photon sphere virtually remain trapped within it as they need to struggle extremely hard to pierce the photon sphere.

Accordingly, the photon sphere itself acts like a virtual event horizon, and no external observer, no telescope, can peer inside the photon sphere. For a rotating black hole or black hole mimicker, the photon sphere gets replaced by a photon ring at the equatorial plane. Thus the so-called image of the compact object in the quasar Messier 87 is, at most, a shadow of the photon sphere of the compact object and is no evidence for any event horizon or any mathematical black hole.

* $R_{\text{Photon Sphere}} = 1.5\, R_s = 3M$

CHAPTER 5

Musings on Relativity

Somewhere, something incredible is waiting to be known – Carl Sagan

KEY POINTS: Three spatial coordinates like length, breadth and height can be combined with time readings to form a mathematical 4-D continuum: 'space-time'. This is essentially a mathematical representation, and 'space-time' need not imply existence *of any material 4-D membrane* or even a mythical 4-D physical entity.

- Unlike Newtonian physics, various observers in relative motion or in different locations of a gravitational field reckon the same spatial and time intervals differently. However, all observers agree on the value 'space-time interval', comprising both space and time intervals.
- For the motion of material particles, space-time interval is +ve (TIME LIKE), which implies properly defined speed is less than the speed of light.
- For the motion of mass-less photons, space-time interval = zero (LIGHT LIKE), which implies light always moves with the fixed speed of light.

- A TIME-LIKE trajectory can only asymptotically approach to become a LIGHT-LIKE trajectory, i.e., the speed of a particle can never attain the speed of light.
- As per Einstein's general relativity, gravity is the manifestation of local curvature of space-time membrane, which in turn is determined by the matter energy momentum.
- At the event horizon of a sufficiently massive black hole, the space-time curvature could be negligible, the same way curvature of a football ground on the Earth appears to be negligible.

Thus space-time curvatures of event horizon of supermassive black holes are negligible, and no quantum gravity effects are expected there.

While we cannot really learn here any general relativity (GR), we can try to get a feel for few central themes in a simple and non-technical manner. For this, it is imperative that first we spend a little time on the special theory of relativity, which is so named because it involves a special type of observers that are moving with respect to one another with uniform velocity *without any acceleration*.

Special Theory of Relativity

As per the historical Michelson–Morley experiment carried out in 1887, the speed of light is the same (in vacuum) for all observers. It is this observational constraint of constancy of speed of light for all observers that mixes up (or messes up) space and time intervals. Suppose a given observer measures a tiny spatial distance dx and a tiny time interval dt. But another observer in relative motion with the first observer will reckon different numerical values of dx and dt.

In other words, spatial interval dt and time interval dt cease to be 'invariant' in special relativity.

Instead, a certain botched up quantity ($+c^2dt^2 - dx^2$) does appear same to all the observers. As if instead of space and time intervals, this mishmash quantity – *space-time interval*– becomes the new *invariant quantity*. We must note here that the *signs of the time and space parts in the space-time interval are opposite*, if one is positive (+), another must be negative (-), and in this one-dimensional (t, x) case, the overall signature of the space-time is (+, -). If we will consider the motion of the particle in three spatial dimensions, then we will have a

SPACE-TIME SIGNATURE = +, -, -, -

- The condition that the material particle moves with a speed that must be less than the speed of light demands that the space-time interval for such a motion is positive. A technical name for the corresponding trajectories of material particles moving with a subluminal speed is **'time like'**.*
- On the other hand, the condition that, in vacuum, mass-less particles like photons always propagate with a fixed speed of light, demands that the space-time interval for light or photons is zero.** A technical name for the

* It is called 'time like' as the time component c^2dt^2 is greater than the space component dx^2.

** $ds^2=dt^2\ (c^2-v^2)=0$, when v=c.

corresponding trajectories of mass-less particles moving with the speed of light is '**light like**'.

- One of the basic rules of both special as well as general theory of relativity is that space-time trajectories must preserve their respective characters. This means that a *time-like trajectory cannot turn light like ever*. Physically this means that *an appropriately defined local speed that is subluminal must always remain so*.

General Theory of Relativity

We know that anything falling freely towards the surface of the Earth does so with an acceleration,* and no motion at uniform speed is possible in the presence of gravity. Thus gravity is intractably linked to acceleration, and all the *inertial frames* of Galilean and special relativity, moving with no acceleration, can be realized only in the absence of gravity. In special relativity, two observers measure different spatial and temporal intervals for the same event only when they are in relative motion, like one onboard a running train and another standing by the railway track.

But, in general relativity, in the presence of gravity, two observers *at two different regions of the gravitational field measure different spatial and temporal intervals for the same event even when they are at rest with respect to one another.*

For example, imagine two observers standing still at the base and at the peak of Mt Everest. Gravitational field due to the Earth is stronger at the base than the same

* On the Earth's surface, this acceleration is $GM/R^2 = 981\ cm/s^2$.

at the peak of the mountain. Physical time intervals for a certain event will be less at the base of the mountain having stronger gravity than what will be reckoned by the observer on the peak.

The locally measured physical time interval is called **proper time interval.**

- Proper time interval is shorter than the coordinate time interval.

On the other hand, the physical spatial interval will be *stretched longer* at the regions of stronger gravity.

Very crudely, the locally measured physical spatial interval is called **proper spatial interval.**

- For attractive gravity, proper distance is larger than the coordinate distance, as if space sags down under gravity.

The fact that in the presence of gravity, the proper spatial and time intervals, in general, vary from point to point or from time to time, unlike the special relativistic case, is manifestation of *warping of space-time by gravity*. The most practical example for the curvature of space-time is the bending of light trajectories around massive objects such as the Sun:

One may naively think that light trajectories get bent as they caress through a space-time warped by the gravity of a star or a compact object.

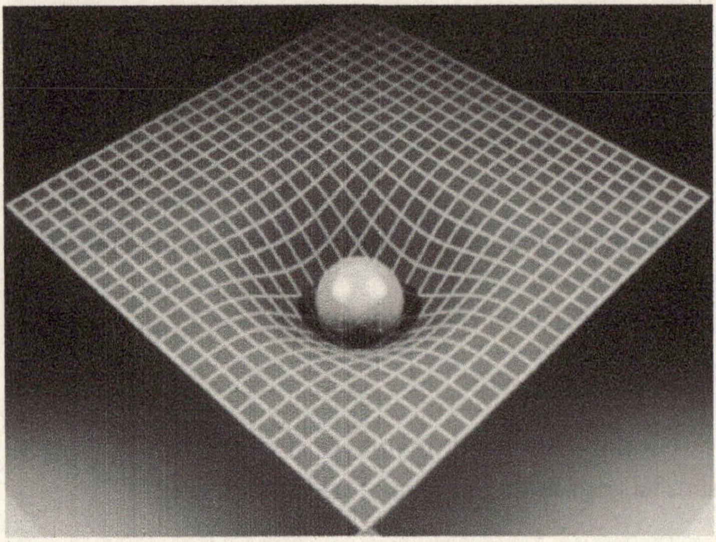

Fig. 12 A popular illustration showing a compact star warping the space around it by its weight (gravity).

Recall here that at the event horizon of a black hole, space-time gets warped so much that light rays can only fall inwards or at the most stay at standstill. And this is the pictorial reason that light cannot escape the black hole.

As per general relativity, the curved space-time structure is directly determined by the matter energy momentum distribution, and by ignoring constants and numerical factors. Einstein's equation for general relativity says:
SPACE-TIME STRUCTURE* = MATTER ENERGY MOMENTUM

* Space-time structure is described by Ricci tensor and its magnitude Ricci scalar, while matter energy momentum depends on density, pressure and momentum of matter.

General relativity demands that the laws of physics are the same not only in uniformly moving inertial frames but also in arbitrary accelerated frames, in the presence of gravity. This statement is loosely encapsulated by the *principle of general covariance*, which also demands that one should be able to use arbitrary coordinates in general relativity. In other words, strictly speaking, there is neither any preferred frame nor any preferred coordinate system.

But we shall also emphasize that, from the viewpoint of physical reality, such an absolute freedom of choice of coordinates may not be justified.

Spherically Symmetric Case

In order to be able to perform analytical studies, physicists often consider problems having spherical symmetry. Consider an isolated star or a galaxy emitting light equally in all directions. In Newtonian physics, the intensity of the light falls off as square of the distance from a spherical source because the area of concentric spheres around the source is given by $4\pi R^2$. In simple terms, this means that if one will measure the intensity of light 10 times farther away, the intensity will diminish by a factor of $10^2=100$. In this sense, the luminosity distance may be called 'area coordinate'.

Though the space-time around this star or galaxy is warped, it turns out that the *intensity of light still falls off in the same inverse square manner* $\sim 1/R^2$.

Thus, in general relativity, R remains the area coordinate or 'areal distance', something akin to a crow-flight path distance above an underlying curved space. However, the problems and paradoxes associated with the concept of a 'black hole' are justified by *replacing this physically significant radial coordinate by exotic new radial coordinates.*

Two Measures of the Strength of Gravity

As per Newton's law of gravitation, 'gravitational acceleration' or 'acceleration due to gravity' of an apple or anything else is well known.* In Newtonian gravitation, it is this acceleration that uniquely defines the strength of gravity.

1. In general relativity too, gravitational acceleration remains one measure of the strength of gravity though its expression gets modified (to be discussed later).

But in general relativity, there is another and more fundamental measure of strength of gravity.

Note that the acceleration due to gravity changes with distance R, and such a spatial variation of acceleration causes *differential or tidal* gravitational acceleration.** For instance, the tides on oceans are caused by the differential gravitational pull on the ocean water due to the moon's gravity.

2. In general relativity, it is this tidal gravitational attraction that is considered to be more fundamental than the direct gravitational acceleration,† and it is related to the *space-time curvature* (K).

* $a = GM/R^2$, where M is mass of the Earth.

** (GM/R^3)

† (GM/R^2)

Quite surprisingly, in the exterior of a spherical object, the general relativistic tidal acceleration or space-time curvature turns out to be same as its Newtonian counterpart.* Then it is promptly seen that the space-time curvature at the event horizon is inversely proportional to the square of the mass of the black hole.** So the more massive the black hole, weaker is the gravity at its surface. It turns out that the space-time curvature at the surface of a supermassive black hole having a billion solar mass is billion times weaker than what is found on the surface on a commonplace star like the Sun. Why is it so?

> Imagine a tiny golf ball whose surface looks highly curved. But a football with a much larger radius looks much flatter. And if we consider a sphere with a very large radius, its surface will look almost flat. That is the reason that a football ground on the surface of the Earth is almost flat. Similarly, for very massive black holes, having very large radii and masses, the space-time curvature or strength of gravity could be negligible.

Implication: There should be no significant quantum gravity or even semi-classical gravity effect near the surface of astrophysical black holes contrary to the assumption made by quantum gravity researchers.

* $K \sim M/R^3$, by setting $G=1$, $c=1$

** $K_H \sim 1/M_{BH}^2 \sim 1/R_s^2$

CHAPTER 6

Black Holes

Exact General Relativistic Solutions

The dimple in his left cheek was ironic – it gave the impression that he was sweet as a cupcake – Elaine Kagan

> KEY POINTS: As per the original Schwarzschild solution, stars cannot contract up to their event horizons, and hence there cannot be a black hole ever. On the other hand, solutions by Droste and Hilbert apparently suggest the existence of mathematical black holes. Yet, Droste and Hilbert themselves cast aspersion on the reality of black holes because of the unphysical behaviour of the pertinent solution in the interior of the black holes where 'space' and 'time' partly swap their roles. Also, some other features of physics become pathological at the event horizon:
>
> While physically measured time intervals become *nil*, as if clocks stop ticking, tiny physical distances appear to get stretched by a factor of *infinity*.

Though later, mathematicians tried to eliminate such pathologies by introducing *new coordinates having no observational connection*, such pathologies silently persist. For example, the very definition of the event horizon as a surface from which even light cannot escape can be ascribed to the *infinite gravitational compactness* of this surface, and no fancy coordinate transformation can hide this fact.

Einstein communicated the final equations of general relativity to the Berlin Academy on 25 November 1915. Immediately, several mathematicians attempted to apply Einstein's freshly formed equation to solve the simplest physical problem, namely, the *vacuum space-time around a neutral point mass*. In Germany, the first person to be successful in this endeavour was Karl Schwarzschild (1876–1916), who communicated this to a journal on 13 January 1916.[1] Ironically, contrary to popular belief, the *original Schwarzschild solution suggested that a star cannot contract* to a radius smaller than what later became known as the Schwarzschild radius $R_s=2M$ (by setting $G=c=1$). For a star of 1 solar mass, $R_s \approx 3$ km.

How could the Schwarzschild solution lead to such a conclusion that would go directly against the black hole paradigm? Well, as mentioned, in general relativity, coordinates are labels and there are lots of (in fact, infinite) choices for 'radial coordinate'. And Schwarzschild's choice of the radial coordinate was such that *the event horizon itself appeared as the origin of the coordinate system.*

This is a hint that *many exotic radial coordinates to be invented by future researchers to consolidate the black hole paradigm may not be physically appropriate even though*, mathematically, one can use any coordinate.

Droste–Hilbert Solution

In 1916, the Ph.D. thesis of an unknown Dutch relativist Johannes Droste (1886–1963), for the first time, used the luminosity distance 'R' to study in detail the motion of particles in the space-time around a point mass.[2] Later, in 1917, the noted German physicist David Hilbert independently published his own derivation of the same Droste metric but being unaware of Droste's detailed research.[3]

However, paradoxically, in a strange historical mix-up, this Droste–Hilbert solution became famous as the 'Schwarzschild solution', while the original Schwarzschild solution was almost forgotten. The latter, however, got highlighted only in some research papers appearing after 1980.

Under the assumption that the mass-point has a finite mass M, the event horizon now appeared as a sphere of radius $R_s=2M$. By omitting this standard angular part and pretending $c=1$, the black hole solution too has the usual format:

Space-time Interval= (Proper Time Interval)^2 – (Proper Spatial Distance)^2

Here the spatial distance has three internal parts: radial distance, angle 1 and angle 2.

Problems with the Black Hole Solution

Though 'space' and 'time' get intimately linked in the wedlock of 'space-time interval' of special relativity, one can still differentiate between the two by noting that while the *sign associated with the time part is always positive*, the same for the *space parts are always negative*. This is similar to the fact that some of the biological features of males and females retain their fundamental differences even after the happiest wedlock. Thus, the signature of special relativistic space-time always is:

SPACE-TIME SIGNATURE = (+, -, -, -)

In general relativity too, special relativity remains valid locally, and accordingly,

+VE Coefficient of Temporal Part = Inherent Signature of 'TIME' -VE Coefficients of Spatial Parts = Inherent Signature of 'SPACE'

For the Droste–Hilbert metric,* this is indeed the case as long as one is outside the black hole. But problems start creeping in if we extend it to the black hole surface or its interior.

Pathological Behaviour at the Black Hole Surface

There are two factors (see footnote *) that convert ordinary time and radial intervals into their respective proper intervals.

But both these factors go haywire or singular at the event horizon.

* Factor for the time part $A = 1 - 2M/R$; the factor for the radial part $B = -(1\text{-}2M/R)^{-1}$. Note, at $R=2M$, these coefficients become 0 and $-\infty$. And for $R< 2M$, they change their signs.

While the one factor becomes zero, the other becomes infinite:

Physically, this suggests that actual time interval becomes zero or clocks stop ticking on the black hole surface. Similarly, any tiny crow-flight radial distance gets *stretched by a factor of infinity.* Such a pathological behaviour suggests that there is a real physical singularity at the black hole surface. Simultaneously, at the black hole surface, one finds:

Space-time Signature = (0, -, -, -) instead of (+, -, -, -).

Pathological Behaviour in the Interior of a Black Hole

If there would indeed be a finite mass black hole, in its interior, the coefficients of the time and radial part would swap their signatures. Thus:

> IN THE INTERIOR OF A BLACK HOLE:
>
> **TIME → SPACE**
>
> **SPACE → TIME**

But even such an interpretation would be *inconsistent* because while the radial coordinate appears to change its original character, the *angular parts continue to retain their original space-like character.*

SPACE-TIME SIGNATURE INSIDE A BLACK HOLE = (-, +, -, -), whereas a complete space-time swapping should have led to a signature of **(-, +, +, +)**.

(i) While physical time intervals become zero on the event horizon, radial distance intervals get stretched by a factor of infinity (metric coefficients become singular).
(ii) Inside the black hole, radial and time coordinates swap their mutual role, as if time becomes the radial coordinate and the radial coordinate becomes time. However, quite inconsistently, angular coordinates continue to retain their space-like character.

Let us summarize the problems associated with the black hole solution:

Gravitational Compactness

The real measure of the gravitational compactness of a star may be gauged by the gravitational redshift of its surface rather than the quantity mentioned earlier.* A photon emitted outwards from a certain source may lose part of its energy during its propagation for a variety of reasons, and this phenomenon in general may be called the redshift of the emitted photon. This is so because as the energy or frequency decreases, the wavelength of the photon increases and its 'colour' gets reddened.

The gravitational redshift may be viewed as loss of energy of photons as they climb up against the gravitational field of a star or compact object, something like a toddler getting exhausted by climbing up a steep flight of stairs.

* (GM/Rc^2)

For a spherical star of radius R and mass M, the gravitational redshift of the photons emitted from the surface is obtained from a well-defined non-linear formula.**

For a star like the Sun whose radius is much larger than its Schwarzschild radius ($R_s \approx$ 3km), the redshift is only around one millionth. For a white dwarf with a mass comparable to the Sun and radius two orders smaller, the same quantity is one part in ten thousand.

Even for a neutron star, which is denser than the Sun by almost a hundred trillion times, one finds $z \approx 0.15$. But if the radius of the compact object will approach its Schwarzschild radius, z shoots up dramatically. And for the black hole event horizon, one will have

z =INFINITE

In such a case, no light will ever leave the event horizon and faraway observers will find it 'black'.

Astrophysical Object	Sun	White Dwarf	Neutron Star	**Black Hole Mimicker****	Black Hole
Order of Gravitational Compactness (z)	One millionth	One part in ten thousand	One tenth	**Could be thousands or even millions**	Infinite (∞)

So, the *physical reason behind why a black hole is black is that its gravitational compactness is infinite.* A black hole mimicker too is almost black because its gravitational compactness is extremely large, may be a thousand, and may be a million.

* $(1+z) = (1- 2M/R)^{-1/2}$

** For a black hole mimicker, $R = 2M(1+e)$, $z = 1/\sqrt{e}$. And for a black hole, $e=0$.

Further, beneath the event horizon, light rays must necessarily hurtle radially downwards. Thus the region within the black hole is a *trapped region* and all imaginary surfaces there are *trapped surfaces*.

The black hole we spoke about is known as the *Schwarzschild black hole*, and most astrophysicists, particle physicists and even quantum gravity researchers using this term may not be aware that the corresponding solution is actually due to Droste and Hilbert.

This neutral point mass at R=0 obviously has infinite density and pressure. More importantly, it is a *gravitational singularity because the space-time curvature* becomes infinite at* R=0.

Mathematical insights by Roy Kerr in the 1960s led to the discovery of the exact solution for a spinning black hole. However, for the sake of simplicity, we shall mostly consider the spherical Droste–Hilbert black holes in this book.

* $K \sim M/R^3$

CHAPTER 7

Critique and Consolidation of the Black Hole Paradigm

The scientist is not a person who gives the right answers; he's one who asks the right questions – Claude Lévi-Strauss

KEY POINTS: Space-time structure at the event horizon appears to be pathological as while the locally measured proper time intervals become zero, proper lengths get stretched infinitely. This is the reason Einstein, Eddington, Hadamard, Max von Laue, Marcel Brillouin and many founding fathers of general relativity considered black hole solution to be unphysical. Several authors such as Painleve, Gullstrand, Eddington showed that, apparently, such pathological behaviour of the event horizon might be removed if one would shift from conventional Hilbert coordinates to appropriate different space and time coordinates. Ironically, all such authors remained skeptical about physical validity of such attempts. In particular, Hilbert too remained skeptical as often the transformation

> process to such new coordinates themselves could be plagued with pathologies.
>
> The ultimate coordinate system which is believed to have brought out the complete inner space-time regions associated with a black hole is known as Kruskal Coordinates and this is now famous as the Maximal Analytic Continuation of the Schwarzschild solution (actually Hilbert solution). Furthermore, the so-called maximum analytical extension introduces science fiction ideas like 'white hole', 'worm hole' and 'parallel universe' in the black hole space-time when the *original problem involved only a single neutral point particle*".

In the previous chapter, we discussed physical and mathematical oddities associated with the Droste–Hilbert solution, which leads to the idea of mathematical black holes:

1. While physical time intervals become zero on the event horizon, radial distance intervals get stretched by a factor of infinity (metric coefficients become singular).
2. Inside the black hole, radial and time coordinates swap their mutual role, as if time becomes the radial coordinate and the radial coordinate becomes time. However, angular coordinates continue to retain their space-like character.

Here, we shall discuss how the mathematical idea of black holes got consolidated by the 1960s, despite objections raised by several leading physicists right from 1916.

Hilbert, whose solution suggested the mathematical existence of black holes as well their pathologies, had warned that the mathematical transformations that might remove such pathologies should not suffer from pathology themselves. However, Hilbert's valid objection was ignored then, and even now, after 103 years, the black hole paradigm keeps on ignoring such arguments. Indeed, mathematical and physical pathologies are hidden by introducing new coordinates, which themselves become pathological at the event horizon.*

Here, we recall six founding relativists who voiced their opinions against the reality of the 'Schwarzschild singularity':

1. Jacques Hadamard (1865–1963) was a French mathematician who made major contributions in number theory, complex function theory, differential geometry and partial differential equations. In 1922, he too raised the issue that the metric coefficients of the Hilbert solution become singular at R= 2M, implying exact black holes *should not form.* And Einstein jokingly referred to this as the *Hadamard catastrophe.*
2. In the same year (1922), Cornelius Lanczos (1893–1974) expressed his doubts about the reality of the R=2M Schwarzschild singularity. Lanczos was a famous mathematician who is credited with the removal of singularity in the de-Sitter solution, which is of paramount importance in cosmology.
3. Meanwhile, Aurther Eddington, one of the best theoretical astrophysicists ever, came out with the maiden comprehensive book on general relativity in 1920. And Eddington wrote:

* All such new coordinates involve a component: log (1-2M/R) which becomes infinite at R=2M.

'There is a magic circle (R= 2M) *which no measurement can bring us inside.*'

4. In 1921, Max von Laue (1879–1960) studied the motion of light around a black hole. He was probably the first to note that the light appears to become standstill at the event horizon, which he thought was unphysical. Accordingly, he opined that *such a surface should not form.* Laue had already won the Nobel Prize in Physics in 1914 for his discovery of the diffraction of X-rays by crystals.
5. In the same year (1921), Paul Painleve (1863–1933) and Allvar Gullstrand (1862–1930) introduced radically different coordinates which rendered the static space-time around a point mass appear non-static. This was something like viewing a static situation from the viewpoint of a freely falling observer who is in accelerated motion. Though the singularity at the Schwarzschild surface gets removed in these new coordinates, Painleve and Gullstrand were unhappy about the ambiguity of the Hilbert metric.
6. Marcel Brillouin (1854–1948) was a famous French physicist. In 1923, he studied this problem of gravitational field of a point particle using a coordinate that was different from the one used by Hilbert (R).[1] Like Schwarzschild, he too found that the point particle of supposed finite mass (singularity) at the heart of a black hole actually corresponds to a material sphere rather than a point. Accordingly, he concluded that there really cannot be any 'point particle' in general relativity, that is, *there cannot be any object whose radius is smaller than its Schwarzschild radius.*[2]

Interestingly, by critically analysing various proposed solutions of the vacuum Schwarzschild solution, in 2007, Luis Bel concluded that Brillouin's solution is 'the only case that satisfies all the equivalent physical constraints'.[3]

In 1930, the Japanese physicist Yusuke Hagihara (1897–1979) studied the motion of particles around black holes in a 120-page long article.[4] He too concluded that the R=2M surface should not ever be arrived at.

On the other hand, the researchers who first 'removed' the singularity of the Hilbert metric were Paul Painleve (1863–1933) and Allvar Gullstrand (1862–1930), though ironically they themselves complained about the 'ambiguity' of the Hilbert metric. Interestingly, Gullstrand was primarily a very famous ophthalmologist and had won the Nobel Prize in Physiology or Medicine in 1911. Somewhat ironically, the next person to invent a new radial coordinate that removes the Hilbert metric singularity by abandoning R and T was none other than Eddington himself.[5] He, however, did not mention that his transformation removes the singularity and, in all probability, it was just an exercise in passing.

Additionally, an initial major support in favour of the black hole interpretation of Droste–Hilbert solution came in 1932 from Georges Lemaitre (1894–1966).[5]

Just like what Painleve and Gullstrand did, Lemaitre too found a new coordinate system which rendered the black hole interior appear non-static.[6] Only by forcing this non-staticity in a situation that was originally a time-independent static one, he could remove the metric singularity at R= 2M.

As mentioned in the 'Preface', in 1939, Oppenheimer and Snyder presented an exact solution for formation of black holes in continued gravitational collapse.[7] And this became one of the biggest milestones for the black hole paradigm.

However, it is well known that Einstein never accepted the idea of black holes, and his 1939 paper concluded that continued gravitational collapse should not produce black holes.[8] By the time Einstein had passed away in 1955, a new crop of mathematical relativists had emerged who established the black hole paradigm by sweeping the original physical objections under the carpet.

The ultimate coordinate system that is believed to have brought out the complete inner space-time regions associated with a black hole is known as Kruskal coordinates after its inventor, the mathematical physicist, Martin Kruskal.[9] The Kruskal solution apparently suggested novel features for black holes in addition to the original ones:

Original Black Hole	A vacuum exterior in the universe.	A vacuum interior with an ultimate sink (singularity).
Kruskal Black Hole	In addition, a **parallel** exterior universe.	In addition, a White Hole, a **time reversed** form of a black hole from which matter gushes out spontaneously.

As if you are originally in a room in which a dead beetle is falling to the ground, and from which you can see the sky illuminated by the Sun. But after wearing coloured magic glasses, you discover, an additional room which is upside down and in which the dead beetle is flying upwards. Also, from its exterior, now you see: Not the Sun but another star, may be, the Alpha Centauri. But once you remove the coloured glasses, you return to the drab reality, a dead beetle on the floor.

Indeed, it must be borne in mind that parallel universes and white holes pop up only when *one abandons the physically significant* luminosity distance and *adopts the extremely convoluted* Kruskal coordinates. While the luminosity distance indicates real crow-flight distances in the real world, the Kruskal coordinates *cannot be connected to any physically significant measurable quantity*.

Thus any imaginary extensions of black hole space-time might be devoid of any reality and might be an artifact of unphysical coordinates.

Final Consolidation of the Black Hole Paradigm

By the end of the 1960s, most mathematical physicists asserted that the singularity at the event horizon is a *mere coordinate singularity*. One of the main arguments for such an assertion is:

- Pathologies of space-time appearing for the Hilbert solution (one factor becoming infinite while another going to zero) can be removed by using Kruskal-like coordinates.
- More importantly, space-time curvature* appears to be finite at the event horizon (by presuming that masses of the black holes are finite and non-zero).

* $K_{EH} \sim 1/M_{BH}^2$

Further, in the 1970s, the singularity theorems of Stephen Hawking and Roger Penrose conveyed the impression that even for realistic gravitational collapse, formation of gravitational singularity is inevitable. Finally, the confirmation that Cygnus X-1 and many other X-ray binaries contain stellar mass black holes practically propelled the black hole paradigm beyond the realm of any questioning.

CHAPTER 8

Yet More Critique of the Black Hole Paradigm

If you tell the truth, you don't have to remember anything – Mark Twain

KEY POINTS:

- The coordinate transformations that endeavour to remove pathologies of the event horizon may be unphysical and even mathematically unacceptable.
- By original premises black hole solution is the 'static', ultimate resting place of massive stars. But all such transformations render the interior of the black holes as *non-static*, which is a self-contradiction.
- Time-like trajectories of particles may turn Tachyon like in black hole interiors in contradiction to relativity.
- The massive star may radiate out its entire original mass–energy before becoming a black hole.
- Indeed, mathematical black holes may be mass-less. If so, the massive black hole candidates cannot be mathematical black holes.

> • Some prominent names whose work suggested that there may not be any true black hole are Paul Dirac, W. McCrea (former president, Royal Astronomical Society), W.H. Menzel (former director, Harvard Observatory), E.T. Newman, N. Rosen, L. Bel, W.B. Bonnors, F. Cooperstock and J.V. Narlikar.

Even after the black hole paradigm got well entrenched in the 1960s, more than twenty noted or at least mainstream general relativists or astrophysicists went on raising various objections against the black hole paradigm primarily on the following grounds:

> 1. The new coordinates introduced to remove black hole pathologies are rather unphysical. They render an originally static scenario (a single point mass with no motion) into a time dependent one.
> 2. The black hole interior region itself is unphysical and should not be realized in real world.

Surprisingly, most general relativists and quantum gravity researchers working on black holes are not aware that many noted general relativists have raised such objections against the concept of black holes even after the corresponding paradigm got established by 1960.

1. Paul Dirac

• No point particle, no true black hole

It was Paul Adrian Maurice Dirac (1902–1984) who laid the foundations for a new general formulation of quantum mechanics, which could successfully incorporate special relativity and spin of electrons. He did so by 1928, at the young age of 26. He is also the founder of quantum electrodynamics, a relativistic theory of the classical electromagnetic field, and was awarded the Nobel Prize in Physics in 1933. From 1932 to 1969, Dirac was the Lucasian Professor of Mathematics at Cambridge, a chair originally held by Isaac Newton. In general, he is considered one of the finest theoretical physicists ever.

Dirac questioned the very concept of a 'point particle' in general relativity the same way Marcel Brillouin had questioned it way back in 1923:

> The mathematicians can go beyond this Schwarzschild radius, and get inside, but I would maintain that this inside region is not physical space...I feel that the space inside the Schwarzschild radius must belong to a different universe and should not be taken into account in any physical theory. So from the physical point of view, the possibility of having a point singularity in the Einstein field is ruled out. Each particle must have a finite size no smaller than the Schwarzschild radius.[1]

These comments clearly show that Dirac ruled out the physical existence of mathematical black holes. His argument is essentially same as that of Einstein, Schwarzschild and Droste that no star or object can shrink down to its Schwarzschild radius.

2. William Hunter McCrea

- True black holes may be massless

Sir William Hunter McCrea, FRS (1904–1999), was the doyen of British astronomy.

He was president of the Royal Astronomical Society from 1961–1963, president of Section A of the British Association for the Advancement of Science during 1965–66 and knighted in 1985. McCrea also won the Gold Medal of the Royal Astronomical Society in 1976 In 1928, he had discovered that the Sun is made of almost 75 per cent hydrogen and 24 per cent helium, with the remaining 1 per cent being other elements. Before this, many people thought the Sun consisted mostly of iron.

He was not only a famous astrophysicist but also deeply interested in general relativity and cosmology. This insightful paper by McCrea suggested that black holes may not form in gravitational collapse because of the inevitable dramatic emission of radiation immediately before the formation of R=2M surface.[2]

By virtue of the aforementioned comment, McCrea may be the first physicist who theoretically predicted the occurrence of cosmic gamma-ray bursts, the most powerful explosions in the cosmos, which will be discussed in a later section.

He wrote, 'A condensation of exactly the singular radius could not, however, be formed in finite time', as if he also envisaged eternally collapsing objects rather than black holes as the final end product of gravitational collapse of massive stars.

Furthermore, by his comment that 'the gravitational binding energy of a particle added to a body of this radius exactly cancels the proper mass of the particle' he also envisaged that the asymptotic black hole that could form after eternal collapse may be of zero mass–energy: $E= Mc^2 =0$, or $M=0$.

3. Elizabeth Hilton

- Event horizon is a physical singularity

Elizabeth Hilton was doing her Ph.D. under the supervision of William McCrea in the University of London in the early 1960s. As a part of her dissertation, she wrote a gem of a paper that argued that the Schwarzschild singularity is a genuine physical singularity even though there are coordinate transformations that try to hide this singular behaviour.[3]

4. Allen Janis, Ezra Ted Newman and Jeffrey Winicour

- True that black holes may be mass-less

Ezra Ted Newman (1929–) is a famous American general relativist. In 1968, he and his two co-authors published a paper entitled 'Reality of the Schwarzschild Singularity' in *Physical Review Letters*.[4]

These authors admitted that as long as the contracting star is larger than its Schwarzschild radius, there is no problem in having a compact object of arbitrary large mass. But once one would conceive it to have shrunk to its Schwarzschild radius, then suddenly, its mass may drop to zero. Physically, this implies that the star must radiate out its entire original mass energy before becoming an exact mathematical black hole.

5. Luis Bel

- Schwarzschild surface is a point: M=0 for true black holes

Luis Bel (1942–), a senior European general relativist is known for the 'Bel–Robinson' tensor that attempts to envisage gravitational field energy as a sort of electromagnetic field energy. In 1969, Bel published a paper with a startling result.

The black hole surface, which is supposed to be a sphere, is actually a point (a sphere of zero radius).

Since the radius of a black hole sphere is twice its mass, Bel's result implies that a true black hole has zero mass and not any finite mass contrary to what is believed in the black hole paradigm.[5]

Bel argued that the extension of the Schwarzschild to non-static ones carried out by Finkelstein and Kruskal are meaningless since there is no interior at all for a mass-less black hole. Nevertheless, the all-powerful black hole paradigm decided to ignore it.

6. Nathan Rosen

- Event horizon is a physical singularity

Nathan Rosen (1909–1995) was a highly noted American-Israeli physicist who had been a long-time collaborator of Einstein. He is famously known for his work on quantum mechanics leading to the Einstein–Podolsky–Rosen paradox. Rosen too could not accept the reality of black holes despite exact solutions. In 1970, he wrote: 'We have here a discontinuity in the geometry in its dependence on R, for R = 2M. The standpoint adopted here is that in nature only particles occur for which R is larger than 2M.'[6]

Later, in 1985, he rejected the idea that the Kruskal coordinates really remove the 'Schwarzschild singularity',[7] saying that they involved coordinate transformations that have singularity at R=2M, believing that if we want the field of a particle at rest, we must *accept the existence of the Schwarzschild singularity.*

7. Fred Cooperstock

- Event horizon is a physical singularity

Fred Cooperstock (1940–2018) was qualitatively different from usual mathematical relativists, and to him, general relativity is a vital tool to unravel real, subtle physics. He was a professor in the Department of Physics, University of Victoria, Canada, and was an emeritus professor there since 2006.

His paper co-authored with Junevicus mostly reviewed the arguments of various researchers that Schwarzschild singularity has a genuine singularity.[8] With reference to various attempts to remove the Schwarzschild singularity by complicated coordinate transformations, they wrote,' We *reject the notion that these transformations remove the* R=2M *singularity*. The transformations themselves are, with various combinations, singular, complex or undefined on R=2M or the interior region.'[9]

8. Donald Howard Menzel

- M=0 for true black holes and so-called black holes are superstars

Donald Howard Menzel (1901–1976) was one of the first theoretical astronomers and astrophysicists in the

US. He discovered the physical properties of the solar chromosphere, the chemistry of stars, the atmosphere of Mars and the nature of gaseous nebulae. The minor planet '1967 Menzel' was named in his honour. Returning to Harvard after the war, he was appointed as acting director of the Harvard Observatory in 1952 and promoted to full director during 1954–66. In between, from 1946 to 1948, he was the vice president of the American Astronomical Society and also acted as its president during1954–56. Menzel was given the John Evans Award of the University of Denver in 1965. After his death, in 2001, Harvard-Smithsonian Center for Astrophysics hosted 'Donald H. Menzel: Scientist, Educator, Builder', a symposium in honour of his hundredth birthday.

Menzel's paper entitled 'Superstar and the Black-Hole Myth' claims that the radius of a black hole turns out to be $R_s=0$. Accordingly, so-called 'black holes should not be true black holes, and instead we can have red holes, infrared holes or even radio holes – but not black holes.'[10]

His paper concludes: 'Many of today's relativists are trying to explore the interiors of black holes, where both time and space appear to possess some peculiar, complex properties. In my opinion, *such studies have got nothing whatever to do with physics.*'[11]

9. Ernst Julius Öpik

- No true black hole ever forms: Black holes a myth?

Ernst Julius Öpik (1893–1985) was an Estonian astronomer and astrophysicist who spent the second half of his career (1948–1981) at the Armagh Observatory in

Northern Ireland. He won the J. Lawrence Smith Medal from the National Academy of Sciences in 1960, the Kepler Gold Medal from the American Association for the Advancement of Science & Meteoritical Society in 1972, the Gold Medal of the Royal Astronomical Society in 1975 and the Bruce Medal in 1976. The asteroid 2099 Öpik is named in his honour. Like Menzel, Opik completely rejected the idea of black holes in a paper titled 'Black Holes – A Myth?', despite being aware of the discovery of massive compact objects that could not be cold neutron stars. He argued that there is no firm evidence that the so-called black hole candidates are true black holes.[12]

10. Venzo De Sabbata and K.T. Shah

- Since gravity may not escape black holes, so-called black holes may not be real black holes

Venzo De Sabbata is a fairly well-known Italian theoretical physicist. In 1978, he and his co-author K.T. Shah raised an interesting question 'Can Gravity Escape Black Hole?'.[13] In quantum gravity, gravitational field is mediated by gravitons, and since nothing can escape the event horizon, one wonders whether the gravitational effect of the point singularity can escape. They too argued that the fact that the position coordinate R and time coordinate T seem to swap their roles inside the event horizon suggests that it is a true space-time singularity *and not a mere mathematical fictitious singularity due to bad choice of coordinates.*

11. Ronald Gautreau

- Black hole concept should be re-examined

Ronald Gautreau is very much a mainstream general relativity expert and often focuses research on the basics of general relativity with a pedagogical appeal. In 1999, in a paper titled, 'Incompleteness of the Kruskal-Szekeres Spacetime', he questioned the idea that the Kruskal metric reveals the complete picture associated with black holes. Way back in 1980, he had raised a somewhat similar question. In these two papers, he suggested that the concept of black holes be re-examined.[14]

12. Leonard S. Abrams

- Event horizon is a physical singularity, no collapse beyond event horizon

In the 1980s, Leonard S. Abrams (1924–2001) probably became the first researcher who reminded the world that the so-called black hole solution is due to Hilbert and not Schwarzschild. He also showed that as far as mathematics is concerned, Schwarzschild's solution, which showed that no star could contract up to its Schwarzschild radius, is more appropriate than Hilbert's paper.[15]

More importantly, Abrams contested the black hole interpretation on the basis that *gravitational acceleration diverges at the black hole surface* and this appears to be a very valid objection.

Subsequently, several other general relativists like S. Antoci and D.E. Liebscher rejected the black hole paradigm by banking on Abram's research and also by pointing out that *the Kruskal coordinates lead to a space-time that is different from that of a point mass* and hence not admissible.[16]

13. William Bowen Bonnor

- Event horizon a physical singularity; extensions of Schwarzschild solutions unphysical

William Bowen Bonnor (1920–2015) was a noted general relativist and served as a professor at the University of London for decades. In his 1992 paper in the respected journal *General Relativity and Gravitation*,[17] he practically rejected the idea of black holes because of inherent fundamental inconsistencies. This paper 'Physical Interpretation of Vacuum Solutions of Einstein's Equations' addressed not only the contradictions associated with the vacuum Hilbert solution but also several other exact general relativity vacuum solutions.

In the concluding section, Bonnor writes: 'The *Schwarzschild surface is a real singularity and the coordinates should end there.* Certainly something physical happens at R=2M, so this is an arguable case.'[18]

Bonnor also completely rejected the Kruskal extension of the Schwarzschild metric, which suggests worm holes and parallel universes within the black hole, writing 'though mathematically complete, it does not make physical sense'.[19]

14. M.S. Borkar and T.M. Karade

- Event horizon is a physical singularity, no exact black hole

M.S. Borkar and T.M. Karade were lecturers in the department of mathematics at Nagpur University in India. Though their recent paper against the black hole paradigm 'On Singularity of Spherically Symmetric Space Times', published in Indian journals, has remained unnoticed, it is worthwhile to take note of it as they claim that their proof is *exact*, subject to the validity of their definition of physical singularity. This work is an extension of a 1975 paper by Karade that had rejected the idea of black holes on the lines of Hilton, Rosen and other researchers who had earlier shown that the event horizon appears to be a physical singularity.[20]

15. S.I.Chermyanin

- Event horizon coincident with central singularity, M=0 for true black hole

In a paper, 'A New Type of Solution of the Schwarzschild Problem for a Point-Source', the Russian author S.I. Chermyanin[21] claimed that the *Schwarzschild surface (sphere) is actually a point* whose implication is that a true black hole has M=0.

16. N.N. Fimin and V. M. Chechetkin

- All extensions of Schwarzschild metric unphysical, no exact black hole

In 2009, two other Russian authors, N. N. Fimin and V. M. Chechetkin too pointed out fundamental inconsistencies in the black hole paradigm[22] in a paper titled, 'The Collapse of Matter and the Formation of Black Holes: Conceptual Aspects'.

Some excerpts from this paper:

'This is confirmed by the fact that, when the process of the collapse is considered (in a realistic formulation of the problem), the possibility emerges that objects such as *black holes* (in their classical treatment) *cannot be formed at all*.'[23]

'Our preliminary qualitative analysis shows that the Schwarzschild-Hilbert and Kruskal metrics probably display a set of *non-physical attributes and cannot be realized under real conditions*.'[24]

17. A.A. Logunov, M.A. Mestverishvili and V.V. Kiselev

- Event horizon a physical singularity, true black holes not possible

Anatoly Alekseyevich Logunov (1926–2015) was a leading Russian theoretical physicist, an academician of the USSR Academy of Sciences and Russian Academy of Sciences. He remained the vice president of the Academy of Sciences of USSR for a long period (1974–1991) and was awarded the Bogolyubov Prize in 1996. His co-author, Varley Kiselev is a noted theoretical particle physicist from the Institute of High Energy Physics, Protvino, Russia, having 4,800 citations for his research.

In 2004, A.A. Logunov, M.A. Mestverishvili and V.V. Kiselev published this interesting preprint which was later published in a journal: 'Black holes: A prediction of theory or phantasy?'[25]

This paper convincingly showed that the physical speed of a test particle attains the speed of light at the event horizon irrespective of the coordinates used. In addition, these authors also mentioned that the *time-like world line of a test particle would turn light-like* in this limit.

Later, in 2012, the first two authors of the paper published more papers claiming black holes are not actually allowed by general relativity.[26]

18. Rainer Burghardt

- Event horizon a physical singularity, no exact black hole

Rainer Burghardt is a senior general relativist from Austria. In several of his works, he has claimed that the event horizon is a physical singularity and thus true black holes should not form and collapse should continue eternally.[27]

19. Jayant Narlikar and Thanu Padmanabhan

- No true black holes, but only quasi-black holes

Jayant Narlikar is a noted cosmologist and a long-time co-worker of the great British astrophysicist Fred Hoyle. He is also the Founder-Director of the Inter-University Centre for Astronomy and Astrophysics, a world-class research institute at Pune, India. Thanu Padmanabhan, originally a Ph.D. student of Narlikar, too is a well-known scholar and researcher in the area of gravitation. In 1988, they published a highly insightful paper titled 'The Schwarzschild Solution: Some Conceptual Difficulties', which questioned the black hole paradigm and suggested that these so-called *black holes should be approximate or quasi-black holes instead.*[28]

Like many other authors, Narlikar and Padmanabhan too argued that the black hole solution is ambiguous because in the black hole interior (1) original space and time coordinates unphysically swap their roles and (2) a space-time originally defined as static appears to be non-static. They may be the first relativists to use the term 'quasi-black holes': 'the discussion of physical behavior of black holes, classical or quantum, is only of academic interest. It is suggested that problems related to the source could be avoided if the event horizon did not form and that the universe only contained quasi-black holes.'[29]

CHAPTER 9

Ocean of Confusion in 'Black Hole Interior'

I don't want to believe. I want to know – Carl Sagan

KEY POINTS: The properly defined local speed of a material particle attains the speed of light at the event horizon and then becomes superluminal in the black hole interior. The explanations offered to avoid such conclusions are not sustainable because the observers who claim to detect subluminal motion in the black hole interior may themselves be moving with superluminal speeds. Indeed, many general relativists have considered the possibility of existence of fictitious superluminal particles, 'tachyons' in the interior of black holes. In order to avoid such physically embarrassing scenes, some relativists have hypothesized that it is the interior space of black holes, and not the test particles, which hurtles down with superluminal speeds. We reject such an unphysical hypothesis. The ultimate way out would be the realization that there cannot be any true black holes.

We have already pointed out mathematical and physical riddles associated with the concept of a black hole. However, the black hole paradigm grew by simply ignoring such critiques and proofs. Despite the mathematical dressings, the black hole paradigm opened up a virtual Pandora's box of confusions and contradictions that continue to remain unresolved even today. One such confusion is about the speed of a free-falling particle at the black hole surface and also in its interior.

Speed at the Event Horizon

The speed of a particle free falling on earth or any star from far away is known since the time of Newton.* Quite surprisingly, infinitely more complicated general relativity too yields *exactly the same expression for the speed of a free-falling particle*. Black hole proponents feel comfortable with this exact general relativistic result as long as it is applied outside the event horizon of a black hole. This is so because the expression tells us that the speed of the infalling particle is subluminal as required by general relativity. However, they get jittery when this expression is used at the event horizon. Why? Because it shows that the particle will attain the speed of light, which is strict 'no, no' in general relativity. And they try to wriggle out of this uncomfortable result by pleading that you cannot define any speed at the event horizon (by using this rule) because there cannot be any fixed observer at the event horizon.

*$V = \sqrt{(2GM/R)}$

For appreciating this objection, let us first recall that when we assign a speed to a falling apple, the speed is measured by an observer sitting fixed on the surface of the Earth or hovering around the instantaneous location of the apple. Similarly, when we quote a certain speed of a running car, we do so with respect to fixed objects such as a milestone or a checkpost.

And though there cannot be any observer sitting pretty on the event horizon, it is not difficult to see the unreasonableness of the foregoing plea. Suppose there is an observer sitting just above one trillionth of a centimetre above the event horizon. She may find that the infalling particle has a speed that is equal to the speed of light within a part of one trillion. One can carry forward such a proposition indefinitely and infer that the speed of the infalling particle would indeed approach the speed of light at the event horizon.

Accordingly, long ago, two Italian relativists F. Salzman and G. Salzman argued that the event horizon may be a physical singularity: 'These results suggest the possibility that even in the Schwarzschild problem *the singularity at the event horizon may have a deeper significance* than has traditionally been accorded to it.'[1]

Note the speed of the infalling apple will, however, differ from the known formula, if the speed is measured by an *observer who herself is falling down instead of hovering at the instantaneous position* of the apple. And indeed, by inventing such an accelerated reference frame, in 1973, Allen I. Janis[2] claimed: 'No, speed of the free-falling particle remains sub-luminal even at the event horizon.'

This claim was nonetheless rebutted by two other Italian relativists G. Cavalleri and G. Spinelli in 1977.[3] They pointed out that Janis's prescription results in subluminal speed because *it is measured by an observer whose velocity approaches the speed of light.*

Much later, two Spanish relativists Paulo Crawford and Ismael Tereno revisited this issue.[4] In a desperate bid to protect the black hole paradigm, somewhat like a royal diktat, they declared that the *velocity measured by any fixed observer is meaningless.* As per Crawford and Tereno, if we are measuring the speed of a free-falling apple, it must be measured by another *free-falling apple.*

However, in view of curved space-time, in general relativity, for velocity or acceleration measurement, both *the observer and the test particle must be at the same spatial location all the time.* In other words, the apple measuring the speed of another apple must keep falling together side by side and not be situated at different heights. But at the same location, two free-falling apples always have the same speed. Hence, by this diktat, the speed of a free-falling particle is always zero, even at the event horizon. Therefore, the diktat of Crawford and Tereno becomes null and void.

Tachyons in Black Hole Interior?

As we have seen, unless one measures the speed of a free-falling particle by another side-by-side free-falling particle, the speed of the particle would indeed acquire the speed of light at the event horizon. Then irrespective of any details, the speed of the particle *must exceed the speed of light inside the event horizon.* However, as we all know, let alone material particles, the speed of even photons or light cannot ever exceed the speed of light anywhere. But there is a catch.

While general or special relativity dictates that the speed of material particles and photons cannot overstep the speed limit, mathematically, there could be an imaginary elementary particle, nicknamed tachyon, which always moves faster than light. In fact, it would require an infinite amount of energy to slow down a tachyon to the speed of light.

Indeed, several research papers have been written to show that matter would behave like tachyons inside a black hole.[5] However, this fantasy about tachyons inside black holes can be rejected on two solid grounds:

1. We know that all the particles we know of have either positive masses (electron, proton, neutron) or zero mass (photon). There cannot be any particle in the real world with negative masses, say minus 4 gm (-4). An infinitely absurd and physically meaningless proposition would be to think of particles having 'imaginary' masses. This is so because an imaginary number is the square root of a negative number and is not definable or measurable. For instance, the square root of plus 4 could be either +2 or -2.* But there cannot be any square root of minus 4, except for mathematical studies. *And tachyons acquire their superluminal speed, by virtue of their masses being imaginary.*
2. Even if momentarily, we accept that there could be tachyons, a free-falling apple made of electrons, protons and neutrons, which are objects with positive masses, cannot ever turn into tachyons having imaginary masses.

* + 4 = (+2) x (+2) = (-2) x(-2)

Apple Falls or the Space Falls?

Many general relativists quietly understand that the speed of a free-falling particle would exceed the speed of light inside a black hole. They also realized that such an unacceptable result cannot be explained away by fantasizing that material particles somehow metamorphose into tachyons inside the black holes. In search for an honourable escape route, a novel model for the black hole interior was hypothesized: the river model of black holes.[6]

In this model, the apple is not at all moving on its own inside the black hole. On the other hand, the apple is stuck up in a *space that itself is hurtling down with superluminal speed in the interior of the black hole!*

Suppose a traffic cop catches a speeding car for violating the speed limit. But the car driver pleads innocence: 'But my car has not moved at all; *it is the road underneath which has been running at a tearing speed!*'

Well, though such a plea would be rejected immediately, there is an iota of reasonableness in it: the road is made of physical matter having finite density (not vacuum), and in principle, it can move.

But vacuum is no matter (at least in classical physics), no mass–energy. Then how can it move and that too with a superluminal speed? And if it would be fancied as some sort of matter, then rules of general relativity must be applicable to it. Hence, under no circumstance, can space move superluminally.

Also, as per the black hole paradigm, not only the event horizon but also the black hole interior (barring the central singularity) is a *perfectly normal region, as normal as the exterior vacuum space outside the black hole.* OK, OK!

But then, *why is space not tumbling down outside the black hole too?*

And why do we at all require laws of gravitation to understand the fall of the apple?

Why can we not simply postulate that the apple is not falling anywhere but rather is stuck in a space which is rushing towards the Earth?

But, then, why is the tree itself not rushing towards the Earth? And why stop at apple? Why are air, clouds and the sky too are not glued to the background space and not tumbling down to the surface of the Earth?

May be an honest introspection would show that it is not space that is falling down anywhere, *but it is the assumption of a black hole interior that is crumbling.*

CHAPTER 10

Time Reversal Symmetry Forbids Black Holes

To hide a lie, a thousand lies are needed – Unknown

KEY POINTS: Einstein equations remain unchanged if positive time is replaced by negative time. Thus, one should be able to run a film on matter hurtling down to a black hole singularity backwards to see matter gushing out of the same singularity, a scene known as a 'white hole'. But matter cannot emerge out of singularity and move outwards through trapped regions. Thus, time reversal symmetry forbids formations of (1) event horizons, (2) trapped regions and (3) black holes.

In order to escape such harsh physics facts, general relativists hypothesized that matter hitting the singularity may emerge out of a white hole in a parallel universe. Indeed the Kruskal extension of original black hole space-time hints at the existence of white holes and parallel universes within black holes. But both the radial and the temporal Kruskal coordinates become infinite (singular) at the event horizon, and the entire story appears to be a mathematical jugglery, which many relativists have rejected. Thus, even a century after the mathematical black hole solution, black hole interior continues to be an ocean of confusion. Are black holes indeed associated with white holes, wormholes and parallel universes? Does space move like a river inside a black hole? Do black hole interiors contain unseen degrees of freedom or even matter with strange properties? There is no clarity over such questions. Nonetheless, all such speculations are in direct contradiction with the fundamental definition of black holes by which a black hole represents the *static vacuum space-time around a single point mass.*

Think of a film on matter inexorably hurtling down towards the central singularity of a black hole, formed supposedly by the 'prediction' of the Einstein equations of general relativity.

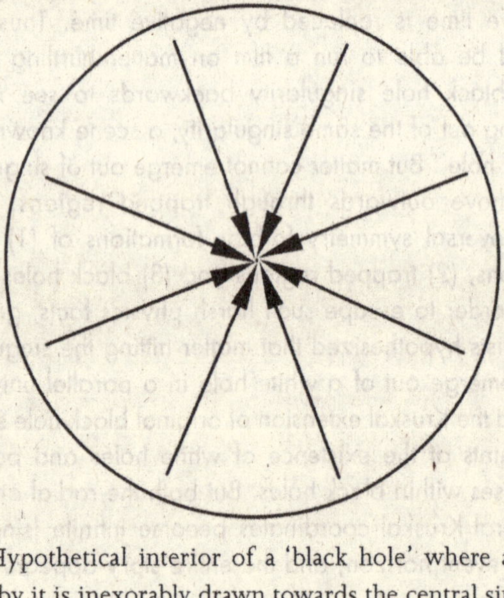

Fig. 13 Hypothetical interior of a 'black hole' where all matter captured by it is inexorably drawn towards the central singularity.

But Einstein equations obey time-reversal symmetry even on a macroscopic scale and not merely on microscopic sub-atomic scales. In the present context, this implies that, in principle, we must be able to run the above referred film *backwards* and discover a queer object where matter is gushing out of the gravitational singularity and flying outwards.

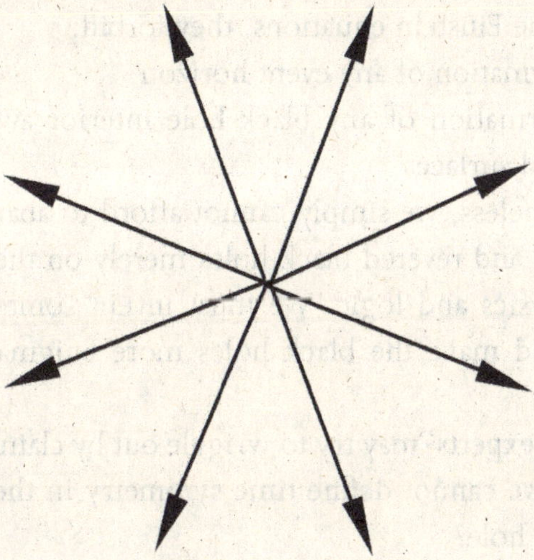

Fig. 14 Sketch of a hypothetical "white hole" which spews off matter from a singularity, but **does not allow** any infall of matter or even light.

Such an object, a time-reversed avatar of a black hole is known as white hole.

Therefore, if Einstein equations allow the formation and existence of black holes, they should also allow the formation and existence of white holes. Indeed, on paper, white holes do exist.

But while the *motion of matter accreting towards a black hole or any other compact object may get reversed in the form of jets and winds* (*run the film backwards*), no matter, no light, can emerge out of the singularity and head towards the event horizon.

In other words, while white holes may exist in isolation, there cannot be any white hole within a black hole.

Therefore, unfortunately, the film on *accretion of matter onto the singularity cannot be run backwards* in violation of the time symmetry of the Einstein equations. Thus if we really honour the Einstein equations, they forbid:

- the formation of any event horizon
- the formation of any black hole interior awash with trapped surfaces

Nonetheless, we simply cannot afford to abandon our cherished and revered black holes merely on the basic of naïve physics and logic. We must invent some way out that would make the black holes more enigmatic more charming.

Some 'experts' may try to wriggle out by claiming that, may be, we cannot define time symmetry in the interior of a black hole?

But why?

If the black hole interior is a non-singular place, why can we not define time symmetry there? Do Einstein equations cease to exist in the interior of a black hole?

More ingenious experts may *invent a parallel universe* within the black hole and then claim that the matter overshooting the singularity in our universe can very well emerge as a 'white hole' in a 'parallel universe'.

After all, the Kruskal solution, which is credited with exploring the entire interior space-time of a black hole, does suggest the existence of

- a white hole as well as
- a parallel universe.

However, note that the exotic and complex inferences about the innards of the black hole are manifestations of the introduction of exotic and complex coordinates that inexorably distort the original physical reality: *A black hole solution is space-time around a single point mass.*

More importantly, both the Kruskal coordinates go wild, become infinite, at the event horizon* because of a certain factor they contain. Thus, even mathematically, the use of the Kruskal coordinates is not justified in the first place.

Suppose you are seeing your image in front of a large life-size mirror. If the mirror has a smooth plane surface, your image will mimick you truthfully. But in case the mirror is fractured and undulated, then, it might appear that:

- Your limbs are fractured
- Your skin is wrinkled
- Your face is contorted

According to an Internet article by Mathew Francis, as of 28 April 2016, 'The interior is *nature's biggest secret*, enshrouded by a barrier that lets everything in but nothing out...The interior of a black hole isn't merely an inaccessible region of the cosmos. It's a laboratory for the most extreme physics: the strongest gravity and the most intense of quantum processes.'[1]

He goes on to say that it is for this very reason that physicists, even with the lack of means to test their ideas, are intensely interested in discovering what happens inside. Nevertheless, most of them are reasonably certain that any

*The factor is log (1- 2M/R) = -ve Infinity at R=2M.

knowledge of the interior would require an amalgamation of quantum physics and general relativity.

Since space and time apparently swap their roles inside a black hole, sometimes it is also profoundly claimed that the black hole singularity is not at a given point but is associated with temporal position. However, black holes arose from an exact solution of a point mass sitting at a *given place*, the origin of the radial coordinate, and it is this point mass that turns out to be the *singularity*. Any statement that a point is not sitting at a place but at the origin of time unfortunately appears to be not only gibberish but also *in direct contradiction with the original scenario.*

Now view a blog 'Quantum Frontiers' by John Preskill (1953–) who is the Richard P. Feynman Professor of Theoretical Physics at the California Institute of Technology (Caltech). Specifically, look at Preskill's question: 'I have a multiple choice question for you. What's inside a black hole?

(A) An unlimited amount of stuff.
(B) Nothing at all.
(C) A huge but finite amount of stuff, which is also outside the black hole.
(D) None of the above.'[2]

According to him, the first three answers appear absurd, boosting the credibility of (D). However, most participants at the 'Rapid Response Workshop' on black holes that he attended were advocating some version of (A), (B) or (C), with 'varying degrees of conviction'.

But recall here that as per general relativity, *a black hole arises from a vacuum solution* marked by absence of any matter.

Thus, if not for the pointmass, B appears to be the correct answer: 'Nothing at all'.

But black hole proponents, unwittingly and yet in a blatantly self-contradictory manner, fantasize about unknown structures inside black hole! Note, since by definition, even outgoing light rays must hurtle towards the masspoint of a black hole, no effect or no quantum gravity considerations can support any structure inside a spherical black hole. But it is hard to argue this when both the authors and referees of reputed journals indulge in such fantasies. A portal called the Daily Galaxy[3] even reported, in January 2013: 'From the "X Files": "Advanced Civilizations may live inside Supermassive Black Holes"', based on a research paper by V. I. Dokuchaev.[4]

Note, even if white holes could exist, they too would violate the time symmetry, because, the film on matter gushing out from a white hole cannot be run backwards as nothing, not even light, can fall within a white hole. Thus time symmetry forbids the existence of both black holes and white holes.

CHAPTER 11

No Real Theoretical Evidence for Black Hole Formation

Truth is stranger than fiction, but it is because Fiction is obliged to stick to possibilities; Truth isn't – Mark Twain

KEY POINTS: On face value, Oppenheimer and Snyder did show that if a star having uniform density would undergo free fall, it would turn into a black hole. But such a free fall is possible only when one ignores all real-life physics effects like pressure, pressure gradient, viscosity and outward flow of heat and radiation. In fact, Oppenheimer and Snyder mentioned that 'Physically, such a singularity would mean that the expression used for the energy-momentum tensor does not take account of some essential physical fact which would really *smooth the singularity out*.' They further stressed that 'Further, a star in its early stage of development would not possess a singular density or pressure; *it is impossible for a singularity to develop in a finite time*.'*

* J.R. Oppenheimer, H. Snyder, 'On Continued Gravitational Contraction', Physical Review, 56, (1939), p. 455

> Indeed, it has been shown that the Oppenheimer and Snyder collapse is an empty mathematical exercise. All such real-life physics effects can be absent only for vacuum and not matter. Hence, in reality, they never showed the formation of any black hole or any singularity.
>
> Instead, for realistic continued gravitational collapse, the collapsing stars keep on getting hotter and hotter, and there is tentative theoretical evidence that they end up as ultra-hot balls of plasma.

For a moment, let us consider the gravitational collapse of a spherical star in good old Newtonian gravitation. First of all, all stars possess kinetic pressure due to the random motion of their atoms/molecules/ions. In addition, stars have heat and radiation. Thus the forces acting on a section of the stars have several aspects:

(i) *Attractive* force due to its own gravity
(ii) *Repulsive* pressure or gradient-induced buoyancy force, which is related to random motion of gas particles
(iii) Various dissipative and resistive forces due to *viscosity*
(iv) Heat and radiation transport (if the cloud is indeed contracting, as per the Kelvin–Helmholtz process)

However, if we are interested in finding an exact solution for the collapse process, we must *ignore all resistive forces* arising from (ii), (iii) and (iv). In other words, pressure must be set to zero: and this is known as the *dust approximation*. Unlike a real gas having pressure, for an assumed *dust*, there are no random motions. So, naturally, 'dust' is always in a state of free fall.

Ignoring all physical effects and using pure Newtonian physics, one can find that the gas cloud having mass M and an initial radius R should collapse to a point (singularity).* Oppenheimer and Snyder too could solve the general relativistic gravitational collapse equations only after throwing away all the crucial physics. And surprisingly, they *obtained exactly the same expression for the time required for collapse* (as seen by an observer moving along with the dust, i.e., comoving observer).

In fact, the expression for free fall speed too is exactly same in both the cases.** Thus *when one ignores pressure, viscosity and radiation forces, at least in this case, general relativity almost reduces to Newtonian gravity!*

> If we ignore pressure and heat, the Sun should collapse to a point in about 27 minutes. But it is known that by virtue of the Kelvin–Helmholtz process, *even in the absence of any nuclear fusion at its core, the Sun would keep on radiating for almost 9 million years!*

Oppenheimer–Snyder Paper Actually Said 'No Black Hole'

Oppenheimer and Snyder admitted that they set pressure = 0 only for *mathematical tractability and not because a star will be pressure-less once it begins its contraction following the exhaustion of nuclear fuel at its core.*[1] They also admitted that the mathematical singularity in their paper arises because they threw away all physics for the sake of an 'exact solution': 'Physically,

* $t_{sing} = \sqrt{(R^3/2M)}$, where we have ignored a numerical factor of $\pi/2$.

** $v_{ff} = \sqrt{(2M/R)}$

such a singularity would mean that the expression used for the energy-momentum tensor does not take account of some essential physical fact which would really *smooth the singularity out*.'[2]

Finally, they wrote that in realistic cases, even within the context of general relativity, there should be no singularity: 'Further, a star in its early stage of development would not possess a singular density or pressure; *it is impossible for a singularity to develop in a finite time*'.[3] In fact, it has been explicitly shown that an Oppenheimer–Snyder collapse is a mathematical illusion as it corresponds to dust density approaching zero.[4]

It is so unfortunate that most general relativists ignored this crucial physics discussion by Oppenheimer and Snyder, and instead got carried away by the mathematics pertaining to an absolutely unrealistic assumption of a free fall. It is certainly one of the greatest scientific ironies that this paper is credited with the final proof about black hole formation.

In contrast, my research has highlighted the important role played by gas pressure in slowing down gravitational collapse.[5] Thus, in a strict sense, there is no theoretical evidence that the gravitational collapse of massive stars can give rise to finite mass black holes.

Radiative Collapse

As a star undergoes gravitational contraction, its *negative* gravitational energy keeps on growing in magnitude. Then in order to *conserve the total energy*, the star has to generate an equal amount of *positive* energy. While part of the released positive energy is used in heating up the star, the rest must be radiated away. Thus physical gravitational collapse must always be accompanied by due emission of radiation, may be in the form of photons and neutrinos.

In the general relativity context, the inevitability of radiative collapse was first highlighted by me in 2006,[6] where I concluded that *radiation-less mathematical collapse should tacitly correspond to no collapse*, because zero pressure condition is realized only for zero density. Indeed later, I could show this explicitly for collapse of an assumed uniform density sphere, which has been studied for almost fifty years.[7]

Fortunately, there are relatively more physical studies of radiative gravitational collapse. In a paper entitled 'Radiating Fluid Spheres in General Relativity',[8] Bayin probably first gave hint that it may be possible to have quasi-static radiating fluid spheres as the end product of continued collapse, something like the radiating supermassive stars considered by Hoyle and Fowler in the 1960s. Later, research done by several other authors too has suggested the possibility of having quasi-static *radiating fluid spheres as the end product of continued gravitational collapse.*[9]

> For instance, the paper by B.C. Tewari, a senior professor and relativist from Kumaun University, offered the model for a supermassive star having 22 million solar mass, a luminosity of 200 trillion times that of the Sun. While such a radiating star cannot be strictly static; it is quasi-static and hence has a very long yet finite lifetime.[9]

Recently, Tewari and his co-workers have presented examples of a likely *horizon-free eternal collapse*: 'Since, for this class of models, the collapse begins at infinite past and continues in the finite present, such models may be considered as examples of "Eternal Collapse".'[10]

Further, it has been tentatively found that the central engines of quasars might be super-massive relativistic radiation pressure supported stars or Eternally Collapsing Objects.[11] Thus, at least, in principle, it might be possible that the physical gravitational collapse of massive stars leads to the formation of ultra-compact hot ball of plasma in lieu of any black hole.

CHAPTER 12

Pillars of the Black Hole Paradigm Crumbled

An expert is someone who knows some of the worst mistakes that can be made in his subject, and how to avoid them – Werner Heisenberg

KEY POINTS: Contrary to the foundational premises of the black hole paradigm,

- A physically significant measurable quantity 'acceleration due to gravity' blows up at the event horizon, which indicates that it is a physical singularity.
- A free-falling observation can very well detect the event horizon by measuring a certain quantity that becomes zero at the event horizon. This shows that the event horizon is no 'coordinate effect' and indeed a physically significant unique surface (physical singularity).

The black hole paradigm insists on the following:

(i) The event horizon is a perfectly normal region where no singular or special physical events occur. Even the fact that there cannot be a static observer at the event horizon was earlier blamed on the defect of the Hilbert radial coordinate R rather than on any genuine singular physical effect.

(ii) Since the event horizon is such a normal surface without any physical oddity, no free falling observer crossing it can ever detect it.

But both these assertions, on the strength of which the black hole paradigm had shrugged off critiques against itself since 1916, were found to be false by the early 1980s. Unfortunately, these landmark results appeared as insignificant publications in relatively unimportant journals and were either overlooked or eventually ignored.

Acceleration Diverges at the Event Horizon

Why can nothing, not even light, escape the black hole surface? The physical answer to this question came only in 1981, almost sixty-five years after the notion of black holes arose when an innocuous-looking article appeared in *The American Journal of Physics.*[1] This paper pointed out that for a spherically symmetric static body, in the general relativity case, the Newtonian acceleration due to gravity gets enhanced by a factor of $(1+z)$, where z is the gravitational compactness.*

As emphasized earlier, at the event horizon, one has $(1+z) =\infty$. Accordingly, the *surface gravity at the event horizon diverges (becomes infinite).*

This result cannot be shrugged off by the convenient plea that there cannot be any observer sitting at the event horizon for any measurement. But

* $(1+z) = 1/\sqrt{(1- 2M/R)}$

1. There can be static observers arbitrarily close to the event horizon, say, trillionth and trillionth of a cm above. The observers will find that the acceleration is indeed blowing up.
2. The gravitational redshift/compactness of the event horizon is measurable and infinite.
3. The acceleration appears as a scalar invariant, which is independent of the coordinates used.

Conversely, this is the reason we must impart an infinite upwards thrust to keep an observer static at the event horizon. This is the physical reason that there cannot be a static observer there. This is also the physical reason that even light cannot escape the event horizon.

> Therefore, the reason that there cannot be a static observer at the event horizon is really not any defect of the radial coordinate R but due to the fact that *the acceleration due to gravity becomes infinite at the event horizon.* Since surface gravity is a measurable quantity, *its divergence indicates that the event horizon is a physical singularity.*

Event Horizon Very Much Detectable

Another 'strong' pillar of the black hole paradigm fell apart in 1982 in view of a seemingly insignificant research note.[2]

This paper showed the existence of the scalar invariant, now known as the *Karlhede invariant*, related to the space-time curvature. In the exterior of the black hole, this invariant is negative. But at the event horizon, it turns zero. Further, inside the black hole, it becomes positive.

> A free falling observer can *very well detect the event horizon* by measuring the zero value of the Karlhede invariant.
>
> Thus, one of the main pillars of the black hole paradigm crumbled with the publication of this harmless 'research note'.

Later, it became known that there were at least two more such invariants that can enable detection of the event horizon. Further, such invariants exist for all varieties of black holes, like spinning charged black holes.[3]

There is one 1990 research paper that reported that the general relativistic equivalent of Newtonian forces diverge at the event horizon.[4] Such a divergence shows the unphysical singular character of the black hole surface, and it is very much anticipated as the surface gravity of a black hole is infinite.

In 1989, Thanu Padmanabhan showed that an important quantity (*phase space volume*) responsible for the thermodynamical properties of a star *would blow up if the star would ever contract up to its Schwarzschild radius.*[5]

CHAPTER 13

Non-occurrence of True Black Holes

The intellect has little to do on the road to discovery. There comes a leap in consciousness, call it intuition or what you will. The solution comes to you and you don't know how or why – Albert Einstein

KEY POINTS: During 2000–02, I published two research papers that for the first time claimed to offer proof that that general relativistic gravitational collapse inhibits the formation of exact black holes. My papers contain three independent parallel treatments:

1. If a material particle would ever hit any event horizon, its time-like path would turn light like, which is prohibited.
2. The only exact solution of black hole formation involving pressure-less matter is an illusion. Such a pressure-less matter is never formed, and mathematical black holes formed in such a collapse are mass-less. Therefore, so-called black holes must be only quasi-black holes.

> 3. If any trapped surface or event horizon forms during stellar collapse, again, the matter-like paths of stellar material would turn light like.
>
> While proof (1) and (2) were correct (see 'Technical Note'), (3) was confusing and *prima facie* erroneous. Proof (3) involved the result of an observer sitting by a given stellar material.
>
> I removed this confusion later and offered the correct proof in 2004.

We have seen that, starting from Einstein, more than two dozen noted general relativists have been reluctant to accept the idea of mathematical black holes possessing event horizons and singularities. But as of 1998, no one had given a precise reason as to

1. Why can there not be a finite mass true black hole?
2. Why must physical gravitational collapse avoid the formation of true black holes?
3. Why may gravitational collapse not yield any true black hole despite the exact Oppenheimer–Snyder solution?

Yet, I decided to explore such issues when I was working in isolation. I had hardly studied general relativity ever, was not a member of any general relativity society and had never attended any conference or workshop on general relativity. The primary agenda of my institute, the Bhabha Atomic Research Centre (BARC), was research on nuclear science and technology, and it only pursued observational gamma ray astronomy in a modest way. In fact, the research in theoretical astrophysics started by me in Kashmir in the late 1980s was often frowned upon, and others were discouraged to work with me.

Note that while the event horizon of a black hole is a static and eternal feature, there is a concept of the formation of a dynamic, running, non-permanent horizon within the collapsing star, known as 'apparent horizon'. Like the event horizon, the region within an apparent horizon too contains trapped surfaces from within which not even light can move outward. *Accordingly, it was believed that if a massive star would collapse into a black hole, the associated cosmic explosion would be much weaker than a typical supernova event.*

The original motivation behind my research was to understand the origin of cosmic gamma-ray bursts (GRBs) whose energy output could be even a thousand times more than that of supernovae explosions (under the assumption of isotropy).

This is what goaded me to introspect whether trapped surfaces and black holes (with finite mass) are really allowed by general relativity. While thinking so, I was fully aware that such a line of questioning would not only isolate me from the world ruled by the believers but also quite possibly endanger my career as a professional physicist. Indeed, the then BARC Physics Group bosses almost finished off my career, and I was asked to work for reactor physics or defence projects.

Note that in 1939, Oppenheimer and Snyder's dust collapse implicitly suggested the formation of trapped surfaces sometime during the free fall collapse of the dust ball.

Inspired by this example of free-fall dust collapse, in the late 1960s, noted mathematical physicist Roger Penrose (1931–) introduced the idea of the formation of trapped surfaces *for all cases of continued general relativistic gravitational collapse.*

Thus, without any justification, he tacitly assumed that even realistic gravitational collapses that involve various resistive effects like pressure gradient, viscosity, heat generation, heat flow and radiation flow must also qualitatively behave like super-idealized dust collapse.

Later by 1970 or so, Roger Penrose, Stephen Hawking and Robert Geroch established 'singularity theorems', *under the assumption that continued gravitational collapse must lead to formation of trapped surfaces*. Under this crucial assumption, singularity theorems showed that continued gravitational collapse too must lead to the formation of gravitational singularities, as is believed to exist within black holes.

Though most astrophysicists think that there is a proof for the formation of trapped surfaces, in reality, there is none; *it is merely a grandiose assumption*. This has been admitted by Charles Misner, Kip Thorne and John Archibald Wheeler[1]. Similarly, Weinberg too wrote: 'However, it is not known whether a real massive star will actually develop a trapped surface.'[2] In the same context, he added: 'A realistic discussion… would require that we consider the effects of radiative energy transport, neutrino energy transport, turbulence, nuclear forces, magnetic fields, and above all rotations.'[3]

It is also interesting to note the comments made by Marcus Kriele, a mathematical relativist from the Fields Institute for Research in Mathematical Sciences, Canada. He pointed out that there is no proof for the occurrence of trapped surfaces and 'under normal circumstances such a trapped surface can only occur inside the black hole region. Thus the *singularity theorems seem to be inapplicable for predicting the formation of a singularity before a black hole forms*.'[4] Kriele's comments essentially mean that:

> Penrose and Hawking *actually assumed what they set out to prove,* by assuming the most crucial part of the proof, namely, the inevitability of the formation of trapped surfaces!

My Research on the Non-occurrence of Trapped Surface

In 1998, I submitted two preprints in *Physical Review Letters* claiming that trapped surfaces should not form in physical gravitational collapse and cosmic gamma rays are super powerful explosions associated with the birth of horizon-less massive compact objects.[5] Though they were rejected, the comments by the referees were mixed and not disparaging at all. The fact that these preprints appeared reasonably convincing may be gauged from the fact that they were later cited by some of the leading astrophysicists.[6]

In order to get my arguments cross-checked, I sent my preprints to Prof. P.C. Vaidya (1918–2010) who had pioneered research in physical gravitational collapse by formulating the Vaidya metric, which describes the exterior space-time of a star undergoing radiative collapse. His landmark research got published way back in 1951. Vaidya is known to be one of the pioneers of the golden age of general relativity and is also one of the founders of the journal *General Relativity and Gravitation*.

He is equally famous for his simplicity and integrity and for being a true Gandhian. Later in his life, he became the

Fig. 15 Prof. Prahalad Chunnilal Vaidya (1918–2010).

vice chancellor of Gujarat University and would arrive at his office by riding his bicycle and wearing a dhoti. Since we had never met before in any capacity, I was ready for the possibility that he might not respond to my request for critical comments at all.

Surprisingly, his reply came early. Vaidya received my letter on 2 May 1998 and posted his reply on 4 May. His essential comment was that I was on the right track and he did not see any flaw in my application of general relativity.

Having received this very positive feedback from a pioneer, I wrote a long manuscript that attacked the problem not only from the angle of gravitational collapse but also from other related directions. In 1999, I submitted three hardcopies of this fairly massive manuscript to *Foundations of Physics* by postal mail. However, I got no response from the editor despite two reminders.

After three months, as a last resort, I wrote to one of the members on the editorial board of the journal. This board member was none other than the celebrated theoretical physicist Gerard 't Hooft, and he promised to talk to the editor. It is only after this nudge from 't Hooft that the editor eventually wrote back to me.

He said that though he had sent my manuscript to several referees, no one responded. But he promised that he would make fresh endeavours to have it reviewed. Simultaneously, he suggested that I should resubmit the manuscript to *Foundation of Physics Letters*. Seven referees reviewed the manuscript, and the editor accepted it for publication only after two referees endorsed it. And it was published online on 2 December 2000.[7]

This preprint was noted by innumerable readers while it was online for almost one-and-a-half years even before its publication. Once it was accepted, it received much more traction, and I received positive and even congratulatory comments from several general relativists and astrophysicists. However, two famous American physicist bloggers even derided me as a 'crackpot'. In 2002, another paper extending this work was published in the same journal, which insisted that the final state of continued gravitational collapse should be quasi-static ultra-compact objects whose size should practically be equal to those of theoretical black holes of equivalent mass, which should keep on contracting indefinitely to asymptotically attain the exact black hole state.[8]

However, I realized later that as far as the central proof about the non-formation of trapped surfaces is concerned, there was a crucial confusion in all my preprints and papers. The proof involves a quantity that is the rate of change of the area radius of the star with comoving proper time. Here, I was following a famous 1965 research paper written by R.W. Lindquist, R.A. Schwarz and the revered C.W. Misner.[9] Equation 3.2 of this paper *expresses this contraction speed (U) as a total rate of change*. But, in reality, this quantity actually involved only a partial rate of change. And this erroneous expression had misled me. Yet, I fortuitously got the correct result as, from the viewpoint of an observer sitting at a fixed location by the stellar matter,* U indeed behaved like a total derivative. It was only in 2004 that I could publish a perfectly correct proof.[10]

Meanwhile, Leiter and Robertson claimed to offer the same result by using a different and less general treatment.[11] Much later, I got this proof published in a peer-reviewed journal:[12]

1. In this new proof, I essentially showed that if any apparent horizon would form, the matter-like motion

* For a R=fixed observer dR(r,t) =0, where r and t are comoving coordinates moving with the star material. Then it turns out that:

at a fixed R(r,t), $dr/dt = -(\delta R/\delta t)/(\delta R/\delta r)$ and $(dr/dt)^2 = [(\delta R/\delta t)/(\delta R/\delta r)]^2$. Here, δ denotes partial differentiation. And thus my original 2000 result remains valid despite my initial confusion.

of the stellar material would turn light like. Since this is not allowed, no apparent horizon, no black hole can ever form as seen by any observer.

2. However, mathematically speaking, a mass-less black hole can form only asymptotically, after infinite time with respect to any observer. This is the same way an electron may attain the speed of light, following hypothetical eternal acceleration.

In other words, continued general relativistic collapse of sufficiently massive stars should continue indefinitely and lead to eternally collapsing objects rather than exact black holes.

Einstein equations remain unchanged if one would replace +t by −t, i.e., they obey the time reversal symmetry. Accordingly, one must be able to conceive of situations where matter and light, inexorably hurtling inwards inside a trapped region, are able to run outwards even from a *singularity*. But by the very definition of event and apparent horizons, not even light can move outwards inside a trapped region. Therefore, contrary to mathematical hypothesis of Roger Penrose, Einstein equations should not allow the formation of any event horizon, any apparent horizon, any trapped region, and finally any black hole. My research confirmed this by removing trapped surfaces.

Does Raychaudhri Equation Predict Formation of Black Holes?

The singularity theorems of Roger Penrose and Stephen Hawking rely on some generic results of evolving self-gravitating matter derived by the noted Indian relativist Amal Kumar Raychaudhuri (1923–2005) in 1955[13]. Raychaudhuri showed that the trajectories of free falling self-gravitating matter tend to come closer and closer irrespective of non-uniformity and asymmetry (shear) of the matter distribution. In essence this is a restatement of the known fact that gravitation remains attractive even in all complex situations. In particular if one would ignore all resistive effects arising from (a) buoyancy force due to pressure gradient; (b) viscosity, heat and radiation flow; and (c) magnetic field, the free-falling matter would hit a gravitational singularity in a finite time.

Nonetheless, as admitted by Raychaudhuri himself[14], his result is almost equivalent to what one would obtain from Newtonian gravitation. In effect, this result is similar to the fact that both Newtonian gravity and general relativity (apparently) suggest that a pressure-less ball of dust collapses to a singular point in exactly the same comoving time; and general relativity (GR) almost reduces to Newtonian gravity when one ignores the physical effects (a-c) (See Chapter 11). On the other hand, when one would include any such real life complexities (a-c), there may be no singularity formation either in Newtonian gravity or GR.

In 2006, a Greek relativist, Christos Tsagas studied the gravitational collapse of pressure-less dust embedded with magnetic field[15]. He found that there is a component of magnetic stress that not only opposes the gravitational attraction but could eventually prevent formation of any singularity. It is of utmost importance here to note that gravitational *singularity may be avoided by some tangible classical effect* (here, magnetic stress) and not necessarily due to any unknown and speculative Quantum Gravity effect.

Thus as far as real life physical gravitational collapse is concerned, both the singularity theorems as well as Raychaudhuri equations have no or little utility.

CHAPTER 14

Static Black Hole Alternatives

The unexamined life is not worth living – Socrates

KEY POINTS: My initial preprints and papers showing the non-occurrence of exact black holes, published during 1998–2002, were noted globally if not acknowledged. Following this, several researchers came up with models for black hole alternatives. However, they could think of models that are strictly static ones. But since standard physics cannot yield static compact objects more massive than neutron stars, these authors were compelled to offer highly speculative and exotic models. One of the prominent static models for a black hole alternative is the 'gravastar', while another is the 'dark energy star'. Such models hypothesize that immediately before the formation of black holes, stellar matter undergoes strong unphysical phase changes and transforms itself to *negative pressure* vacuum or extreme Bose–Einstein condensate. Similarly, it has also been hypothesized that stellar matter made of protons, neutrons, electrons and photons somehow transform themselves into bare elementary strings and the star turns into a 'fuzzball'. The fuzzball model, however, does not explain how a fuzzball resists the infinite pull of gravity. All such models tacitly assume the occurrence of extreme quantum gravity phase transitions immediately before the event horizon formation. This assumption, however, is unjustified because both density and space-time curvature near the event horizon can be arbitrarily small for supermassive black hole candidates.

Indeed, till date, nobody could explain how such exotic *static* models could be formed in gravitational collapse.

My preprints and papers published during 1998–2002 claimed to have proven the non-existence of exact black holes for the first time. I offered three parallel lines of proof to drive home the same point. In fact, one of them was confusing and, in a strict sense, incorrect, which, however, was corrected later. Most mainstream general relativists, even within India, would never admit that many aspects of my research were novel and at least convincing in many ways. Yet, 2002 onwards, several authors argued that black holes are unphysical and offered models of black hole alternatives. Of course, none of them ever cited my papers, which would certainly be below their dignity.

However, I have no hesitation in citing them and discussing their interesting research below.[1]

Gravitational Vacuum Condensate Stars (Gravastars)

All the stars, all the matter, we know of possess positive pressure, which contributes to gravitational attraction. But mathematically, one can imagine a fluid whose gravity is repulsive. In 1917, Einstein was compelled to hypothesize that vacuum has an inherent repulsive property in order to impart stability to his model of a static universe. Such a repulsive vacuum has an extreme requirement: its pressure is not only negative but also, in magnitude, equal to the mass–energy density of vacuum. In contrast, the positive pressure of air in a room could be one trillion times lower than its mass–energy density. Since 1998, such a fictitious repulsive and invisible energy, possessing extreme negative pressure, has been known as 'dark energy', and cosmologists hypothesized its existence in order to explain supposed accelerated expansion of the universe.

Following this cue, in 2002, Pawel O. Mazur and Emil Mottola proposed that the so-called gravastar model, which is a bubble of repulsive Dark Energy, has zero temperature.[2] On the surface of this bubble, there is an ultra-thin layer of ultra-relativistic matter straddling the location of the event horizon $R \approx 2M$. While for the interior bubble, the pressure is equal to the negative of its density,* for the ultra-thin material layer, pressure is equal to the positive of its energy density.** The anti-gravity repulsive action of the negative pressure of the dark energy bubble supports the weight of the overlying layer of matter.

Mazur and Motolla envisaged that the vacuum bubble having negative pressure is the result of Bose–Einstein condensation. But there is no model of gravitational collapse that can convert stellar matter comprising electrons, protons,

* $P = -\rho c^2$

* $P = +\rho c^2$

neutrons and radiation into dark energy having negative pressure. Furthermore, Bose–Einstein condensations are regularly studied in laboratories, and they never create *any negative pressure or convert matter into vacuum.*

Indeed, there is no model of gravitational collapse that suggests the formation of gravastars.

Dark Energy Stars

In 2005, George Chapline proposed that the dark energy stars[2] are quite similar to gravastars. Chapline insisted that general relativity must break down near the R≈2M surface, and there will be a lot of new physics that would cause quantum phase transition. He began with an exotic, almost wishful thinking: 'If one visualizes the vacuum as analogous to the ground state of a condensed matter system and ordinary matter as analogous to excited states of this system, then it follows that the atoms in the condensed matter system must move without collective rotation.'

Later Chapline suggested that the behaviour of space-time in dark energy stars is very similar to superfluids, a kind of fluid that has no electrical resistance at all. But I severely criticized the hypotheses of Chaplin in another preprint in the same year.[3]

Fuzzballs

String theory proposes that the fundamental constituents of subatomic particles, including the force carriers, are composed of incredibly tiny one-dimensional strings,and it *denies* the existence of point particles. *If so one would expect string theory to inhibit the formation of black holes or any other singularity. But ironically string theory interprets several solutions as black hole states possessing due singularities.*

In 2005, Samir D. Mathur of Ohio State University proposed that the so-called black holes are not vacuum at all but a non-singular ball of strings.[4] The classical radius of a fuzzball is exactly the same as that of a black hole even though the surface is irregular or fuzzy on the scale of Planck length. Even assuming that string theory indeed allows such a singularity-free black hole alternative, there are severe problems with the fuzzball proposal:

- For any massive static configuration, there must be sources of negative pressure or other resistive agents. But the fuzzball proposal does not even address this crucial issue let alone resolve them.
- Most importantly, how does matter, during gravitational collapse, comprising protons, neutrons and electrons, turn into a ball of tangled elementary strings near the event horizon? Such a pure quantum gravity state is marked by the incredibly high Planck temperature,* which is roughly *trillion times larger* than the highest energy attained by the most powerful man-made accelerator, namely, the *Large Hadron Collider.*

Should the star not detonate itself under such strong radiation pressure much before it can attain such an incredible temperature, which may be necessary for elementary strings to be in the open?

For all such models, one must pose the following question: For conventional quantum gravity arguments, strong quantum fluctuations can happen only near the

* Around 10^{30} K

singularity at spatial dimensions close to the Planck length,* an incredibly tiny distance, almost a billionth trillionth trillionth of a centimetre. Thus there is no basis for the hypothesis that super-strong quantum fluctuations occur near the event horizon.

Accordingly, we conclude that the ideas of gravastars, dark stars and fuzzballs are unphysical and inconsistent.

We know that as per the black hole hypothesis, matter falling within a black hole may emerge out in a parallel universe through its interior white hole. Such a combination of a black hole and a white hole is broadly known as a 'wormhole'. Sometimes, in desperate search for black hole alternatives, which are even more exotic, more unreal than black holes, wormholes too are invoked. But most general relativists admit that wormholes are nice only for science fiction and cannot occur in reality.[5] This is the reason we do not discuss this topic any further.

* $\sim 10^{-33}$ cm

CHAPTER 15

Why Eternally Collapsing Objects (ECOs)

And a heaven in a wild flower, Hold infinity in the palm of your hand, And eternity in an hour – William Blake

> KEY POINTS: As mentioned earlier, the gravitational collapse of massive stars can result in a perfectly static compact object like gravastar or dark energy star if one assumes mysterious quantum gravitational phase transitions. But no such unphysical effects are there in real life. Further, since no apparent horizon or trapped surface is formed, continued collapse must, mathematically, approach the formation of $E=Mc^2=0$ black holes. But since at the event horizon of a M=0 black hole, stellar matter would turn light like, even such a black hole is not allowed. Hence, the collapse of massive stars must give birth to eternally collapsing objects (ECOs).
>
> As the contracting star would dip below its photon sphere, sooner or later, the gravitationally trapped radiation would attain its Eddington value and the outward radiation pressure would halt the contraction.

Nonetheless, infinitely slow shrinking would continue indefinitely towards the M=0 black hole state. So instead of a vacuum black hole with a central point singularity, the massive star ends up as an ultra-hot ball of fire/plasma. And stellar mass ECOs are locally so hot that they are balls of quark-gluon plasma, a molten state of protons and neutrons. This result may be inevitable because trapping of own radiation beneath the photon sphere is the *only generic general relativity effect associated with continued collapse.*

My later publications[1] correctly showed that in order that stellar matter keeps moving like 'matter' and not like light, *the radius of any spherical section of the star must always be larger than the horizon radius.**

Therefore, if the star is assumed to collapse all the way to a point mass having zero radius, the gravitational mass of the star too must reduce to zero. Such a final state (R=0, M=0) would correspond to the formation of the event horizon (R=2M=0) of a zero mass black hole.

But even the formation of a zero mass black hole is not allowed in order to ensure that *matter can never move like light*. Thus, at the most, a zero mass black hole can form only *asymptotically* and never in practice. In other words, continued gravitational collapse must be eternal, unless some static compact object like a white dwarf or a neutron star is formed.

Thus, irrespective of all details, continued collapse of massive stars must result in ECOs.

* Radius > 2 x Mass; R > 2M. Therefore, if Radius →0, one must have M→0 too.

And the asymptotic ultimate state will be a zero mass black hole: $E=Mc^2=0$.

A most natural question here will be:

How can a star of finite size keep on contracting eternally?

Look, when we say that a star has a radius of R, we mean that its surface area is $4\pi R^2$. In Newtonian physics, where the space-time is *flat*, this would immediately mean that the physical depth of the star too is R. But this is not so in the *curved space-time* of general relativity. In the presence of the attractive gravity of the star, *the physical or actual depth of the star is larger than the externally perceived radius R.* Crudely, this is like the fact that the actual distance between two towns on a hilly terrain is always larger than the crow flight distance between them.

Let us revert to the radial part of the space-time structure around a black hole:

Space-time Interval = $(\text{Proper Time})^2 - (\text{Proper Distance})^2$

So if an element of a tiny *crow flight* distance is 'dR', the actual radial or proper distance is larger than dR by a certain factor.* It is easily seen that as one would approach the event horizon, *this space-stretching factor will become infinite.* In fact, this was one of the pathologies associated with the surface of black holes. However, here we are concerned with the *space-stretching factor within the star*, and it is likely that this factor too would turn infinite if one would attempt to dive all the way down to the singularity at (R=0), as if, *an infinite depth may be lurking within all physical objects preventing them from being singular ever.*

* Factor is $\sqrt{(1-2M/R)}$

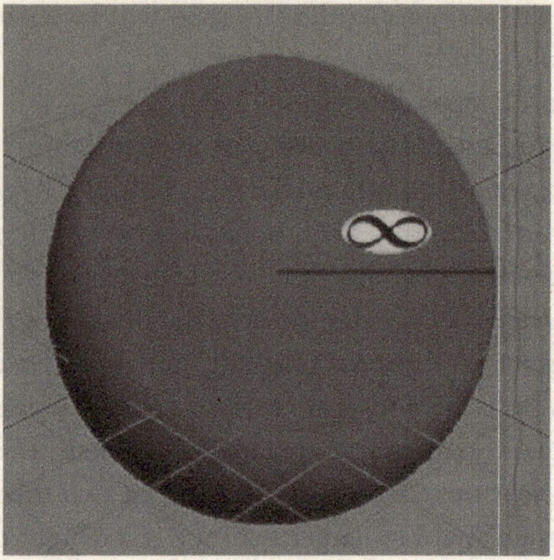

Fig. 16 As if infinite physical depth is hibernating inside any object, which would wake up if it would be compelled to collapse into a 'point'.

How Can an ECO Form?

Black hole alternatives like wormholes, gravastars and fuzzballs are strictly static and cold objects. The space-time exterior to them is a perfect vacuum with no heat no radiation. In contrast:

> An ECO is an ultra-hot ball of fire or plasma, which, in a strict sense, is always contracting and emitting radiation at an infinitesimally slow rate. However, for all practical purposes, it is a static object like an ultra-compact version of the Sun. And it is held against its own intense gravitational pull by its equally intense outward radiation pressure.

Before we appreciate how ECOs are formed, we revisit the idea of the gravitational compactness of a star in terms of its gravitational redshift (z). While for the Sun, the compactness is only of the order of a millionth, a neutron star has a compactness ~0.1. As we think of regions much more compact than a neutron star, first we have the photon sphere. The gravitational compactness on the boundary of the photon sphere* is 0.732. Within the photon sphere, photon trajectories mostly spiral inwards and their chance of escaping out is almost negligible. This chance of escape keeps on further dwindling as photons approach the event horizon where all motions necessarily turn inwards. Ultimately, the most compact region is the event horizon possessing an infinite gravitational compactness. Therefore, the journey from the photon sphere to the event horizon is an infinite trek.[2]

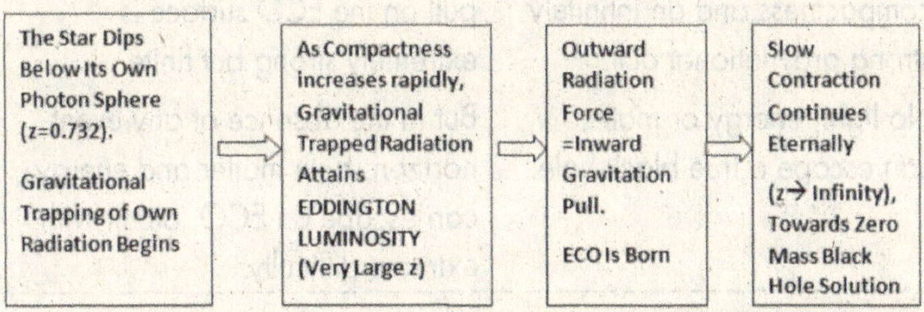

At this stage, the total energy density of the stellar matter density will get overwhelmed by the radiation density.[3] By using such results, it has been estimated that the mean local temperature of an ECO of 10 solar mass** is around 20,000 billion kelvin. At such temperatures, even neutrons and protons melt into a soup of quarks and their binding agent

* $R=3M$

** $T \approx 600\ \text{MeV}\ \sqrt{(M_{\odot}/M)}$ where $M_{\odot}$ is mass of the Sun gluons. In other words, stellar mass black hole candidates are likely to be balls of *quark-gluon plasma.*[4]

The observed lifetime of an ideal ECO could be billions of years, and it keeps on increasing with its compactness. Since black hole formation corresponds to infinite compactness, an ECO can never become a true black hole. The crucial differences between an ECO and a true black hole are as follows:

Mathematical Black Hole	Eternally Collapsing Object (ECO)
A black hole is a vacuum except for its central singularity.	An ECO is a ball of extremely hot plasma (ionized matter). There is no singularity at its centre.
A black hole has only an imaginary surface, which has an infinite gravitational compactness and an infinitely strong gravitational pull.	The gravitational compactness of an ECO is extremely large but finite. Similarly, the gravitational pull on the ECO surface is extremely strong but finite.
No light, energy or matter can escape a true black hole.	But in the absence of any event horizon, both matter and energy can escape an ECO, albeit with extreme difficulty.

Indeed, an ECO is an unstable state and is vulnerable to unpredictable instabilities. It is because of such unpredictable instabilities that an ECO is likely to undergo various eruptions unlike a *cold* neutron star. And this may be the reason that the so-called black hole X-ray binaries *are much more violent than their neutron star counterparts.*

Accordingly, ECOs are much better suited to explain explosive flaring activities from so-called astrophysical black holes than the mathematical vacuum black holes.

CHAPTER 16

Why Magnetospheric Eternally Collapsing Objects (MECOs)

We can know only that we know nothing. And that is the highest degree of human wisdom – Leo Tolstoy

KEY POINTS: All astrophysical plasma invariably contain some seed magnetic field (B), and the number of magnetic lines of force threading a star remains constant during its gravitational contraction. Thus, if the radius of the star will contract 10 times, the closeness of the lines of force will increase 100 times. In other words, the magnetic field strength of the star will increase by a factor of 100. This is the reason that neutron stars with only R ~10 km have B ~ 1 trillion gauss (on the surface of the Sun, B ~ 1 gauss). If the plasma further contracts towards its event horizon, general relativistic effects would give rise to additionally stronger magnetic fields. Hence, ECOs, almost as compact as black holes, are bound to be magnetospheric ECOs or MECOs. Faraway observers, however, see much weaker magnetic fields due to the strong gravitational compactness of MECOs. In 2006, there was a press release by the Harvard-Smithsonian Center for Astrophysics that claimed that the so-called supermassive black hole in the quasar QSO 0957+561 is a MECO in view of its strong dipole-type intrinsic magnetic field. The relatively strong magnetic fields found around many astrophysical black holes can be readily understood by realizing that they are actually MECOs.

The neighbouring magnetic fields of some *MECOs can, however, be weaker if they have unusually large surface gravitational compactness.*

Though astrophysical plasma is quasi-neutral, it can generate some seed magnetic field due to relative motions between ions and electrons driven by localized rotations. If the plasma is highly conductive, then the number of magnetic lines of force threading a given cross-section remains conserved. So whenever an astrophysical plasma contracts, the magnetic lines of force are squeezed together, and the field strength increases as the inverse square of the radius, i.e., if the radius decreases by a factor of 10, the field increases by a factor of 100.

This is essentially the reason that a newborn neutron star having a radius of around 10 km gets endowed with a magnetic field of hundreds of billions of gauss. Since ECOs are much more compact than neutron stars, they can easily have a stronger magnetic field. General relativistic effects further enhance this magnetic field during contraction of the star near a would-be event horizon, as was first suggested by the great Russian theoretical physicist Vitaly Ginzburg in 1964.[1]

Consequently, ultra-compact ECOs of stellar masses can easily possess magnetic fields as high as ten thousand trillion gauss.

Accordingly, Stanley Robertson, Darryl Leiter and I rechristened the astrophysical ECOs as *magnetospheric eternally collapsing objects* (MECOs).

> *There have been indirect and relatively more direct evidence that many astrophysical black hole candidates possess intrinsic magnetic fields. Such evidence suggests that the so-called astrophysical black holes could be MECOs.*

Indirect Evidence for MECOs

Here, we briefly discuss that some of the observations associated with the so-called stellar mass black holes may be better understood by realizing that they are actually MECOs.

In high-energy astrophysics, two kinds of X-ray binaries are of special importance:

1. neutron star X-ray binaries (NSXBs) and
2. black hole candidate X-ray binaries (BHCXBs).

The luminosities of some NSXBs may suddenly increase by a factor of thousands for a few days. Such sudden transient behaviour is understood in terms of a *tug of war between the*

- outward magnetic pressure of the neutron stars and
- the inward ram pressure of the accreting plasma.

Surprisingly, most BHCXBs too are transient. But since true black holes devoid of any intrinsic magnetic field *cannot exert any outward magnetic pressure*, there cannot be any such tug of war. Accordingly, there is no real cogent explanation for state transitions in BHCXBs.

But Robertson and Leiter attempted to explain the changes of spectral states of both NSXBs and BHCXBs occurring over periods of several years on *a common platform by assuming the BHCXBs to contain MECOs instead of black holes.*[2]

Also, many NSXRBs and BHCXBs emit radio waves apart from X-rays. There is a certain relationship between the radio and X-ray luminosities of the two apparently *distinct classes of binaries*. Yet, surprisingly, this relationship is practically the same for both the cases. *This suggests the existence of some intrinsic similarity between the physical nature of variable NSXBs and BHCXBs.* Robertson and Leiter also explained this almost common relationship between the radio and X-ray luminosities of BHCXBs and NSXBs by proposing that the former contains magnetized compact objects (MECOs) like the latter (NS).[3]

More Direct Evidence for MECOs

For a non-magnetized black hole, the inner radius of the accretion disk is located at 3 Schwarzschild radii ($3R_s$). However, if the compact object is a strongly magnetized MECO, its magnetic field can push the accretion disk much beyond, the same way a magnetized neutron star can push the accretion disk away. Indeed, a similar effect was inferred for the following quasar.

In 2006, Rudy E. Schild of Harvard-Smithsonian Center for Astrophysics and his co-workers[4] presented evidence that

> The inner edge of the accretion disk of the quasar QSO 0957+561 appearing as a bright luminous ring is located at *35 Schwarzschild radii*, when for an un-magnetized black hole, it should have been only at *3 Schwarzschild radii.*

In view of the importance of this landmark observation evidence, on 25 July 2006, the Harvard-Smithsonian Center for Astrophysics issued a press release (No. 06-21) entitled 'New Picture of Quasar Emerges'. Here are few excerpts from this press release:

> 'This quasar appears to be dynamically dominated by a magnetic field internally anchored to its central, rotating supermassive compact object,' stated Schild.
>
> 'Our finding challenges the accepted view of black holes,' said Leiter.
>
> 'We've even proposed a new name for them – Magnetospheric Eternally Collapsing Objects, or MECOs, a variant of the name first coined by Indian astrophysicist Abhas Mitra in 1998.'

Later, a similar inner structure was found in another quasar Q2237.[5] Further, studies of 55 more quasars too indicated the presence of inner magnetic field-controlled structures, similar to the one found in QSO 0957.[6]

Such studies suggest that all quasars may contain MECOs in lieu of black holes. The detailed physics of X-ray emission and radio emission from Sgr A*, the black hole candidate at the centre of our galaxy Milky Way, may too be well understood in the MECO paradigm.[7]

CHAPTER 17

Have True Black Holes Been Detected?

It is not that I'm so smart. But I stay with the questions much longer – Albert Einstein

> KEY POINTS: Both true black holes and their mimickers possess photon spheres outside them, which behave like virtual event horizons. Accordingly, no faraway telescope can peek inside the photon sphere. Therefore, contrary to the claims made, the 'image' released by the Event Horizon Telescope (EHT) may contain the shadow of the photon sphere and not any event horizon. Similarly, some of the 'ring down' features of gravitational signals recorded by LIGO-Virgo correspond to vibrations of the newly formed photon spheres (or photon rings).
>
> Some of the accreting neutron stars display occasional X-rays bursts resulting from the nuclear fusion of accreted matter on their hard surfaces. But accreting black hole candidates do not undergo any such explosion. Apparently, this confirms that the surfaces of black hole candidates

are event horizons. But matter accreting on a gaseous or liquid MECO would merge with it without accumulating on the surface. Thus, the absence of such bursts is no unique evidence of any event horizon.

We shall briefly dwell on four aspects that claim to have offered direct evidence for the existence of event horizons and, hence, true black holes. It will be found that all the claims are either misleading or incorrect.

1. EHT Has Presented an Image of an Event Horizon

The radius of a black hole mimicker is larger than a black hole of the same mass by a miniscule fraction of one thousand or one million and will hence appear almost equally black to a faraway observer. In Chapter 4, we have already discussed that the central dark circle contained even in the sharpest image of the shadow of a supposed black hole or black hole mimicker would be the shadow of their photon sphere, which is 50 per cent larger than either of them.

This is so because the gravitational field of the black hole or black hole mimicker becomes already so strong at 50 per cent Schwarzschild radius away from their surface, that is, at R=3M, that light rays or photons can move in closed unstable circles. Within the photon sphere, gravity naturally is even stronger, and photons are likely to fall inwards and remain trapped. Accordingly, *the photon sphere acts like a virtual event horizon and appears as a dark sphere.*

Now you may think that the shadow of the black hole or black hole mimicker should then have a radius of 3M. No, it appears even larger. Why?

Because light coming from behind the black hole or black hole mimicker gets bent away by the strong gravity of the photon sphere, the way *concave lenses* diverge away incident light rays. It turns out that, because of gravitational lensing, the shadow of the photon sphere acquires a radius of $3\sqrt{3}$ M, which is approximately 2.6 times larger than the event horizon.[1]

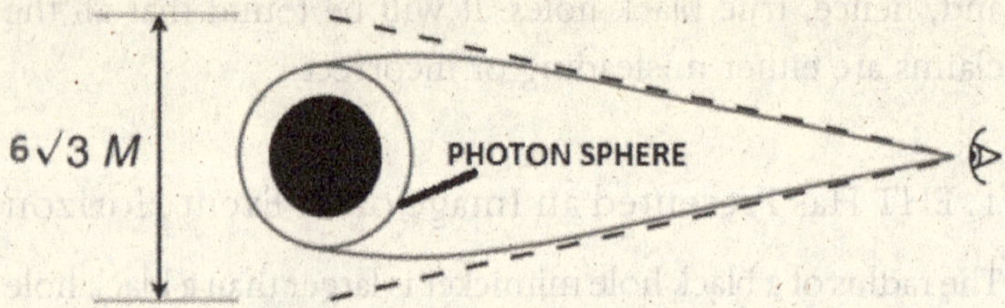

Fig. 17 No telescope can peer below the Photon Sphere of a black hole or its mimicker. Thus a telescope can at the most detect the shadow of this photon sphere. Further the shadow gets enlarged by a factor of $\sqrt{3}$ due to concave lens like bending of light by the strong gravity of the photon sphere.

For a rotating black hole, the photon sphere gets replaced by a photon ring at the equatorial plane. Therefore, the EHT may have released the enlarged shadow of a photon sphere or photon ring and no shadow of any black hole or even its mimicker. From such a shadow, *it is fundamentally impossible to distinguish between a black hole and a black hole mimicker.*

2. LIGO Confirmed Evidence of Event Horizon?

The detection of gravitational wave signals from an event (GW150914) recorded on 14 September 2015 by the Laser Interferometer Gravitational Wave Observatory (LIGO) is a milestone in observational astronomy. This was announced on 11 February 2016 and presumably became the most publicized science news in recent times.

It is expected that the newly formed event horizon resulting from the merger of two compact objects should 'ring', that is, oscillate in shape between a distorted, elongated and flattened spheroid. As this ringing process gets damped, the resultant gravitational waves show a characteristic *ring down* feature. The LIGO observations indeed detected such a ringdown feature in the final gravitational wave burst, which apparently gave a direct evidence of event horizon of the coalesced black hole.

Following this publicity blitzkrieg post 11 February2016, I received more than two-dozen queries from my young Facebook friends. Some of them were quite disparaging and implied that the conclusion of my research papers claiming the non-existence of event horizon had bitten the dust.

During 14–15 February 2016, I happened to interact with a LIGO theoretician Nathan Johnson-McDaniel, who was a postdoctoral fellow at the International Centre for Theoretical Sciences, Tata Institute of Fundamental Research, Bengaluru, India. I congratulated the LIGO team profusely for its success and told them that I had a special reason to be elated – the crucial Indian contribution behind the LIGO data analysis and other associated theories.

But I also insisted that the detected signal must be due to the merger of some quasi-black holes and not due to true black holes possessing event horizons. Initially, Johnson-McDaniel tried to ward off my arguments. Next, he tried to educate me on why black holes are already well established.

Eventually I dragged him to the core argument—the proof about the non-existence of finite mass black holes and their likely alternatives. I sent him a detailed email to this effect on 15 February 2016. But following this, *I never heard back from him.*

However, two months after this, *Physical Review Letters* published the result of a numerical study of the merger of not only black holes but also black hole mimickers (quasi-black holes).[2] This study showed that the main burst of radiation during the early ring down phase is only associated with the vibration modes of the newly formed *photon sphere* (R=3M) and *does not depend* on whether or not the space-time has a horizon (R=2M).

In short, LIGO did not detect any event horizon either in 2015 or later.

3. Non-occurrence of X-ray Bursts at Black Hole Surfaces

Neutron stars in X-ray binaries rip off matter from their companion star and draw it towards their surfaces. Under the intense gravitational grip, the piled up accreted matter develops extremely high temperature and density. Occasionally, such hot and dense plasma may undergo runaway thermonuclear chain reactions or nuclear fusion. As a result, astrophysical neutron stars may occasionally radiate intense flashes of X-rays and soft gamma rays. Typically, such an X-ray burst may radiate the energy released by the Sun in a month in a matter of 10 seconds.

However, astrophysical black hole candidates never undergo such X-ray bursts. Astrophysicists explain such non-occurrence of X-rays bursts by arguing that astrophysical black holes have no hard surface and no matter can accumulate and pile up there.[3]

Such an argument would indeed go against the models of horizon-less compact objects, which are assumed to have 'hard surfaces' like gravastars and fuzzballs. In contrast, MECOs are ultra-hot balls of fluid (gas or liquid) *without any hard surfaces. Matter accreting onto them simply merges with the liquid body of MECOs instead of piling up on its surface.* Hence, the non-occurrence of X-rays bursts from accreting black hole candidates is no evidence against MECOs.[4]

4. No X-Ray Pulses from Astrophysical Black Holes

Accreted plasma, upon heating a neutron star surface, creates X-ray 'hotspots'. As these X-ray hotspots rotate with the neutron star, the X-ray beams too pulse with the same period. Hence, accreting neutron stars are also called X-ray pulsars.

In contrast, X-ray beams from accreting (so-called) black holes do not pulse at all. Astrophysicists usually explain such non-pulsation by arguing that there cannot be any hotspot on black holes as they have no surface at all.

However, while a neutron star gravity is reasonably strong (gravitational compactness ~0.1), the gravity on a black hole mimicker could be thousand or million times stronger (compactness: thousand to million). As a black hole mimicker rotates, it drags the surrounding space-time along. But the rate of rotation of the surrounding space-time falls off rapidly as one moves away from the surface of a black hole mimicker. Consequently, even if the X-ray emission is pulsed at the surface of a black hole mimicker, the pulsation will get completely *smeared away from the surface*.

Thus non-pulsation of X-rays from astrophysical black hole candidates is no evidence that they are true black holes having no physical surface.[5]

Finally, it may be pertinent to recall the wise comments by three European astrophysicists, M.A. Abramowicz, W. Kluźniak and J.P. Lasota, who very much believe in the existence of true black holes:[6]

> Recently, several ways of obtaining observational proof of the existence of black-hole horizons have been proposed. We argue here that such proof is *fundamentally impossible*: observations can provide arguments, sometimes very strong ones, in favour of the existence of the event horizon, but they cannot prove it. This applies also to future observations, which will trace very accurately the details of the spacetime metric of a body suspected of being a black hole.

CHAPTER 18

Fall of the Black Hole Paradigm

It is during our darkest moments that we must focus to see the light
– Aristotle

KEY POINTS: The black hole paradigm may have fallen through because of the following reasons:

- The black hole paradigm asserts that the event horizon is a perfectly normal surface and no physical quantity associated with it can be infinite. But the acceleration due to gravity, a physically significant quantity, indeed becomes infinite there. In fact, all other forces too blow up there, which suggests that the event horizon is a physical singularity. The very fact that measurable gravitational redshift of the event horizon is infinite and nothing, not even light, can escape it had already suggested that the event horizon is a physical singularity.
- The black hole paradigm asserts that the event horizon is such a normal surface that a free-falling observer can never detect it. But in 1982, it was shown that a free-

falling observer *can very well detect the event horizon* by noting the change of sign of a measurable physical quantity (Karlhede invariant) at the event horizon.

- The black hole paradigm fell when my papers showed that the trajectory of a material particle would turn light like if it would ever arrive at the event horizon.
- The black hole paradigm fell with my proof that no apparent horizon, no event horizon, no trapped surface can form in the gravitational collapse of massive stars.

The black hole paradigm assumes that a black hole is a sphere having an arbitrary large mass and radius. But there are several independent proofs showing that a mathematical black hole is point of zero mass and zero radius. Following such proofs, the black hole paradigm falls. Therefore, the so-called black holes must be horizonless compact objects.

The Droste–Hilbert solution, which is at the core of this paradigm, is very nice as long as the radius of a spherical star is larger than its Schwarzschild radius even by a tiniest amount. But in case one would imagine the star to have shrunk to a point (and yet retain a finite mass), the solution displays singular or pathological features at the black hole surface.

Yet, the black hole paradigm got established on the basis of the following arguments:

1. Black holes are physically acceptable because the apparent pathologies at the black hole surface can be removed by several coordinate transformations.

2. All measurable quantities remain finite at the black hole surface. Since, there is nothing unusual or dramatic happening at this surface, a free falling observer cannot detect it despite the presence of apparent singularities.
3. The space-time curvature on the black hole surface is finite.
4. Oppenheimer and Snyder showed that general relativistic gravitational collapse leads to the formation of trapped surfaces and black holes.
5. The singularity theorems of Penrose and Hawking show that continued gravitational collapse must lead to space-time singularities.

And here we repeat some of our earlier arguments countering the above arguments.

How can R ever be a 'bad coordinate' when out of all the radial coordinates invoked for black holes, R is the only one that has a profound physical significance as the luminosity distance? It would be utter physical nonsense to claim that luminosity falls off inversely as of the square of the time.

Furthermore, the original problem of involving a single masspoint is static. But the exotic coordinates that are introduced to remove pathologies of the black hole surface and its interior make the scenario time dependent. While mathematically, everything may be okay, physically, this is an unacceptable self-contradiction.

Removal of singularities from the black hole surface is fallacious. This is so because all of them become singular at the event horizon by virtue of the presence of a factor,* which becomes

* The factor is log (1-2M/R), which becomes minus infinity at R=2M.

minus infinity at the event horizon, *whose singularity such coordinates claim to hide.*

> Accordingly, all such coordinate transformations are unphysical, and the pathological behaviour of the event horizon is genuine. In other words, the event horizon is a physical singularity and no 'coordinate singularity'.

More importantly:

- In 1981, it was highlighted that the *surface gravity of a black hole* (or acceleration due to gravity) *diverges.*[1] Since this surface gravity is a scalar, no coordinate transformation can remove its divergence. Furthermore, the divergence of the acceleration at the event horizon is directly related to the occurrence of *infinite gravitation redshift* of the same surface. This reconfirms that the event horizon is a physical singularity and not a mere coordinate one.
- In 1982, it was found that one can very well *detect the event horizon* by noting that the Karlhede invariant, a scalar made of space-time curvature tensor, becomes zero at the event horizon.[2]
- The only exact analytical solution for the formation of *exact black holes* is due to Oppenheimer and Snyder. They obtained this solution only after burying all physical effects associated with gravitational collapse: viscosity and dissipation, heat and radiation transport, and eventually no pressure at all. They admitted that 'Physically such a singularity would mean that the expression used for the energy-momentum tensor does not take account of some essential physical fact which would really *smooth the singularity out.*'[3]

My papers have indeed shown that *the exact solution for black hole formation is an empty mathematical fallacy* as the mass of the pressure-less dust is tacitly zero (M=0), when the black hole paradigm requires it to be arbitrarily large. If one would still insist for mathematics, dust collapse actually continues *eternally* from the viewpoint of not just faraway observers *but all observers.*[4]

Black Hole Paradigm Fails as Mathematical Black Holes are Mass-Less

My research papers have offered several independent proofs that the gravitational mass of mathematical black holes is zero and not finite. One of my attempted proofs involved the 170-year-old rule of coordinate transformations, according to which the area of, say, a tiny square depends on the ordinary multiplication: length x breadth = breadth x length. But it turns out that this rule tacitly involves vector-like multiplications and not ordinary multiplications. Then that particular proof gets invalidated. However, the other independent proofs to this effect remain valid, and let me summarize them[5]:

- During 2000–02, my papers showed that if a material particle would approach the event horizon, its matter (time)-like trajectory would turn light like in violation of general relativity. Therefore, there must not be any event horizon ever.[6] However, in case, one swears by the exact black hole solution, then, the resolution would be that a neutral black hole must be of zero mass. This is so because
    1. *it requires infinite time to form such a black hole with respect to any observer and*

2. if one would still assume the existence of a zero-mass black hole, *the test particle will require infinite time to reach its surface.*

- In other words, the test particle will never reach the event horizon even by its own clock readings, and its trajectory will preserve its matter-like character.
- More importantly, our publications showed that forget event horizon, no apparent horizon can form during gravitational collapse in order that stellar material continues to move in a matter (time)-like trajectory unlike photons.[7] This requirement means that the radius of any section of the star must always be larger than twice the mass–energy contained within it. In turn, this demands that in case the star is assumed to shrink to a point, its gravitational mass too must shrink to zero.

Other authors too had suggested a somewhat similar result in the past.

- In 1960, in a classic paper in *Physical Review Letters*, Arnowitt, Deser and Misner, showed that by accounting for all pervasive self-gravitational interactions, the total energy of a 'point charge' is solely due to its electric charge.[8] Therefore, the mass of a neutral point particle having no charge should be zero.

In 1968, this was also tacitly suggested by Janis, Newman and Winicour[9]:

> As long as one is outside the event horizon, the so-called Schwarzschild sphere is a sphere. But as soon as one approaches the event horizon, it appears to crush into a point.

They concluded their paper with the following comments:

'It is clear that if our truncated Schwarzschild metric is to be considered as the physical solution corresponding to a spherically symmetric point mass, then the entire question of gravitational collapse beyond the Schwarzschild radius becomes meaningless.'[10]

- In the following year (1969), Luis Bel came up with the same result that the Schwarzschild surface behaves like a 'point singularity'.[11] Since a *point has zero radius*, this implies that the Schwarzschild radius, which is twice the mass of the black hole, is zero. This in turn means that mathematical black holes have zero mass.
- When a black hole has *zero mass, the space-time curvature* indeed becomes infinite at its event horizon.*

And this directly implies that the so-called black holes having huge masses are only black hole mimickers or quasi-black holes.

* ($K_H \sim 1/M^2$)

CHAPTER 19

Basic Failure of Black Hole Astrophysics

Once you eliminate the impossible, whatever remains, no matter how improbable must be the truth – Arthur Conan Doyle

KEY POINTS: The launching of relativistic radio jets, often found with accreting astrophysical black holes, requires the presence of fairly strong twisting magnetic fields at their bases. But astrophysical black holes have no intrinsic magnetic field, and the magnetic field generated by the accretion flow may be negligible. On the other hand, the launching of relativistic jets from X-ray binaries (like Circinus X-1) having modestly magnetized spinning neutron stars is much better understood. Because of their huge gravitational compactness, stellar-mass MECOs too may behave as modestly magnetized spinning neutron stars and, accordingly, can naturally explain the phenomenon of launching of relativistic jets.

The origin of gamma-ray bursts (GRBs), the most powerful explosions in the cosmos, is associated with the formation of black holes. This is self-contradictory as black hole formation was earlier associated with very weak supernovae. In particular, it is assumed that massive stars collapse to become spinning black holes surrounded by massive accretion disks. Then GRBs are explained by assuming that the entire massive disk accretes onto the black hole in a matter of only ~ 10s. There is little justification for such a drastic assumption.

Alternatively, it is assumed that the magnetic field of the newly formed disk may be ultra-magnetic ~ thousand trillion gauss. The GRB jet is produced by the Blandford–Znajek model, which assumes that the black hole effectively turns into a pulsar as disk magnetic field lines thread it. The same mechanism is also invoked to explain launching of jets from quasars. But the Blandford–Znajek model is just wishful thinking. A black hole is vacuum and not any conductor or magnetized pulsar. The external magnetic field cannot get organically connected to vacuum black hole or any insulator in the absence of electrons. On the other hand, one can get away from all such theoretical and mathematical deceptions, by replacing the black hole by a MECO, which can indeed act like an ultra-relativistic pulsar.

All astrophysical objects we know of have their own magnetic fields, be it planets, stars, galaxies or compact objects like white dwarfs and neutron stars. Much of the fascinating astrophysical phenomena associated with such astrophysical objects are directly related to the existence of *intrinsic magnetic fields* of such objects.

In contrast, the fictitious astrophysical black holes are the only objects that are devoid of any magnetic field. This is so because astrophysical vacuum black holes have no charges, currents or turbulences, and even the central point singularity is removed from the universe by the supposed event horizon.

True, all astrophysical flows including the one in the accretion disk are endowed with imbedded magnetic fields. But such flow magnetic fields are naturally negligible compared to the same of the underlying magnetized object that is causing the accretion, like the Earth, white dwarf or neutron star. The magnetic field at the inner accretion disk is dominated by the magnetic field of such magnetized objects.

With this introduction, let us now highlight some of the road blocks high-energy astrophysics comes across by assuming that the black hole candidates are mathematical vacuum black holes.

Jets from 'Black Holes' Remain Unexplained

Highly collimated outflow of matter or plasma is ubiquitous in astrophysics. Though the formation of jets is not understood properly, there is a broad unanimity that magnetic fields do play an important role in their launching. While non-relativistic jets may be understood as an ordinary hydrodynamic process, relativistic jets found in association with neutron stars and black holes are believed to be of complex magneto-hydrodynamic origin. Magnetic fields play a crucial role in launching, accelerating and collimating astrophysical jets.

The tentative contours of magnetic field lines around such jets of ionized matter are indicated in the following illustration:

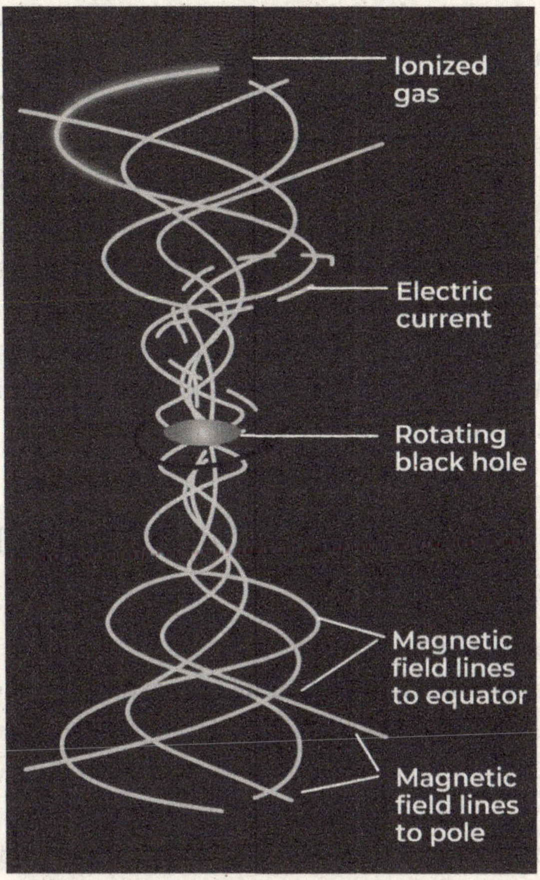

Fig. 18 Artist's impression of the contours of magnetic and electric of a relativistic jet ejected by a spinning black hole or its mimicker.

For jet confinement and propagation, we require an appropriate rotating central compact object that can twist the surrounding magnetic lines of force. But in 1973, two Russian astrophysicists, N.I. Shakura and R.A. Sunyaev, carried out the most in-depth research on the physics of black hole accretion disks and concluded that[1]: 'Hence, within the disk, the field is most likely to be *chaotic and of small scale.*'

Therefore, the magnetic field lines associated with the accretion disks may not possess an organized magnetic field structure strong enough to twist the magnetic field lines and launch relativistic jets. Such launching of relativistic jets from the proximity of a compact object and its subsequent confinement by large-scale twisting magnetic field lines can be far better understood if the compact object is a spinning magnet instead of an unmagnetized black hole or black hole mimicker.

Failure to Understand the Power Supply of Jets

In order to explain the energy budget of relativistic jets, it may not be sufficient to assume that part of the accretion power somehow gets channelized into jets. One may need an additional reservoir of power to explain jets. Accordingly in 1977, Blandford and Znajek(B-Z) claimed that in the presence of an accretion disk, a black hole acts as a spinning, conducting massive magnet, something like a pulsar.[2] But while pulsars are

1. *excellent conductors* and
2. possess *strong intrinsic magnetic fields*,

Black holes have (1) zero conductivity and (2) zero magnetic fields.

But the B-Z model assumed that a black hole, spinning in the ambient weak magnetic field of its surrounding disk, develops an induced magnetic field, and somehow acts like a pulsar. This landmark paper, which every other astrophysicist swears by, begins with the following sentence: 'When a rotating black hole is *threaded by magnetic field lines* supported by external currents flowing in an equatorial disc, an electric potential difference will be induced.'[3]

In the foregoing sentence, what does 'threading by field lines' mean? To seek an answer, let us revisit the concept of electromagnetic induction.

Electromagnetic Induction

Well, in 1831, the celebrated British physicist, Sir Michael Faraday (1791–1867), discovered that when a *conductor (not an insulator)* moves in an external magnetic field, it develops an electric voltage gap or potential difference across its ends or between the centre and the boundary. Thus electromagnetic field gets induced in the conductor even in the absence of the application of any direct electric field.

It became known later that this phenomenon of electromagnetic induction is related to the *motion of the free electrons* inside the *moving* conductor and the generation of an induced electric field under the influence of the external magnetic field.*

The conductor gets *organically connected* to the exterior magnetic field as the *dense free electrons of the conductor* get tied up with the exterior magnetic field by microscopic Lorentz forces. In contrast, the density of free electrons in an insulator is almost zero. Thus, even if the exterior magnetic

* Lorentz force on the free electrons.

lines may penetrate an insulator, it does not experience microscopic Lorentz forces. Hence, there is *never any organic connection of a moving insulator with the exterior magnetic field.*

Thus, even though exterior magnetic field lines thread both a moving conductor and an insulator, it is only the former which really develops induced electromagnetism. Therefore, the assumption that rotating black holes can develop induced electromagnetism merely because they are threaded by exterior magnetic field lines is incorrect.

While insulators may still have few free electrons (almost zero conductivity), *a classical vacuum has not a single free electron, and its conductivity is an absolute zero.*

Thus, a spinning vacuum cannot develop any induced electromagnetic field. Even the virtual electron positron pairs momentarily popping up and getting annihilated in a quantum vacuum cannot generate any net free charge. Therefore, the idea that vacuum uncharged black holes can develop induced electromagnetism and act as some sort of pulsar may be *the greatest theoretical 'deceit' in astrophysics.*

How did this 'deceit' get established as a pioneering development in black hole astrophysics? The answer is that, by virtue of the innocuous assumption that a rotating black hole must turn into a conductor merely because exterior magnetic field lines can thread it. This *single assumption quietly metamorphoses a vacuum black hole into a conductor.*

Why do all astrophysicists laud this assumption instead of introspecting about its unphysical nature? Because it saves and suits all. Without tacitly assuming black holes as conductors, black hole astrophysics would crash. Who would like to set his or her own house on fire?

I could spot only one intrepid astrophysicist who dared to question this business of energy extraction from black holes: 'Energetic astrophysical jets have always been associated with relatively strong large-scale magnetic fields that extract energy from the rotation of a central black hole and its surrounding accretion disk. This natural association does not answer the fundamental question –*what is the origin of the large-scale magnetic field* [in black holes]'?[4]

Further, even if we momentarily assume that there is some induced magnetic field at the event horizon of a spinning black hole, its kinetic energy cannot be harnessed unlike the case of a spinning neutron star or a pulsar. Why?

A pulsar is a rigid body and if some external experimenter could drill a hook at its surface, he can tap the entire kinetic energy of the pulsar. But *black hole being a vacuum and not a rigid sphere*, an external observer has no direct/rigid access to the rotational kinetic energy of the entire black hole.

We may note here that the singularity within a rotating black hole is a rotating ring, which is the source of all matter and kinetic energy. Therefore, in order to harness the rotational kinetic energy of a black hole, *electric currents must be able flow out of the ring singularity towards the exterior* of the black hole. But by definition, nothing, no light or current, can flow out of the central singularity. Hence, *the supposed kinetic energy of a black hole cannot be harnessed even if one would assume the existence of an induced magnetic or electric field on the event horizon.*

The Blandford–Znajek mechanism itself was refurbished later by introducing the *membrane paradigm* which was built by blurring the physics and general relativity by means of wishful artifacts *like feigning the existence of a physical conducting membrane having finite redshift in place of an event horizon.* This was done by *stretching* the event horizon outwards to suppress the physically singular behaviour of the event horizon.[5]

However, the authors of this paper admitted that

> The mental *deceit* of stretching the horizon is made mathematically viable, indeed very attractive, by the elegant set of membrane-like boundary conditions to which it leads at the stretched horizon.[6]

The phrase 'mental deceit' is the only objective aspect in this elaborate description of this entire issue of electromagnetic energy extraction from spinning black holes.

My Interaction with Roger Blandford

I was fortunate to be able to discuss about the Blandford–Znajek model with none other than Roger Blandford when I attended the 19th Texas Symposium on Relativistic Astrophysics at Paris in 1998. Apart from being a famous

Fig. 19 Reception desk of 19th Texas Symposium on Relativistic Astrophysics held in Paris in 1998.

astrophysicist and international science administrator, Blandford happens to possess a very charming personality.

At the end of the talk, I walked up to him with some trepidation but mustered enough courage to essentially tell him that his mechanism of energy extraction from spinning black holes cannot work despite impressive mathematics behind the same because black holes are the worst insulators without having a single free electron.

With a charming smile, he reminded me that there had been lot of work on the *membrane paradigm*. In particular, he asserted that black holes do possess an electrical resistance of 377 ohms, which proves that they can behave like conductors. Hence, one should be able to extract energy from spinning black holes.

Before we proceed, we must recall that impedance is a sort of generalization of electrical resistance for the propagation of alternating currents and electromagnetic waves. Incidentally, the *impedance of vacuum** is the ratio of electric and magnetic fields of electromagnetic radiation travelling through free space, which has a value of 377 ohms.

Thus I politely replied that 'I'm sorry but the 377 ohms you are referring to is *not* any resistance associated with the flow of current.' On the other hand, 377 ohms is the *impedance* of the vacuum, and is related to the flow of light or any electromagnetic waves in vacuum. *This precise value 377 ohms confirms that event horizon is vacuum and not any physical surface or any conductor.*

* $Z_0 = E/H = 377$ ohms, where E and H are magnitudes of the electric and magnetic fields.

Blandford had to leave for another session in another room, and I am thankful that he entertained a small discussion with me.

Failure to Understand the Central Engine of Gamma-Ray Bursts

The physics of cosmic gamma-ray bursts (GRB), the biggest explosions of the universe, certainly cannot be understood by hypothesizing that these events are related to the birth of black holes from which nothing can escape. Indeed before 1995, birth of black holes was believed to result in only 'failed supernovae', which are much-weakened versions of the standard supernovae, associated with birth of neutron stars.

Accordingly, the weak supernovae model got tweaked to explain the origin of cosmic bursts, which could be hundreds of times more powerful than supernovae. And there are two variants:

1. The collapsar model assumes that a black hole is born along with a massive disk around it. Then it hypothesizes that almost the entire disk gets accreted onto the BH in mere 10–100s.[7] A significant fraction of the kinetic energy associated with the crashing disk results in an ultra-powerful neutrino–anti-neutrino beam whose mutual annihilation results in electron positron pairs and eventually GRB.
2. But how can the entire disk crash and vanish in few seconds? If it were possible, how can all accretion disks around white dwarfs, neutron stars and black hole candidates survive for billions of years? Thus the collapsar model is highly improbable.

3. In the related Hypernova model,[8] the origin of GRBs is explained by invoking the direct conversion of the spinning kinetic energy of the black hole or its disk into the electromagnetic beam. But this model needs to assume the existence of disk magnetic fields that could be 1,000 times stronger than that of young neutron stars. The Shakura and Sunayaev paper referred to earlier had concluded: Black hole disk magnetic field should be 'many orders smaller than' 100 million gauss.[9] In fact, the proponent of this model, Bodhan Paczynski himself wondered: 'It is not clear how a super strong field is generated, even though it has become popular in theoretical papers over the last few years.'[10]

Thus one can easily rule out the hypernova model of GRBs.

Indeed, till date (2020), it is admitted that the actual mechanism for GRB launching is hardly understood. One relatively more promising model to explain GRBs is in terms of the spin-down kinetic energy of a newborn magnetar, which indeed may possess 1,000 trillion gauss magnetic fields. On the same note, GRBs may be better explained by considering the burst of energy released associated with the formation of a MECO and the subsequent radiation caused by its spin-down luminosity.

CHAPTER 20

Tentative Evidence against True Black Holes

Even strength must bow to wisdom sometimes – Rick Riordan

KEY POINTS: There could be eruptions from the accretion disks of both neutron stars and so-called black hole X-ray binaries. But unlike neutron stars, there cannot be any massive eruption from the close vicinity of a black hole. Yet, NASA reported a massive coronal outburst from the close vicinity of the so-called supermassive black hole named Markarian 335 in 2015. This is a contradiction and is best explained in terms of a coronal mass ejection from the magnetized plasma of a supermassive MECO.

If the black hole binaries indeed contained true vacuum black holes that have no matter or magnetic field, which can only suck matter, they are expected to be much quieter and steady emitters compared to their neutron star counterparts that can undergo eruptions from their magnetospheres. But the fact that black hole X-ray binaries are much more variable and turbulent suggests that they contain MECOs, ultra-hot, ultra-magnetized balls of plasma.

In the same vein, all reports about 'burping' and 'belching' from 'black holes' show they are MECOs and not true vacuum black holes.

A spinning neutron star has a magnetosphere full of energetic charged particles responsible for many lively high-energy phenomena. In contrast, a black hole has no magnetic field, no matter, no charged particles; it is just a vacuum from which nothing can escape. Of course, both can have conducting accretion disks around themselves. In particular, accretion flow close to a black hole is expected to be a radial free fall in a gravitational field. In contrast, for an accreting neutron star, plasma can interact with the neutron star's magnetic field.

Thus one would expect systems containing neutron stars to be much more turbulent than the black hole systems. But in reality *the reverse is found*. The so-called black hole X-Ray binaries are vulnerable to dramatic explosions and eruptions. This suggests that the so-called black holes may be MECOs, which are ultra-magnetized balls of fire. In view of their ultra-strong magnetic field, MECOs could be much more turbulent than the Sun, which undergoes flares and coronal mass ejections. Some of the astrophysical observations tend to support this proposal.

Burp and Belch from 'Black Holes'

Google will give you a number of results if you search for 'black hole burp'. By 'burp', astrophysicists imply a sudden burst of high-speed winds from the vicinity of black holes.

But let us consider a *Newsweek* report of 16 January 2018: 'How Does a Black Hole Burp? Belching Supermassive Black Hole Has Big Implications for Physics'.[1] This report endeavours to explain the origin of such 'burps':

> *Intense gravitational and magnetic forces surround black holes.* These can pull in large amounts of matter, creating a veil of dust and gas. As the greedy black hole feasts on this nearby gas, some is expelled in a powerful kind of burp. Each 'burp' is really an outflow of high-energy particles, which astronomers can observe using X-ray images.

However, a more natural explanation for such outbursts could be *in terms of the coronal mass ejections* (CMEs) from *the supermassive* MECO. Though a supermassive MECO is expected to spew out a burst of plasma as its CME, the ejected plasma could combine faraway to generate neutral molecules or the CME can hit the disk, which in turn may burp ultra-fast wind. Similarly consider the news report titled 'Black Hole Shoots Bullets' (*Sky &Telescope*, 11 January 2012):

> Two bullets of high-energy material seen shooting into space in 2009 from H1743-322 may help astronomers understand how black holes create the powerful jets sometimes observed streaming out from their poles.[2]

All such *burping* and belching can certainly be much better explained in terms shooting of plasma balls from a MECO than from a black hole.

Burst of Corona from a 'Black Hole'

X-ray flares from black hole systems are very commonplace, and these systems are much more violent than their neutron star counterparts. Here, we recall one particular X-ray flare detected in September 2014 by NASA's explorer missions Swift and the Nuclear Spectroscopic Telescope Array or NuSTAR, which became the talk of the town. For the first time, it was found that the X-ray flare was triggered by a burst of corona from *close to the black hole* candidate weighing about two hundred million solar masses in the AGN Markarian 335.[3]

A *corona* is essentially a haze of energetic electrons found around the disk and the central black hole candidate. What causes the corona, however, is not known. Now, let's look at a popular science report on this important finding, 'NASA Observes Object Coming Out of a Black Hole for the First Time Ever', which says: 'Commonly held belief and scientific proof holds true that black holes suck matter in rather than spewing them out. But NASA has just found some curious evidence around a supermassive black hole named Markarian 335.'[4]

The natural resolution for this puzzling observation would be the realization that *black holes* in black hole binaries are MECOs, balls of ultra-magnetized *ultra-hot plasma, which are vulnerable to unpredictable eruptions all the time in the form of winds, flares and coronal mass ejections, an act that a neutron star cannot do.*

CHAPTER 21

Direct Evidence against True Black Holes

Even strength must bow to wisdom sometimes – Rick Riordan

KEY Points: Since black holes possess no intrinsic magnetic field, the ambient magnetic field is expected to be negligible compared to dynamic flow energy density. But in the past few years, there has been almost direct evidence for much stronger magnetic fields around many astrophysical black holes. And this constitutes *direct evidence against true black holes*. In the desperation to explain the origin of such unusually strong magnetic fields, two wishful assumptions have been made:

1. Accretion flow around black holes somehow gets stalled by an outward magnetic pressure. But since an uncharged black hole exerts no outward magnetic pressure unlike a neutron star and the magnetic field embedded in the *flow cannot arrest itself*, this assumption is completely erroneous.

2. Even if the black hole devours the accretion flow, there cannot be any accumulation of any plasma (or anything) near the event horizon. Yet it is assumed by the theorists of black holes that somehow the magnetic fluxes of past flows, which vanished inside the black hole, get accumulated outside the black hole to give rise to a strong exterior magnetic field. This idea is almost metaphysical: a person is dying, body is perishing, but the soul is left behind to do unfulfilled tasks. This analogy apart, as per Ampere's law, the magnetic field generated by a charged flow/current at a given instant is proportional to the strength of the *current at that instant and not on accumulated past history of the flow.*

By definition, astrophysical black holes have no magnetic field and they cannot push away their accretion disk even by an inch. Thus the inner disk of the accretion disk is located at 3 Schwarzschild radii, when the same for young neutron stars are located far away by virtue of the enormous outward magnetic push of the neutron star. In Chapter 16, we discussed that there are observations that the inner disk of the quasar is located at 35 Schwarzschild radii, implying that the so-called black hole in this quasar is actually a MECO. A similar feature was observed in many other quasars too. But in this chapter, we shall highlight direct evidence for the existence of unexpectedly strong magnetic fields around astrophysical black holes.

We recall again a key point from the pioneering study on black hole accretion disks by Shakura and Sunayev: 'The energy of the magnetic field in the disk evidently *cannot exceed the thermal energy* of the matter.'[1]

This means that the black hole magnetic field is always negligible compared to any dynamically important value unlike the cases of strongly magnetized neutron stars or MECOs. In particular, for stellar mass black holes, inner disk magnetic field is expected to be lower than a million gauss.[2] But in 2003, it was found that the value of the magnetic field at the inner edge of the disk of Cygnus X-1, which had apparently confirmed the existence of black holes in 1975, is around 100 million gauss.[3]

Since such a strong magnetic field cannot be explained in terms of a black hole, the Russian astrophysicists Yu. N. Gnedin and his co-workers speculated that Cygnus X-1 may contain a 'charged black hole' whose rotation has generated this strong induced magnetic field.[4] However, such a speculation is baseless because astrophysical black holes are charge-less as the astrophysical plasma is overall neutral.

On the other hand, such a result can be *most naturally explained by realizing that the compact object in Cygnus X-1 is a MECO* and not a black hole. Of course, such an admission would be blasphemy, and somehow, the preprint that reported this high value of Cygnus X-1 magnetic field remained a preprint and never got published in a reputed journal.

In recent years, astrophysicists have carried out more accurate direct measurement of magnetic fields around astrophysical black holes. Such detections often throw out unexpected surprises.

- *Sagittarius A** is the black hole candidate at the centre of our galaxy and has an estimated mass of around 4 million solar mass. Following this, in 2015, astrophysicists declared that: 'Our measurements provide direct evidence of *ordered magnetic fields* in the immediate vicinity of Sgr A*, firmly *grounding decades of theoretical work.*' They went on to state, 'A dynamically important magnetic field was recently found near the Galactic Centre black hole. If this is common and if the field continues to near the black hole event horizon, disk structures will be affected, *invalidating assumptions made in standard models...* These fields obstruct gas infall.'[5]

All active galactic nuclei are believed to be powered by supermassive black holes at their hearts. During 2014–15, the presence of unusually strong magnetic fields was detected in the vicinity of the so-called black hole candidates of

- AGN PKS 1830−2[6] and
- 76 supermassive black hole candidates and various quasars.

The above-referred paper, on the 76 supermassive black hole candidates mentioned, 'We conclude that the jet-launching regions of these radio-loud galaxies are threaded by dynamically important fields, which will affect the disk properties.'[7]

Recall that real black holes have no magnetic fields, and they can never affect disk properties unlike neutron stars possessing strong intrinsic magnetic fields.

Also, have a look at the titles of some Science News on the unexpected strong magnetic fields around astrophysical black holes:

- Are Black Holes Magnetic? (Dated 15 August 2013)[8]
  Of course, the honest answer is NO.
- Our 'Magnetic' Black Hole (Sky & Telescope, 3 December 2015)

This was about the discovery of magnetic fields around the black hole candidate Sgr A* in our galaxy: 'So essentially, the astronomers are seeing tangled, turbulent magnetic fields cavorting right near where gas takes its final plunge in past the event horizon.'[9]

We remind the readers that black hole disk magnetic fields are (1) chaotic and on a small scale and (2) much weaker than dynamically important strengths.

Thus, certainly, the best way to explain all the above listed observations is in terms of the dynamically important magnetic fields of spinning MECOs getting tangled and turbulent by interacting with the embedded magnetic field of the infalling gas.

Can Embedded Magnetic Field Arrest the Accretion Flow?

It is trivial to see why the magnetic field *embedded within the flow*, strong or weak, *cannot halt the flow*. This is so because a real magnetically arrested disk is a result of *two opposing effects*:

Left Arrow = Outward pressure due to the intrinsic magnetic field of the central compact object

Right Arrow= Inward ram pressure of the flow

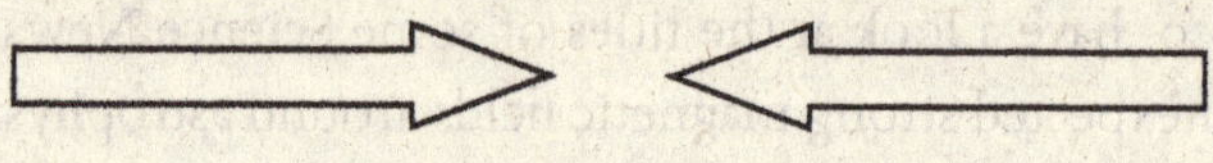

Such magnetically arrested flow can be conceived only when the *compact object has a strong magnetic field* such as neutron stars or MECOs, and the location of the inner disk is determined by *two opposing effects*.

In contrast, any magnetic field carried by the flow *becomes part of the right arrow* and not of the left one. Therefore, for a black hole, *the left arrow is absent and hence there is no magnetically arrested flow*. Rather naively, we may give the following analogy:

> A passenger on board a running train cannot slowdown the train by pushing the train, that too pushing it in a direction the train is moving.

Therefore, the presence of an unusually large magnetic field at the inner accretion disk can be explained only by realizing that the inner compact object is highly magnetized and is not a mathematical black hole.

Can the Magnetic Field Keep on Accumulating around Black Holes?

Even twenty years ago, no article, research paper or science journalist would claim the existence of dynamically strong magnetic fields around black holes. Everybody was happy with the classic paper by Shakura and Sunyaev,[10] which suggested that the magnetic fields around astrophysical black holes are negligible and NOT dynamically important.

However, subsequently, as observations suggested evidence for significant magnetic fields around black holes, attempts were made to explain such unusually strong magnetic fields by pure wishful hypotheses.

Thus, in a desperate attempt to address this issue, in 2003, R. Narayan, I.V. Igumenshchev and M.A. Abramowicz[11] hypothesized that strong magnetic field gets *accumulated* around the black hole owing to the entire previous history of accretion flow: '*We assume that a significant amount of poloidal* magnetic flux has collected in the vicinity of the black hole as a result of the cumulative action of the accretion flow*, and that the magnetic field is dynamically dominant.'

They further assumed that the accumulated magnetic field could even arrest the gas inflow by truncating it at a magnetically arrested disk. But is there really any justification for such a hypothesis?

> These authors hypothesized that the all the past accretion flow, which had already sunk and got lost within the black hole, left its embedded magnetic field behind outside the event horizon. As if, *even though a person is dead, his/her soul remains alive outside the body!*

Such an analogy apart, it is easy to see the complete unscientific nature of such a hypothesis. To this end, let us recall Ampere's law by which

> magnetic field strength *(at a given moment) generated by a flowing electric current* is proportional to electric current *(at the same moment)*.

Therefore, the strength of magnetic field at a given location *cannot be determined by the previous history of the current flow*.

* Roughly, the Earth's 'poloidal' magnetic field lines are somewhat vertical and passing through the poles. In contrast, 'toroidal' magnetic field lines are horizontal and parallel to the equator.

Since the existence of such strong magnetic ambient fields cannot be explained by the black hole paradigm, some authors have even speculated that galactic centres harbour balls of *magnetic monopoles.*[12]

What is a monopole? The bar magnet we see is basically a dipole having two poles: north and south. So it is dipole. In nature, there is no magnet with only one pole, and monopoles are only a wild theoretical speculation. No astronomical body can be a collection of monopoles. For instance, be it the Sun, a white dwarf or a neutron star, they all behave like magnetic dipoles. Indeed, the black hole candidates too primarily behave like dipoles. Therefore, the existence of unexplained strong magnetic fields around black hole candidates is best explained in terms of MECOs, because out of the proposed black hole alternatives, only MECOs have strong intrinsic (dipole) magnetic fields.

Hence, all things considered, the existence of strong magnetic fields in the vicinity of the so-called black holes is direct evidence that these compact objects have strong intrinsic magnetic fields and are likely to be MECOs.

CHAPTER 22

Scientific Developments Post Research

Physics is, hopefully, simple. Physicists are not – Edward Teller

KEY POINTS: By the 1970s, the black hole paradigm got so solidly entrenched that even the objections by Einstein and Dirac were considered as merely respectable historical babbles. It was only post my 2000–2 *Foundation of Physics Letters* papers that many physicists started questioning mathematical black holes and offered models of black hole alternatives like gravastar, dark energy stars and fuzzballs. From 2004 onwards, even Stephen Hawking kept issuing statements that there may not be any exact black hole, though, even now, nobody really understands what alternative he suggested. As to the study of the gravitational collapse of massive stars, research papers started appearing that claimed that event horizon or black hole formation might be avoided because of loss of mass energy by radiation, something that had been first stressed by this author. Though such studies often invoked obscure semi-classical or quantum gravitational mechanisms for the non-occurrence of true black holes, they avoided mentioning the most transparent physics of MECOs.

My papers claiming no exact black holes can ever exist got published since December 2000. And some of them happened to be in the list of 'most downloaded papers' from journal websites for more than a year. Later one of my 2006 paper was even chosen as one of the highlight publications of the Max-Planck Society, Germany. In the same year, for the first time, the scientific programme of the 11th Marcel Grossmann Meeting on General Relativity, Berlin, included a special session on 'Black Hole Alternatives'. This was also the only time in my life that I could attend the Marcel Grossmann Meeting. I was allotted 10 minutes for my oral presentation, in which I argued why MECOs are the only physically acceptable black hole alternatives. In contrast, Mazur and Mottola, the two conveners of this session, allowed themselves 60 minutes to promote their gravastars.

Earlier, I have mentioned the three popular black hole alternatives, namely, gravastars, dark energy stars and fuzzballs. All these ideas emerged following the publication of my *Foundations of Physics Letters* papers (2000–02). In fact, it is only since 2001 that popular science news reports on the likely non-formation of exact black holes started appearing regularly in the media. We revisit some of them below to show the beginning of a new scenario involving black hole alternatives post 2001.

Popular Science News on Black Hole Alternatives

Here we are only listing the title of the news items in order to emphasize the significance given to black holes and its alternatives in the media over the last two decades. Any reader interested in their content may find the links from the references:

1. 'Is Black Hole Theory Full of Hot Air?' (CNN, 21 January 2002)[1]
2. 'Hawking Changes His Mind about Black Holes' (*Nature News*, 15 July 2004)[2]
3. 'Black Holes Turned "Inside Out"' (BBC, 22 July 2004)[3]
4. 'Black Holes Do Not Exist' (*Nature News*, 31 May 2005)[4]
5. 'Black Holes: Have They Reached Their Use-By-Date?' (SCI GOGO, 6 August 2006)[5]
6. 'Mysterious Quasar Casts Doubt on Black Holes' (*New Scientist*, 27 July 2006)[6]
7. 'A New View of Quasars' (*Universe Today*, 25 July 2006)[7]
8. 'Do Black Holes Really Exist?' (*New Scientist*, 18 June 2007)[8]
9. 'No More Black Holes?' (*Science*, 21 June 2007)[9]
10. 'Stephen Hawking: "There Are No Black Holes"' (*Nature News*, 24 January 2014)[10]
11. 'Do Black Holes Exist?' (*Cosmos & Culture*, 5 February 2014)[11]
12. 'There Are No Such Things as Black Holes' (*Universe Today*, 24 September 2014)[12]
13. 'Black Holes are Actually "Eternally Collapsing Objects" – Indian Physicist Refutes Hawking'(*Daily Galaxy*, 2 November 2014)[13]

14. 'No Such Thing as a Black Hole?' (*Discover*, 26 February 2015)[14]
15. 'Supermassive Black Holes More Fiction than Scientific Fact' (Natural Philosophy Society Blog, 13 May 2015)[15]
16. '10 Strange Theoretical Stars' (listverse.com, 23 October 2015)[16]
17. 'Black Holes Are Ultra Hot Balls of Fire Like Our Sun: Scientist' (*Techtimes*, 30 November 2015)[17]
18. 'Are Black Holes Real?' (*Nova*, 10 March 2016)[18]
19. 'Do Black Holes Really Exist?' (*Science Fiction and Fact Magazine*, University of Washington, 23 September 2017)[19]
20. 'Black Holes DO NOT Exist – They Are WORM HOLES Claims Shock Study' (*Express*, 14 June 2018)[20]
21. 'Physicist Proposes Alternative to Black Holes' (*Sky & Telescope*, 19 March 2018)[21]
22. '5 Stunning Alternatives to Black Holes in Case They Don't Exist' (*TechQuila*, 19 October 2018)[22]
23. 'Black Hole Pretenders Could Really Be Bizarre Quantum Stars' (*Scientific American*, 16 March 2018)[23]
24. 'Black Holes Really Just Ever-Growing Balls of String, Researchers Say' (26 July 2018, Ohio State University).[24]

New Research Papers Questioning Black Holes and Trapped Surfaces

Following the publication of my papers that claimed that the formation of black holes should be avoided due to the loss of mass–energy by intense radiation preceding the formation of the event horizon, several authors used similar concepts. While some authors considering this possibility worked in the framework of classical general relativity, most invoked semi-classical or even tentative quantum gravity for claiming the non-occurrence of black holes. Note 'semi-classical' gravity implies a treatment where gravity is treated as classical like general relativity, but a hypothetical quantum field replaces matter. While the details of the publication of these papers are given in the note[25], it will be interesting to note their titles and the years of publication here to illustrate the point: 'Small, dark, and heavy: But is it a black hole?,' (2009); 'Do Horizons Exist?' (2011); 'Massive Compact Objects in a Quantum Theory of Gravity' (2014); 'Not Quite a Black Hole' (2017)

On the other hand, Corda and Cuesta considered the possibility of the avoidance of black holes due to some new physics, which we are not discussing here. The titles of their papers, with the details in the note[26], are also worth considering: 'Removing Black Hole Singularities with Nonlinear Electrodynamics', (2010); 'Farewell to Black Hole Horizons and Singularities', (2011).

In 1997, when I was struggling to formulate my ideas into papers, I had a few sessions of discussions with Pankaj Joshi, a former professor at the Tata Institute of Fundamental Research. He is a noted researcher, and studies *mathematical gravitational collapse* by ignoring any heat flow and sometimes even any pressure. I am happy to see that later Joshi used the concept that trapped surface formation may be avoided due to emission of radiation in three publications.[27] While the details are in the notes, the names of the articles themselves are of relevance here: 'A resolution of space-time singularity and black hole paradoxes through avoidance of trapped surface formation in Einstein gravity' (2005); 'Quantum Evaporation of a Naked Singularity' (2006); 'On trapped surface formation in gravitational collapse' (2007).

But Pankaj Joshi is not alone to consider the non-occurrence of singularities owing to the loss of mass energy by radiation. Two Spanish researchers, Francesco Fayos and Ramon Torres, have extensively used a similar concept.[28] While the details are in the preceding note, it the titles of their papers are illustrative: 'A class of interiors for Vaidya's radiating metric: singularity-free gravitational collapse' (2008); 'Local behaviour of evaporating stars and black holes around the total evaporation event' (2010); 'On the quantum corrected gravitational collapse' (2015).

Several other general relativists have used the same idea that black hole formation may be inhibited because of profuse emission of radiation.[29] While the details are in the preceding note, their titles are of special interest here: '*Fate of gravitational collapse in semiclassical gravity*, (2008); '*Observation of incipient black holes and the information loss problem*, (2007); *Gravitational Collapse without a Remnant*, (2008); '*Backreaction of Hawking radiation on a gravitationally collapsing star I: Black holes?*' (2014); *The Absence of Horizon in Black-Hole Formation* (2016); *Do event horizons exist?* (2017).

Baccettiet, Mann, and Terno write, 'We demonstrate that when this radiation is taken into account it prevents horizon crossing/formation in a large class of models. We conjecture that *horizon avoidance is a general feature of collapse*.'[30] This argument is made in several other recent papers[31] with titles: 'Horizon avoidance in spherically-symmetric collapse' (2017); 'Role of evaporation in gravitational collapse' (2018).

The essential concept of an ECO is that mathematical black holes are formed only asymptotically, that is, strictly never. This view is not only with respect to a faraway observer, as is the case for a finite mass black hole formation but also with respect to an observer moving with the stellar fluid. A somewhat similar concept has been arrived at in a recent paper. In 'Asymptotic Black Hole' (2017), Pei-Ming Ho writes: 'We find that a generic gravitational collapse asymptotes to a universal configuration which resembles a black hole but without horizon.'[32]

Recall, my proof of the non-occurrence of trapped surfaces and horizons is based on the finding that otherwise matter-like (time-like) trajectories of stellar matter would turn light like. A paper by Mann, Nagle, Terno arrives at a similar conclusion for a very specific case in 'Transition to light-like trajectories in thin shell dynamics' (2018).[33] Overall, such publications not only consider the non-formation or evaporation of the gravitational singularity but some of them also talk about the existence of *horizon-less compact objects*.

As already acknowledged, while most of these papers invoke unknown semi-classical or quantum gravity, my previous papers on the non-formation of black holes are still very much relevant to all of them. Unfortunately, only three of these publications cited one or two of my pertinent papers.[34] May be my contribution in this regard has been recognized in the following Quora answer on some of the milestones on black hole research, which mentions the development of the idea of ECO in 1998 and MECO in 2003.

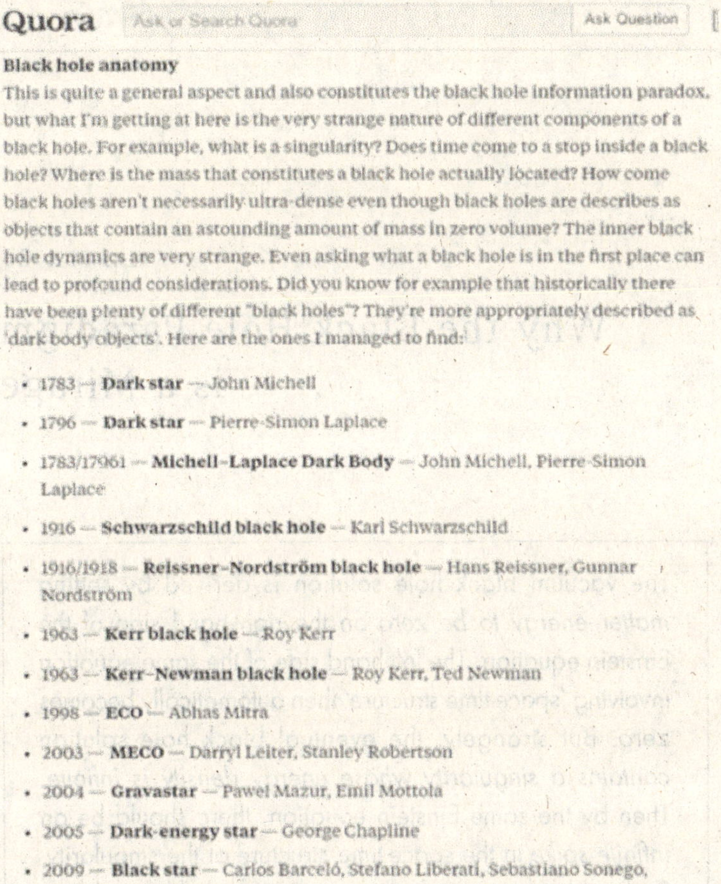

Quora Ask or Search Quora Ask Question

Black hole anatomy

This is quite a general aspect and also constitutes the black hole information paradox. but what I'm getting at here is the very strange nature of different components of a black hole. For example, what is a singularity? Does time come to a stop inside a black hole? Where is the mass that constitutes a black hole actually located? How come black holes aren't necessarily ultra-dense even though black holes are describes as objects that contain an astounding amount of mass in zero volume? The inner black hole dynamics are very strange. Even asking what a black hole is in the first place can lead to profound considerations. Did you know for example that historically there have been plenty of different "black holes"? They're more appropriately described as 'dark body objects'. Here are the ones I managed to find:

- 1783 — **Dark star** — John Michell
- 1796 — **Dark star** — Pierre-Simon Laplace
- 1783/1796[1] — **Michell–Laplace Dark Body** — John Michell, Pierre-Simon Laplace
- 1916 — **Schwarzschild black hole** — Karl Schwarzschild
- 1916/1918 — **Reissner–Nordström black hole** — Hans Reissner, Gunnar Nordström
- 1963 — **Kerr black hole** — Roy Kerr
- 1963 — **Kerr–Newman black hole** — Roy Kerr, Ted Newman
- 1998 — **ECO** — Abhas Mitra
- 2003 — **MECO** — Darryl Leiter, Stanley Robertson
- 2004 — **Gravastar** — Pawel Mazur, Emil Mottola
- 2005 — **Dark-energy star** — George Chapline
- 2009 — **Black star** — Carlos Barceló, Stefano Liberati, Sebastiano Sonego,

Fig. 20 The image of a 2003 Quora page showing few milestones in history associated with black holes and their alternatives.

To recap, innumerable research papers have been published that have discussed why real gravitational collapse may not generate true black holes but also likely black hole alternatives. Though my preprints and papers highlighted such issues, during 1998–2002, most of the later authors feigned ignorance about them.

CHAPTER 23

Why the Black Hole Paradigm is a Mirage

The vacuum black hole solution is derived by setting *matter–energy to be zero* on the right-hand side of the Einstein equation. The left-hand side of the same equation involving 'space-time structure' then automatically becomes *zero.* But strangely, the eventual black hole solution *contains a singularity whose energy density is infinite.* Then by the same Einstein equation, there should be an *infinite spike* in the space-time structure at the singularity. Such a blatant contradiction can be avoided by realizing that (1) there should not be any mathematical black hole. If one still swears by the exact black hole solution, then (2) the mass of the mathematical black hole should be zero. This generic argument rules out the formation of exact rotating black holes too. When mathematical black holes reduce to zero mass black holes, the black hole paradigm reduces to a mathematical mirage, as do all conjectures about weird black hole interiors having white holes and parallel universes. Note, such weird interiors appear mathematically *only when one sacrifices the luminosity distance radial coordinate in favour of exotic coordinates that have no physical relevance.* This is akin to the appearances of distorted and even multiple images of a simple reality in a badly cracked mirror.

Further, all such exotic coordinates become infinite at the event horizon. In other words, they attempt to hide the physical singularity of the event horizon by becoming singular themselves. Hence, the exotic interior black hole space-times projected by such coordinates are merely mathematical mirages.

My preprints and research papers have shown that though the black hole exact solution is very much correct, it is illusory because the gravitational mass of the black holes is necessarily zero and not finite. I arrived at this conclusion from three parallel and independent considerations. However, I was not aware that the same result was suggested or anticipated by some noted relativists way back in 1969. Let me remind again the conclusions by Janis, Newton and Winicour (1968):

'It is clear that if our truncated Schwarzschild metric is to be considered as the physical solution corresponding to a spherically symmetric point mass, then *the entire question of gravitational collapse beyond the Schwarzschild radius becomes meaningless.*'[1]

And pardon me for citing from Bel's paper once more:

> 'A new point of view is presented for which the Schwarzschild Singularity (event horizon) becomes a real point singularity.'
>
> 'For anyone who accepts it, this point of view eliminates any speculation about the physics of objects supposed to have collapsed beyond the Schwarzschild singularity (event horizon).'[2]

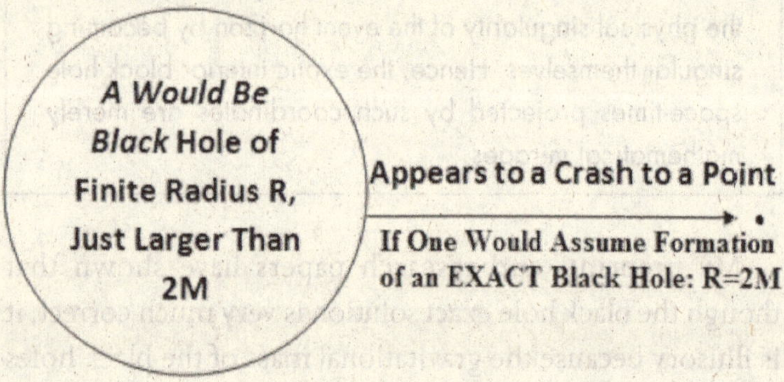

Fig. 21 Pictorial illustration of two landmark papers which suggest while a massive star can contract extremely close to its event horizon, it would appear to crash to a point once it would be assumed that it has become an exact black hole

It is found that not only Droste–Hilbert black hole solution, but even rotating Kerr black hole and charged black hole solutions appear to crash to point singularities if the collapsing matter would acquire even a tiny amount of quantum field.[3]

For a moment, let us ignore all the research papers that have shown or indicated that there cannot be finite mass black holes and, instead, discuss a generic proof. We start by recalling the essence of the Einstein equation:

Space-time Structure* = Matter Energy Momentum

The black hole solution is obtained as a vacuum solution, that is, by ignoring the presence of any matter, energy or momentum. Then the left-hand side of the above equation, by definition, becomes zero:

Space-time Structure= 0
For the entire black hole including R=0

You may think that if the space-time structure is indeed zero,** then how can there be any meaningful solution at all. Well, think of a case where the acceleration of a car is zero. But the occurrence of zero acceleration need not mean the absence of all motions. On the other hand, *zero acceleration only means that the car may be moving at a constant speed.*

Though the black hole space-time structure = 0 even at the central point, the eventual black hole solution leads to the presence of an interior singularity where the space-time curvature is infinite.

The black hole paradigm then ascribes the singularity to the presence of matter possessing infinite density. In other words, at the interior singularity, one must have: Matter Energy Momentum = Infinite. Then, if we return to the same Einstein equation, we will conclude that at the black hole singularity, one must have[4]

* Space-time structure is represented by Ricci tensor and its magnitude Ricci scalar.

** Space-time structure =0, actually leads to Ricci scalar =0.

Space-time Structure = Infinite Spike At the singularity (R=0)

Thus the concept of a black hole leads to a contradiction:

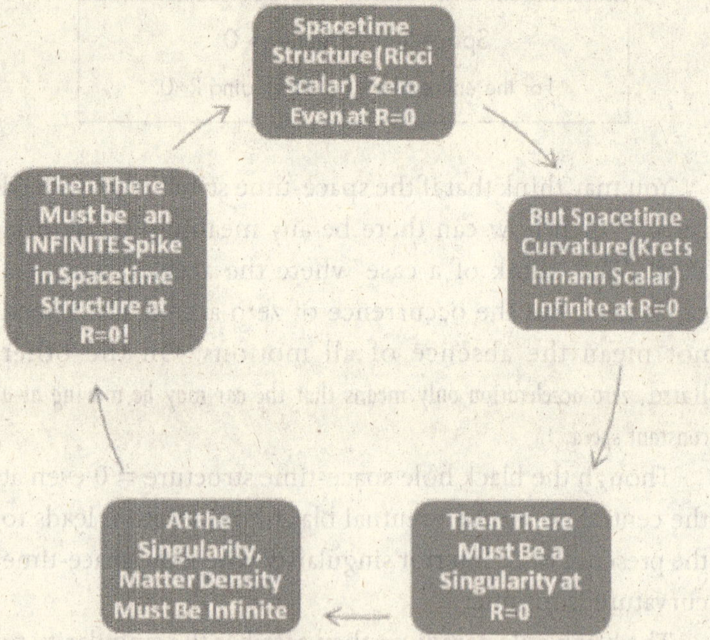

Fig. 22 Fundamental inconsistency in the idea of an 'exact black hole'.

Narlikar and Padmanabhan had highlighted this fundamental inconsistency of black holes long ago in a paper entitled 'Schwarzschild Solution: Some Conceptual Difficulties'.[5] They also deliberated on several other inconsistencies associated with the concept of black holes. For instance, they highlighted the well-known fact that from *the perspective of a distant observer or an astronomer, gravitational collapse proceeds eternally and an exact black hole is never formed.* Accordingly, they concluded that:

> It is shown that inconsistencies arise when we look upon the Schwarzschild solution as the space-time arising from a localized point singularity. The notion of black holes is critically examined, and it is argued that... The discussion on physical behavior of black holes, classical or quantum, is only of academic interest.
>
> It is suggested that problems related to the source could be avoided if *the event horizon did not form and that the universe contained quasi-black holes.*[6]

These days many researchers with a background in quantum gravity also argue that exact black holes should not form and, instead, there should be only horizon-less compact objects.

However, as a rule, they think that as far as classical general relativity is concerned, black holes are very much admissible. They think that the formation of exact black holes may be stalled only by unknown quantum gravitational effects.

In contrast, Narlikar and Padmanabhan effectively concluded that black holes are *inconsistent even within* general relativity. This is what this book has reconfirmed in many ways.

Yet a black hole believer would still argue: 'But black holes are exact solutions of general relativity. How can we rule them out within the same general relativity?'

Well, there is a way out. If we accept that the gravitational mass of the black hole is zero, the space-time structure at the singularity can still be zero despite an infinite spike.*

Note, we arrived at this conclusion from generic arguments without resorting to any mathematics. Hence, this discussion is equally valid for a so-called rotating black hole. In other words, the mathematical rotating black holes too have zero mass, and the so-called rotating black holes are rotating ultra-compact horizon-less compact objects.

White Holes and Parallel Universes within Black Holes?

Though mathematical black holes are points with zero radius and zero mass and they are not spheres of finite radii and finite masses, for a moment, let us revisit the claims that black hole interiors, in addition, harbour white holes and parallel universes too.

One arrives at such inferences when one says goodbye to the only physically significant radial coordinate, the luminosity distance, and invents extremely convoluted Kruskal coordinates having no physical or geometrical significances.

But can physical reality change with change of coordinates?

Can a rectangle change into something else if we change the (x,y) coordinates?

Suppose we have copied the sketch of a flower on a graph paper by plotting the x,y coordinate readings from the original sketch. However, an innovative mathematician

* Ricci scalar ~ M x infinite spike. If M=0, one may still have Ricci scalar =0.

may a draw a semi-logarithmic* sketch of the same plot. And now the *flower would look distorted beyond recognition.*

But will it mean that the flower is actually so distorted? Certainly NO.

Note, if there is a source of light radiating equally in all directions, the intensity of the light falls off rapidly as one moves away from the source.** To be precise, if one would go 10 times further away, the intensity will decrease by a factor of 10^2 or 100. *This is physics.*

Now enters a mathematician. He says no, I am free to use any other radial coordinate for describing the same scenario. Suppose he declares that henceforth, the new distance coordinate is the inverse of R.

As per this new definition, now, *the intensity of the light will rapidly increase as one goes farther away.*†

While such a new law may be alright from a purely mathematical point of view, physically, it is not only erroneous but also nonsense.

Let us think of yet another trivial case where the change of coordinates, at its face value, may distort the physical reality. Suppose there is a tower building of a height of 50 m, and we assign a coordinate:

$z = +50$ m

to its topmost point. Here the + sign indicates that the tower is standing upwards and not downwards.

But suppose, now a mathematician introduces a new coordinate: $u = -z$. The original topmost point of the tower will now get labelled as

* By changing y into log y

** $L \sim 1/R^2$

† $L \sim U^2$

u = -50 m

Will it mean that now the tower is standing upside down? Certainly NO.

And we must give due respect to the original height coordinate z, which was in tune with the physical reality.

Next, imagine, you are standing in front of a badly cracked big mirror. You might invent that

1. Your limbs are broken
2. Your face is contorted
3. You exist as multiple personalities (multiple images)

> And various exotic coordinates perform like such badly cracked mirrors. The exotic worlds presented by them are fake, artifacts of mathematical jugglery.

Black hole experts coolly make a profound statement: In the interior of a black hole, space and time swap their mutual roles. Here I have a poser:

Suppose I found a train with a certain number had arrived at Delhi, and accordingly, I made a statement: This train had left Mumbai at 8 AM and arrived at Delhi at 8 PM. But now somebody points out that there was total shutdown in Mumbai and the train had actually started from Nagpur. But I am not ready to budge, and so I issue a fresh statement:

> Oh no, the train had actually left a *place* named 8 AM at a *time* Mumbai, but nonetheless managed to reach Delhi at 8 PM.

Though mathematically, the above alteration might be acceptable, physically, it is nonsense. And if event horizon is no special place, *why do the radial and time coordinates change their characters only inside and not outside the event horizon?*

If space would indeed turn time like inside the black hole, why do the angular coordinates defining the same space continue to retain their space-like character?

Further, all the exotic coordinates invented to save the black hole paradigm are unacceptable even by mathematical gold standards because all of them become infinite* at the event horizon whose singularity they intended to hide!

Thus a star can never shrink all the way up to its event horizon even by general relativity, as was believed by Einstein, Dirac and at least two dozens noted general relativists. Therefore, the singularities at the event horizon indicated by the luminosity distance are real, and the event horizon marks the end point of the available space and there cannot be any region beneath it. In other words, event horizon marks the origin of the luminosity distance and the mathematical black holes solution corresponds to a point (R=0, M=0) and not a sphere.

*All such exotic coordinates contain a factor: log(1-2M/R), which becomes negative infinity at R=2M.

CHAPTER 24

Towards an Alternative Paradigm

A new scientific truth does not triumph by convincing its opponents and making them see the light, but rather because its opponents eventually die, and a new generation grows up that is familiar with it – Max Planck

KEY POINTS: Almost sixty years after the culmination of the mathematical black hole paradigm, the famous international magazine *Sky & Telescope* wonders what is inside a black hole: 'Wormholes, alternate universes, time warps—we've all heard crazy theories about what happens inside a black hole. So what's the real story?' And admits: 'The short answer is, physicists don't know.' And if the claims about the existence of echoes in the Laser Interferometer Gravitational Wave Observatory's (LIGO) gravitational waves are correct, we may have evidence that the so-called black holes are exotic compact objects (ECOs), having physical surface. Incidentally, I was the first person to coin the acronym 'ECO' (eternally collapsing object). The research on searching for alternatives for black holes/ECOs has entered the mainstream. It is in this sense that the black hole paradigm may have fallen even by the mainstream yardstick. Indeed, on 16 March 2018, the *Scientific American* commented that there are sufficient reasons to seek such alternatives, because black holes raise a host of theoretical problems.

The black hole paradigm silently fell through when several independent proofs suggested that black holes correspond to ultimate ground states of gravitational collapse having $E=Mc^2=0$. The first such proof was due to L. Bel in 1969. The same paradigm fell on observational grounds with the detection of unexplained strong magnetic fields around many so-called astrophysical black holes.

Most ECO models invoke vague semi-classical or quantum gravity ideas, all of which are fundamentally incorrect because both the density of stellar matter and space-time curvature near the event horizon of sufficiently massive black holes could be absolutely negligible. The *only generic* general relativistic effect near the event horizon is the trapping of stellar radiation, which invariably leads to the only model of ECO and its magnetized version MECO. While many researchers are working on non-existent quantum gravity ECO models, many are ignoring the peer reviewed ECO/MECO alternatives, thus pursuing intellectual apartheid, and are reluctant to give any credit to physicists disconnected from the strong international network.

Pioneer Works is a very old cultural centre dedicated to experimentation, education, and production across disciplines, and is based in Red Hook, Brooklyn, USA. Recently, it organized a series of conversations between scientists on scientific controversies and unsolved quandaries, hosted by its director of sciences Janna Levin. This project is supported by Science Sandbox, a Simons Foundation initiative dedicated to engaging everyone with the process of science. On 26 July 2018, it organized its 15th conversation by stating, 'Black holes are gloriously weird.'[1]

Fig. 23 Cover page of a certain issue of 'Scientific Sandbox' published by the Simons Foundation.

Not that this was a serious physics conversation, but nonetheless it acknowledged the fact that black holes continue to be controversial almost sixty years after the mathematical black hole paradigm got firmly established.

But on 28 December 2016, Camille M. Carlisle, the science editor of the famous *Sky & Telescope* magazine, published a really serious article entitled 'What Is Inside a Black Hole?' She began by posing the following question:

'Wormholes, alternate universes, time warps—we've all heard crazy theories about what happens inside a black hole. So what's the real story?' And immediately, she admitted: 'The short answer is, physicists don't know.'[2]

More importantly, a decade before it, in 2008, three European relativists, Rosa Doran, F.S.N. Lobo and P. Crawford, came together to defend the black hole paradigm by claiming that there is no harm if space and time must swap their roles in the interior of a black hole. They also defended the strange coordinate transformations that render an originally static problem into a non-static one. However, they ended up making the following comments for such mathematical tricks: 'The solutions that do away with the interior singularity and the event horizon, although interesting in themselves, *sweep the inherent conceptual difficulties of black holes under the rug*. In concluding, *we note that the interior structure of realistic black holes have not been satisfactorily determined*, and are still open to considerable debate.'[3]

The reason that the interior structure of black holes is not understood almost after a century is because there is no mathematical black hole in the first place. In the previous section, I presented the ultimate proof of it: While the black hole paradigm begins by assuming that the space-time structure (Ricci scalar) is *zero* everywhere including the central point, soon, the black hole paradigm leads to an *infinite spike* in the space-time structure at the same central point. The only face-saver from this contradiction is to realize that the mathematical black hole solution corresponds to zero mass black holes that can never form. Mathematically, a zero mass black hole can form asymptotically, after infinite physical time by all observers, not only distant observers.

In turn, this means that continued gravitational collapse should give rise to horizon-less ECOs and not static singular black holes possessing horizons.

For both a black hole and its mimicker, there is an exterior photon sphere that is 50 per cent larger than them. Gravity is already so strong there that light can move in unstable circular orbits, and no exterior telescope can peep inside it. Thus the photon sphere acts as the 'virtual event horizon'. An exterior telescope claiming to find an 'image' of the black hole or its mimicker can at the most find the inflated shadow of the photon sphere and not the surface of any black hole or its mimicker. For rotating black holes or their mimickers, the 'photon sphere' gets replaced by a 'photon ring'. Hence, one can never distinguish a black hole from its mimicker by any imaging.

Therefore, the claim that the so-called Event Horizon Telescope finally imaged a true black hole, at this point, is the worst distortion of physics, the worst misleading publicity, of this century.

Similarly, a distortion of physics and an equally misleading publicity blitzkrieg was launched in 2016 by claiming that LIGO has yielded direct evidence of 'event horizon'. The 'ring down' feature of the gravitational waves must have arisen from the bell-like vibrations from the newly formed shaky event horizon settling into its ultimate static form. But in reality, since the photon sphere acts as the virtual event horizon, again the 'ring down' feature is the signature of a shaky vibrating photon sphere settling into its ultimate static form.

Gravitational waves generated from the vibration of the newborn unsteady photon sphere travel both outwards, seen as 'ring down' waveform, and inwards. If the underlying newborn compact object would be a true vacuum black hole, it would gulp down all inward-moving gravitational waves. In such a case, external telescopes would not detect any subsequent gravitational wave emission for the given event. But in case, the underlying compact object is horizon-less, the inward-travelling gravitational waves will initially remain trapped between its surface and the photon sphere. However, part of it would soon diffuse out later following repeated reflections from the physical surface. In such a case, there might be a subsequent *echo* of gravitational waves.

There have been some weak evidences for gravitational wave echoes associated with three cases of detection of gravitational waves: GW150914, GW151226, and LVT151012.[4] In comparison, there has been stronger evidence for gravitational wave echoes for the binary neutron star merger event GW170817.[5] Thus the tentative detection of late echoes of gravitational waves might suggest that the compact objects formed by the coalescence of either so-called black holes or even neutron stars might be black hole mimickers having physical surfaces and not vacuum black holes[6] possessing event horizons. Even such instances of tentative evidence have become one of the hottest sub-topics of research, and there may be more than hundred papers that have focused on this issue.[7]

Indeed, few years ago, a new phrase was coined, exotic compact objects (ECO), which broadly refers to all varieties of black hole mimickers and quasi-black holes.[8] Ironically, Vitor Cardoso, who coined this term, never mentioned that this acronym was first used by me twenty years ago (ECO= eternally collapsing object).

Most such authors believe that ECOs must be result of some quantum gravity effect during the preceding gravitation collapse. Instead of honestly saying that gravitational wave echoes from ECOs may reveal that they possess a physical surface unlike black holes, they would still say that ECOs may be black holes but with 'quantum fuzz'; they may also link the black hole mimickers with the legacy of Stephen Hawking even when the latter always remained confused and ambiguous on black hole mimickers. By such twists, they kill four birds with one stone: (1) no blasphemy, begin by paying due obeisance to the black hole paradigm, (2) successfully market obscure but pet quantum gravity, (3) enrich the proposal with the glamour of Hawking and (4) keep the simple but cogent general relativistic alternative MECO at bay.

But can such fictitious quantum gravity objects ever form in the gravitational collapse of massive stars or gigantic gas clouds? No. Why?

> In order to have some miraculous quantum gravity effect for the formation of a black hole mimicker, two factors may be needed:
> extremely large space-time curvature and density of the cloud when it has shrunk almost to its Schwarzschild radius.
> Supermassive black hole mimickers meet none of these fundamental requirements.

It is true that the space-time curvature on the surface of a 1 solar mass black hole mimicker is approximately 30 times larger than the same on the surface of a neutron star. But for a black hole mimicker of 1 billion solar masses, the surface space-time curvature *will be 1 billionth billionth time smaller than the same of a neutron star.*

This is so because the 'space-time curvature' on the surface of a black hole mimicker decreases rapidly as the square of its mass. So the bigger the black hole, the much weaker is the space-time curvature.

This is the reason that even if one would admit the case of 'Hawking radiation a quantum fuzz', this effect is absolutely negligible for all macroscopic black holes. For instance, the evaporation time for a 1 solar mass black hole is 20 million trillion trillion trillion trillion trillion years.*

Also, the mean density of a black hole mimicker too falls off rapidly as its mass increases. Thus while the mean density of a 1 solar mass black hole mimicker is approximately 1,000 times larger than the density of a neutron star, the same black hole mimicker possessing a billion solar mass would be *smaller than the neutron star density by a whopping factor of 1,000 trillion!*

Therefore macroscopic black hole mimickers cannot form due to any fictitious quantum gravity effect.

Some recent studies by William George Unruh (1945–), one of the leading researchers of semi-classical gravity, and his co-workers may be confirming our assertion:

* 2×10^{67} years and this increases fast as the cube of the black hole mass!

> Quantum effects do not play an important role for the collapse of astrophysical objects.[9] In addition, they have concluded that the pre-Hawking radiation cannot prevent the formation of horizon.[10]

Also a recent blog by Paolo Pani, co-author of Vitor Cardoso, admitted that 'None of the Exotic Compact Object models on the market succeeded in reproducing all these properties ... but we know that theoreticians are stubborn and keep trying.'[11]

It seems that they are so stubborn that *they must ignore the mundane but plain vanilla black hole mimicker* ECO/MECO whose formation is suggested by the *generic general relativity effect of trapping radiation*, in favour of exotic quantum gravity fantasies.

But Why MECOs May Be the Only Realistic Black Hole Mimicker?

> It should be clear now that black hole mimickers *must be formed by virtue of some innate generic physics effect* and not because of any quantum gravity effect. The only inevitable generic physics effect when a gas cloud collapses within its photon sphere is that even photons can hardly move outwards. In other words, self-gravity traps the heat and radiation generated within the star or the cloud. Further once the luminosity of the trapped radiation attains its Eddington limit, by definition, rapid gravitational contraction gets stalled. And an ECO is formed.

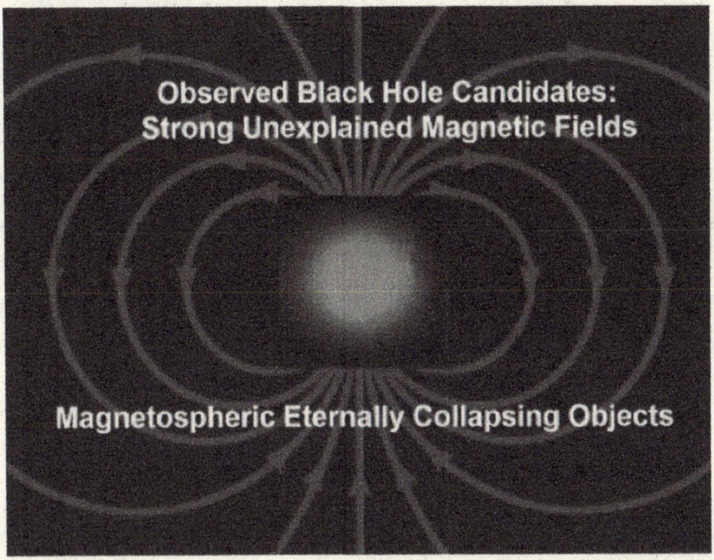

Fig. 24 Artist's impression of a Magnetospheric Collapsing Object.

Whenever an astrophysical plasma ball contracts and its radius decreases, the magnetic field embedded inside it approximately increases inversely as the square of the radius. In addition, there is a general relativistic enhancement of magnetic fields near the event horizon. Hence astrophysical ECOs turn out to be MECOs.

By virtue of this intrinsic magnetic field, a supermassive spinning MECO could be the central engine in some quasars and gamma-ray bursts (GRBs).[12] The vast energy associated with supernova explosions results from the release of gravitational binding energy of newborn neutron stars. Similarly, the binding energy released during the formation of MECOs can foot the bill for the mind-boggling energy budget of GRBs.

Status of the New Paradigm

In the previous chapter, I pointed out that following my paper claiming non-occurrences of trapped surfaces and exact black holes, there have been innumerable high-profile media reports as well as research papers which talk about

1. the non-formation of black holes or
2. the non-formation of trapped surfaces and singularities, and
3. horizon-less compact objects.

These may be seen as the beginning of a new paradigm.

However, at this moment of transition, this paradigm is in a state of utter confusion. Why? Well, unfortunately, physicists have not appreciated the fact that the black hole solution, though correct, is illusory because

- *Blackholes correspond to the ultimate ground state of the collapsing star having* $E=Mc^2=0$ or there should be no mass or energy.
- Also, most astrophysicists are not aware that *there could be radiation pressure supported stars of arbitrary high mass.*

Most astrophysicists may also not be aware that my papers in *Monthly Notices Royal Astronomical Society* have shown that general relativistic radiation pressure supported stars have no lower mass limit either ($M \rightarrow 0$). Nor are many aware that even in classical general relativity, a contracting star must keep on emitting radiation irrespective of the poorly understood and rather mysterious *Hawking radiation.*

In addition to such genuine reasons, there may be treacherous socio-political angles that have frustrated the proper growth of this new paradigm. The research paper that first showed that the maiden LIGO gravitational wave signal could be due to the coalescence of black hole mimickers rather than true black holes was authored by three young European relativists, namely, Vitor Cardoso, Edgardo Franzin and Paolo Pani.[13] Two of them, Vitor Cardoso and Paolo Pani, elaborated on this issue in a subsequent paper in *Nature Astronomy* in 2017.[14] Following this, on 9 September 2017, I sent a congratulatory email to Vitor Cardoso, in which I also explained why MECOs could be the most likely black hole mimickers:

> Dear Dr Cardoso,
>
> First greetings from me for your several important recent papers (i) 2016 PRL paper showing LIGO GW features could be due to Photon Sphere/ring and not due to EH, and consequently be due to BLACK HOLE mimickers.
>
> (ii) Your Nature Astronomy paper where you explore the possibilities of BH mimickers vis-a-vis true BHs.
>
> In the latter, like most of the researchers, you opined that continued collapse cannot be brought to a halt by any classical effect and hence BH mimickers must arise from QM.
>
> However, **like everybody else, here you ignored the fact**, in astrophysics there is a concept of Eddington Luminosity of a compact object at which
>
> Inward Gravitational Pull = Outward Radiation Thrust
>
> Thus by definition, if a collapsing object would attain its Eddington Luminosity, the catastrophic collapse would stop and the star would end in a quasi-static radiation

pressure supported object like the Supermassive stars of Hoyle, Fowler and well described by Weinberg.

A series of peer reviewed papers (MNRAS, MNRASL, New Astronomy, PRD) by me have shown that this indeed happens. Such a hot object has surface redshift z >>> 1 and behaves like a BH mimicker. But they keep on radiating albeit at negligible rate, and form a DYNAMIC SOLUTION contrary to the STATIC BH mimickers.

In addition my papers have shown no trapped surface is formed, hence no Naked Singularity, or no BH ever.

I am sure as an honest physicist, you would consider them with due seriousness when you talk about BH mimickers.

Cheers

Abhas

He replied promptly on 11 September 2017:

Dear Prof. Abhas,

Thank you for your message and for the reference to your works. I was unaware of those developments, but they are very interesting and certainly very useful: we plan on releasing a review on these matters and will make sure to include your results in it.

Sincerely,

Vitor Cardoso

Initially, I thought that he was genuinely interested in learning about such physics issues. Since he promised to include such developments in his review paper, the same day, I sent him links to all the relevant papers and explained the basic physics behind them. Since then, he has written many research papers on this topic. In particular, he has published a 76-page review paper citing 520 references.[15] He cited the cases of all black hole mimickers, howsoever speculative, howsoever unphysical. But he did not touch the case of MECO even with a barged pole after writing 'they are very interesting and certainly very useful' in his email of 9 September 2017.What is more notable is that he *never replied to my emails anymore.*

It is clear from this incident that if the case for the most natural black hole alternative is being ignored, the pertinent reason need be not be of any scientific nature. On the other hand, it could be due to a new form of *intellectual apartheid* by which globally networked elite authors may be thinking: *why should we cite backbenchers who have no global scientific clout, who may never confront us in an international conference and, above all, who will never be the reviewers of our elite papers.*

If the question of a black hole alternative would be settled, the quantum gravity black hole alternatives, pursued by around hundred authors, may end.

Astrophysical Observations may Ring the Truth

What might really decide the true nature of the so-called black hole candidates? Well, it could be precise study of magnetic field patterns around the black hole mimickers in an unprejudiced manner. Fortunately, there are some astrophysicists who do not subscribe to such a prejudice.

A case in point is Dr Andrei Lobanov who is a radio astronomer from Max Planck Institute for Radio Astronomy in Bonn, Germany. His central research topic is to probe the innermost regions of active galactic nuclei (AGN) jets and their magnetic fields, via long baseline radio telescopes. Since 2007, he has given scientific talks at many international conferences, which have highlighted the need for finding out the true nature of the black hole candidates. Here is a slide from one of his talks and has the subtitle: 'Present evidence does not strictly prove existence of black holes'.

In this talk, he is seen to be stressing on the need to distinguish between a true black hole and its alternatives such as boson stars (BS) and MECOs. He also mentioned that a MECO might be distinguished from a black hole by studying the associated magnetic field with the former.[16]

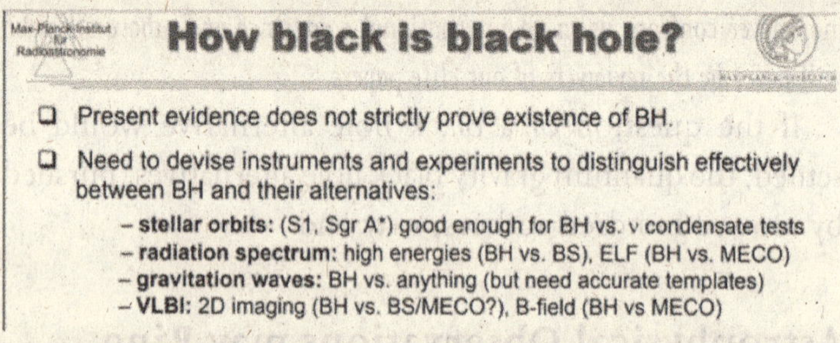

Fig. 25 Screenshot of a presentation by Dr A. Lobanov which discusses MECOs vs black holes.

Also, have a peek at another slide from his subsequent talk.[17] Here, Lobanov discusses the physics of MECO; in particular, he mentions that the dipole magnetic field of a MECO falls off as the cube of distance (see last point of this slide),which might tell whether the so-called black hole is a MECO or not.

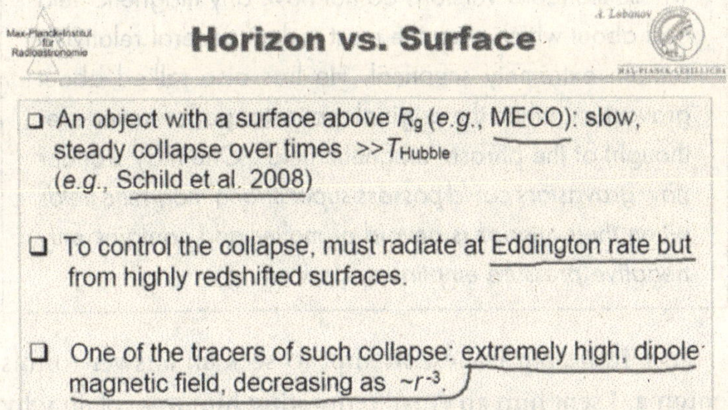

Fig. 26 Screenshot of another presentation by Dr A. Lobanov which mentions a MECO can be differentiated from a black hole by studying pattern of decrease of the surrounding magnetic field.

On 2 March 2017, Lobanov published a research note on this theme in *Nature Astronomy*: 'Beyond the Event Horizon or Altogether Without It'.[18]

About black holes, he posed the question: *But are they also an intrinsic part of our physical reality?*

In this commentary, he emphasized on the fact that, actually, there has been *no evidence for the detection of any event horizon*, and *wrote* 'A broad class of compact horizon-less objects discussed in the recent literature might in fact provide the strongest contestants to the canonical black hole.'[19]

Here he elaborated on his earlier point that the pattern of spatial variation around an astrophysical black hole may reveal whether it is a true black hole or a black hole mimicker.

But somehow Lobanov forgot about MECOs in this *Nature Astronomy* piece. Instead, here he talked about wormholes whose standard versions do not have any magnetic field and about which even the most ardent general relativists remain extremely sceptical. He has also talked about gravastars, when the original gravastar paper never ever thought of the phrase 'magnetic field'. One may wonder *how gravastars could possess super strong magnetic fields when their interior is devoid of matter and contains only negative pressure emptiness, dark energy.*

In a futile but honest attempt to seek an answer to this enigma, I sent him an email requesting him to explain why he blacklisted MECO in his *Nature Astronomy* research note when he had been discussing about the same since 2007. Unfortunately, I have not received any response from him yet.

Deadly Snowball Effect

In addition to such human pitfalls, there may be a genuine fear of getting academically ostracized or at least marginalized if one makes a direct critique against the black hole paradigm. Such manuscripts may never be accepted in respectable peer-reviewed journals, and even if such papers may get published after several rejections, nobody may cite them. The authors of such papers may rarely be invited to conferences or be nominated for academic awards.

Consider the case of Valery Kiselev, who is a senior and excellent theoretical physicist from Institute of High Energy Physics, Protvino, Russia. He co-authored a preprint entitled 'Black Holes: A Prediction of Theory or Phantasy',[20] the abstract of which was just the following line: 'We argue that black holes do not represent a strict consequence of general relativity.'

Though the scientific content of the paper is quite solid, it was mostly ignored and later got published in the Russian journal *Physics of Particles and Nuclei* after two years in 2006. If the world were very logical, one would not expect Kiselev to write any paper that would consider black holes to be on sound physics footing. But later, ignoring his own research, Kiselev did write papers based on black holes: 'Radial Geodesics as a Microscopic Origin of Black Hole Entropy'.[21] This paper was published in the much more prestigious journal *Physical Review* and received five citations as compared to his other one questioning the black hole, which was studiously ignored.

For that matter, consider the insightful 1988 research paper by Narlikar and his erstwhile graduate student Padmanabhan.[22] In this paper, the authors concluded that the discussion of the physical behaviour of black holes is only of academic interest. This paper has not received ten citations, neither Jayant Narlikar nor Thanu Padmanabhan ever cited their own paper in any journal or in any of the several books written by them. Somewhat surprisingly, later, in a U-turn, Padmanabhan fine-tuned his research in such a manner that the concept of black hole event horizon played a crucial role.

Prejudice and Intellectual Intolerance of Some Physicists

Yes, it is these two factors that have always prevented or delayed the dawning of new scientific paradigms. Let me cite three specific incidenct involving the research carried out by me in tandem with Rudy Schild, Stanley Robertson and Darryl Leiter.

1. Sabine Hossenfelder is a theoretical physicist working in the area of quantum gravity. She might be the most open-minded quantum gravity researcher. She is one of the best theoretical physics bloggers ever, in addition she writes lucid in-depth commentaries for *Nature*, *Scientific American* and *Quanta Magazine*. Her popular science book entitled *Lost in Math: How Beauty Leads Physics Astray* published in June 2018 became an international bestseller. Several years ago, when she was not so widely known, she was on my Facebook friends' list.

She had probably posted about one of her blogs concerning black holes. She concluded that as far as general relativity is concerned, the formation of black holes is inevitable and, if at all, some quantum gravity effect may prevent their birth. I made a couple of detailed comments where I told her that black hole formation can be prevented by general relativity and that there may never be any fictitious quantum gravity. I gave her references to my papers in *Physical Review D*, *Monthly Notices Royal Astronomical Society*, *Monthly Notices Royal Astronomical Society Letters* to convince her, as I thought after all she was a rare open-minded theoretical physicist. I was eager to see her response, but after a day or two, I could not track her post at all. Then I discovered that she had quietly blocked me on Facebook. So this is the level of academic prejudice and intolerance of one of the most open-minded quantum gravity researcher.

2. On 25 July 2006, the Center for Astrophysics (CfA), Harvard, issued a press release 'New Picture of Quasar

Emerges' based on the research paper by Rudy Schild, Darryl Leiter and Stanley Robertson, which also made a passing mention of me. This press release highlighted that the quasar Q0957+561 may contain a supermassive MECO in lieu of a black hole. For a true unmagnetized black hole, the inner edge of the accretion disk is located at 3 Schwarzschild radii, but for this quasar, the accretion disk appeared to be pushed far away to 35 Schwarzschild radii by the strong magnetic field of the MECO.

Around the time this press release was issued, Darryl, who passed away in 2011, would often visit Rudy at CfA. There one day he met Ramesh Narayan, Thomas Dudley Cabot Professor of the Natural Sciences and a high-profile theoretical astrophysicist. In several high profile papers, Narayan has claimed that his research has offered cogent evidence that astrophysical black holes indeed possess event horizons. Darryl possessed a childlike simplicity and exuberance.

He spoke freely to Narayan about our MECO research and why black holes cannot be true black holes. May be Darryl requested Narayan to resume this scientific discussion later.

But no such further meeting took place ever. On the other hand, after couple of weeks, in an unthinkable move, CfA *removed its own press release!* So some highly influential high-profile physicist must have convinced the CfA director, Dr Charles Alcock, to remove the press release challenging the black hole paradigm from the CfA site.

It is anybody's guess who that high-profile and influential astrophysicist could be. May be the name of an insignificant yet notorious Indian in a Harvard press release was a bit too much for a high-profile American Indian.

3. The last international astrophysics conference I could attend was in Tata Institute of Fundamental Research (TIFR): 'Jet Triggering Mechanisms in Black Hole Sources' (20–23 January 2016).

I delivered my twenty-five minute plenary talk at the inaugural session: 'Exploring Magnetospheric Origin of Jets for Both Neutron Star and "Black Hole" Systems'. During the evening tea session, I was strolling alone on the beautifully manicured TIFR lawns adjoining the shore of the Arabian Sea. A young man rambled up to me and introduced himself as a Ph.D. student in the Department of Astronomy, TIFR. He told me that he was already aware of the MECO proposal and today he got almost convinced. But he also told me that he would never have the guts to engage his professor in any discussion on MECO, let alone discuss the same in his thesis.

Now anyone should be able to gauge that if theoretical physicists and astrophysicists can be so prejudiced and intolerant, even in the open, against any paradigm that might challenge the black hole paradigm, how neutrally they can act as *anonymous referees* for research papers involving the MECO paradigm.

In 2017, I wrote a research paper based on the content of this TIFR plenary talk along with two co-authors. In the past three years, our manuscript has been rejected by four journals. Though no anonymous referee has pointed out any error or inconsistency in our paper, they rejected it either with open malice or with the plea, 'We already know this'.

Indeed nobody wants to kill the goose that has been laying golden eggs for general relativists, astrophysicists as well as theoretical physicists since the 1970s. Fortunately, in our fifth attempt, we have received some balanced critique from a referee of *Astrophysics & Space Science* where our paper might get published.[23]

On October 22, 2020, an author from Hajipur, Bihar of unknown affiliation has published a long preprint on arXiv criticizing all aspects of ECO research by Robertson, Leiter, Schild and Glenndenning and me during the period of 2000-14.

He has rejected my revised proof for non-occurrence of trapped surfaces by insisting that the contraction speed of the boundary of the star is zero when by definition it is non-zero for contraction. He has refused to accept the concept of 'Eddington Luminosity' which shows that outward radiation pressure can counterbalance the pull of gravity. His ultimate rejection of ECO is based on his claim that profuse emission of radiation leads to violation of the principle of conservation of some quantum numbers. But all physics students and researchers know that emission of radiation does not lead to any such alleged violation.

On learning about it, I submitted a detail rebuttal to arXiv (submit/3462013). Unfortunately, it has not been published even after many days, and I wonder if arXiv moderators are in collusion with this author who claims to 'debunk' 14 years of published peer-reviewed research. So as of now, I have published my rebuttal on another electronic platform academia.edu[24].

Ray of Hope?

There is a famous quote by Oscar Wilde: 'The truth is rarely pure and never simple.' Yet truth has the bad habit of rearing its head sooner or later and may also prove to be the ultimate victor. While I am not foolish enough to even remotely compare myself with Ludwig Boltzmann (1844–1906), we may recall his story. On the basis of kinetic theory involving the random motion of atoms, he formulated a statistical mechanical interpretation of thermodynamics by showing that the concepts of heat and entropy are manifestations of invisible microscopic random motion of atoms. His contemporaries, leading physicists like Ernst Mach, Wilhelm Ostwald and Lord Kelvin, fiercely rejected his formulation. Since influential scientists control the scientific organizations, the Royal Society too disregarded Boltzmann's idea. This happened when Boltzmann already was a very famous physicist, quite unlike me.

By 1906, Boltzmann went into a state of mental depression, which may have been triggered primarily by personal reasons. On 5 September, while on a summer vacation in Trieste, Italy, he committed suicide by hanging himself. But what is more important to note here is that his equation $S= k_B \log W$, where S is the entropy of a thermodynamic system and W is the number of ways in which atoms can be arranged, got recognized as one of the most fundamental ones in physics. Later, his pioneering equation got etched on his bust at his cemetery following his death.

Subramanium Chandrasekhar is certainly one of the best mathematical astrophysicists ever. In 1983, he shared the Nobel Prize in Physics with William Fowler whom I have mentioned in the 'Preface'. Chandrasekhar researched on many outstanding astrophysical problems in his career. However, he may not have won this glory of Nobel but for his landmark, yet simple two-page paper titled, 'The Maximum Mass of Ideal White Dwarfs' written way back in 1931.[25]

As per the NASA Astrophysics Data Service, as of July 2020, this paper has 514 citations, which though impressive may be insignificant compared to the citations of papers on fashionable topics like string theory, dark energy and the black hole information paradox. As to Chandrashekhar's paper, most of these citations started pouring in only after the 1970s. But for the first thirty years, this paper had received only two citations!

We can only hope that science will be practised without any bias, prejudice, elitism, politics and, above all, untouchability. We hope, eventually, science will rise over herd mentality even for potential paradigm shifts. Otherwise, even world-class experiments set up using huge public funds may falter when arriving at crucial scientific truths. For instance, the EHT may never deliver its full scientific potential if the astronomers would analyse its data with a predetermined mindset: *We believe that the astrophysical black hole candidates possess event horizons, and we named our telescope accordingly. We are certain that the EHT will eventually reaffirm our belief. If at all, we may consider black hole alternatives that look exotic and are proposed by influential authors. And we cannot damage our reputation by considering plain vanilla MECOs proposed by a bunch of authors who have no international clout.*

The real name of 'Event Horizon Telescope' should have been 'Photon Sphere or Photon Ring Telescope' because we have emphasized that it is fundamentally impossible to peep below the photon sphere or ring. But a name such as 'Photon Sphere Telescope' would kill half the fun and may even kill the 'confirmations' of having detected a real 'event horizon'. Nevertheless, a recent paper by Daniel Terno, a researcher in semi-classical gravity from Macquaire University, Australia, supports my research results.[26]

The usual black hole folklore *assumes* that during continued collapse, at some undefined, unknown time, a time varying 'apparent horizon' forms and keeps on expanding outwards.

> But Terno shows that the apparent horizon *should not form* in order to ensure avoidance of *unphysical scenarios*. Of course, he could not mention that I was the first to claim the non-occurrence of the apparent horizon.

Indeed, even in 2017, Valentina Baccetti, Robert B. Mann and Daniel R. Terno had argued against the formation of any event horizon.[27]

The bitter fact that the black hole paradigm actually fails to explain the observed astrophysical jets can be perceived from a rare candid admission by two prominent astrophysicists Avery E. Broderick of Perimeter Institute and Avi Loeb of Harvard, who in 2012 were selected as one of the most influential 'People in Space' by the *Time* magazine: 'More embarrassing to astrophysicists is our lack of understanding of black hole jets – phenomena in which the forces near a supermassive black hole somehow conspire to spew out material at ultra-relativistic speeds (up to 99.98 per cent of light speed).'[28]

The black hole paradigm tacitly treats spinning black holes not possessing a single free electron as best conductors teeming with trillions and trillions of free electrons by an innocuous assumption that external magnetic field lines thread the event horizon.

If wishes were horses, anybody could make the same assumption about a spinning ball of the worst insulator and imagine it to turn into the best conductor.

Well, such an embarrassment can be avoided by realizing that the so-called black holes are ultra-magnetized balls of plasma (MECOs). A spinning MECO may act as an ultra-relativistic pulsar and can not only accelerate charged particles by its strong electric field but also collimate the flow into jets by its strong magnetic fields.

In the very long run, science is much more than counting approval ratings. Whether the black hole paradigm has already fallen or not or what is the most reasonable black hole alternative cannot be decided by merely counting the number of citations. One cannot but recall here a famous quote by Galileo Galilei (1564–1642) who is often dubbed as the 'father of modern physics' even though this sounds like an old cliché in the present academic world: 'In questions of science, the authority of a thousand is not worth the humble reasoning of a single individual.'

Despite this suffocating scientific atmosphere afflicted by herd mentality and politics, the truth may be spreading. Consider Mike Row (1962–), a famous American TV host and narrator who has worked for *Discovery Channel, National Geographic* and CNN. In his blog of 12 January 2012, 'Off The Wall: Black Hole of Proof', he writes:

> But it's easy these days to confuse theory with fact. Thanks to countless movies and television shows

> that feature Black Holes as a plot device, and many documentaries that bring them to life with gorgeous CGI effects and dramatic music, a lot of people are under the assumption that Black Holes are every bit as real as the Sun and the Moon. Well, maybe they are, and maybe they aren't. We just don't know.[29]

And before this, he wrote,

> *The existence of Black Holes has never been proven.* Some cosmologists are now convinced they don't exist at all, and the race to prove their actuality has become pretty intense. Why? Because so much of what we think we know about the cosmos depends upon them. In other words, *the most popular explanations as to how the universe actually works, are based upon the existence of a thing that no one has been able to prove.*

Now consider a recent popular article on five weird black hole alternatives in Curiosity: wormholes, fuzzballs, boson stars, gravastars and MECOs.[30]

Black Holes Might Not Exist, So Here Are 5 Weirder Alternatives

Fig. 27 From a blog of Curiosity, last accessed 25 June 2018.

However, a little unprejudiced analysis will show that while the initial four alternatives are not only weirder but also require unexplained unphysical phase transitions of stellar matter, the idea of a MECO though weird is the natural alternative. Why? This is so because the dramatic gravitational trapping of the radiation of a collapsing massive star immediately preceding the formation of any horizon is an inevitable generic effect. This article does state: 'The idea here is that as a collapsing object gets super dense and super hot, the radiation it produces creates outward pressure that prevents its collapse, leaving it as a hot ball of plasma rather than a black hole.'

CHAPTER 25

Epilogue

Rebellion without truth is like spring in a bleak, arid desert – Khalil Gibran

Almost all physicists agree that in the real world, no physically significant quantity can be infinite. If infinities do rear their ugly heads in any theory, then

- the theory may be incorrect,
- it may have been applied by invoking some tacit unphysical assumption or
- it must be replaced by a fundamentally new theory.

To this extent, most physicists implicitly accept that in the real world, there cannot be any true black hole harbouring a singularity at its heart. Further, since acceleration due to gravity becomes infinite at the event horizon, there should not be any event horizon either.

In electromagnetism, we assume the existence of 'point charges' where electrostatic field strength is infinite. But in nature, the smallest particle is electron,which is not a mathematical point charge.

Nonetheless, infinities do occur even in quantum field theories. But such infinities can be eliminated in 'renormalized field theories', which take into consideration the usually ignored effects of various *negative self-interactions*.

Returning to the case of black holes, most physicists think that it is only some quantum gravity or some semi-classical gravity theory that might eliminate event horizons or central singularities. But as far as the event horizon is concerned, no such theory can prevent its formation because, for the cloud of gas that is approaching its event horizon, both the *space-time curvature* near the surface, and *mean density* fall off rapidly with the mass of the cloud and might be much lower than the same on the surface of the Earth or its atmosphere. Moreover, space-time curvature of the collapsing cloud changes smoothly as it would approach its event horizon. Thus no semi-classical gravity or quantum phase transition can really prevent the formation of large black holes. Hence, there should not be any formation of macroscopic quantum black holes or even quantum black hole mimickers. This is not to deny the fact that all macroscopic objects in the universe have a hidden quantum story. For instance, the Sun is ultimately made of electrons, protons and neutrons, all of which are quantum objects. But that does not mean that we must delude ourselves by coining a new term 'Quantum Sun'.

To repeat, the key to quantum renormalization theories is the inclusion of various opposing or negative self-interactions. Gravitation may be the only field theory that is renormalizable at the classical level itself by virtue of its *all-pervasive negative self-gravitational energy*. In fact, long ago, Arnowitt et al.[1] showed that even for an assumed 'point charge', negative self-gravitational interactions ensure that its mass–energy is finite and not infinite. More importantly, the mass of the point charge is proportional to the magnitude of its charge. Therefore, for an assumed neutral point mass having no charge, the mass energy turns out to be zero: M=0. This simple realization eliminates finite mass black holes from general relativity.

Since all semi-classical or quantum gravity effects can be negligibly small near event horizons, the only way to prevent their formation is by exploiting their property for which they are most notorious: nothing, not even light, can escape them. As soon as a star or cloud would contract beneath its photon sphere, the virtual event horizon, the heat and radiation generated within the star start getting trapped by classical gravity and not by any fanciful obscure undefined semi-classical or quantum gravity effect.

Since 'singularities' are often associated with points, one of the motivations behind string theory is the hypothesis that the basic constituents of matter are not point particles but 'strings' having tiny but finite extents. Yet paradoxically, string theorists proudly claim that their theory throws up solutions that should be interpreted as black holes possessing singularities and horizons.

This book has shown why the same generic classical gravity effect should turn contracting massive stars into quasi stastic ultra-hot balls of fire (ECO) and not any vacuum singular mathematical black holes.

Also, it is this same physical process that prevents the formation of mathematical 'point masses' in general relativity. However, quantum gravity theories that *tacitly presume* the existence of finite mass 'point particles' will conclude that gravity is the only theory that is not renormalizable.

On the other hand, now many physicists believe that gravity may be the only theory that cannot be quantized ever because gravity is the structure of space-time and not an interaction the way electromagnetism is. Therefore, the key to the elimination of event horizons must be sought in the framework of good old general relativity only.

If black holes are indeed prediction of the Einstein equations of general relativity, then by definition, black holes must obey the time symmetry of the same equations. Ironically, this would mean, non-formation of trapped surfaces, event horizons, and hence black holes. And this book shows how general relativity ensures this.

Note, the formation of an exact black holes would go against the spirit of general relativity which insists that '*there cannot be any preferred observer*' (Principle of General Covariance) because while a fictitious observer collapsing with a star is believed to perceive formations of the event horizon and the singularity, a *distant astronomer can never see the formulation of the event horizon*, let alone any singularity:

EXACT MATHEMATICAL BLACK HOLE (BH)	ETERNALLY COLLAPSING OBJECT (ECO)
To a distant astronomer, a massive star keeps on contracting eternally towards its event horizon; and no singularity, no exact BH is ever formed. So the star becomes an ECO, a frozen star.	To a distant astronomer, a massive star keeps on contracting eternally. No event horizon, no singularity is ever formed.

However, a *preferred* observer moving with the star dips below the event horizon and soon crashes into a singularity.
So there would be a FUNDAMENTAL DICHOTOMY between the physical realities perceived by an astronomer and a fictitious local observer.

An observer moving with the star too *has the same physical reality*. The star becomes an ECO, a frozen star, without formation of any event horizon and any singularity.
Perfect *unison* between the perceptions of all observers without any fundamental dichotomy.
No preferred observer.

And general relativity keeps obeying the principle of general covariance by ensuring that massive stars collapse into ECOs and not exact black holes.

So, Einstein's intuition that there cannot be any exact black holes in the real world was no intellectual senility, as portrayed by those arguing for the black hole paradigm. Instead, he was correct in his belief.

Nobel Prize for Physics in 2020

Even those readers who may have become convinced by most of the scientific evidences and discussions presented in this book might nonetheless wonder what to make of the fact that Roger Penrose has won the Nobel Prize for Physics in 2020 'for the discovery that black hole formation is a robust prediction of the general theory of relativity.'

But, did Penrose or anyone else really make any 'robust prediction' for the formation of true black holes? As far as exact solutions are concerned, indeed in 1939, Oppenheimer and Snyder[2] apparently showed that a massive star of uniform density would collapse to a true black hole possessing an event horizon provided *all resisting effects arising from pressure or heat flow or radiation or magnetic field would be completely ignored*. Here it is to be noted that all the surfaces in the interior of an assumed black hole are 'trapped surfaces' in the sense that even light pulses must only hurtle inwards towards the singularity. And Oppenheimer and Snyder were compelled to ignore all physical effects because even for an assumed spherical symmetry, there cannot be any exact generic solution for the Einstein equations for gravitational collapse if any single physical effect, for instances, buoyancy forces due to pressure gradient, are to be considered.

In 1965, therefore, Roger Penrose wanted to explore the likely formation of singularities by bypassing the impossible route of solving for the Einstein equations[3]. Instead he developed powerful geometrical arguments to conclude that singularity formation (but not event horizon formation) is inevitable for massive stars even when they are not spherically symmetric at all. However, in order to arrive at this geometrical picture, he required to make several assumptions and most crucial of which was that, sooner or later, collapsing massive stars must develop 'trapped surfaces' *a la* black holes.

And while discussing 'Singularity Theorems', which were fully developed by 1970, in 1973, Misner, Thorne and Wheeler observed that [4]: 'All these conditions, except the trapped surfaces, seem eminently reasonable for any physically realistic spacetime!'

In the preceding year 1972, Steven Weinberg had wisely commented, 'A realistic discussion... would require that we consider the effects of radiative energy transport, neutrino energy transport, turbulence, nuclear forces, magnetic fields, and above all rotations.' [5] Weinberg also wrote there, 'However, it is not known whether a real massive star will actually develop a trapped surface.'

Yet, Penrose tried to justify the assumption of formation of trapped surfaces by arguing that, pressure, by virtue of its tiny mass equivalence (p/c^2) should add to gravitational attraction instead of opposing the same. But the fact is that, even in general relativity, pressure gradient continues to resist gravity as was specifically shown by me a few years ago.[6,7]

Indeed in 1995, the Canadian relativist Kriele made an apt comment[8]: 'under normal circumstances such a trapped surface can only occur inside the black hole region. Thus the singularity theorems seem to be inapplicable for predicting the formation of a singularity before a black hole forms.' Kriele's comments essentially mean that, as if,

> Penrose and Hawking *actually assumed what they set out to prove*; by assuming the most crucial part of the proof, namely, inevitability of formation of trapped surfaces!

In Chapter 11, I discussed that completely pressure-less Oppenheimer and Snyder collapse is a nice mathematical illusion, which never occurs in real life, and mathematically Oppenheimer Snyder black hole has M=0 which never forms.[9,10]

It should be clear by now that, contrary to the citation by the Nobel Committee, neither Penrose nor anyone else has ever been able to present any 'robust evidence' for the formation of true black holes.

Further as discussed in Chapter 13, trapped surfaces as well as event horizon formations are not allowed in order that stellar matter continues to move like 'matter' and never behaves like 'light'[11,12]. And if trapped surfaces cannot form in the simplest spherical case, they also should not form in non-spherical cases where additional sources of resistivity like centrifugal repulsion would be present.

Finally we revert to the very Oppenheimer and Snyder paper which inspired Penrose into claiming inevitability of singularity formation in all cases of gravitational collapse[12]: 'Physically, such a singularity would mean that the expression used for the energy-momentum tensor does not take account of some essential physical fact which would really smooth the singularity out.' In the same page 456, they also wrote: 'Further, a star in its early stage of development would not possess a singular density or pressure; it is impossible for a singularity to develop in a finite time'. And this book has shown that the prophecy of Oppenheimer and Snyder was correct: massive stars should contract eternally without formation of any black hole or any singularity. This book cites about one hundred research papers or research news which talk about problems with the idea of black holes and hence their likely alternatives. It is in this sense that the hallowed black hole paradigm may have silently fallen despite the renewed hype generated by the 2020 Physics Nobel Prize.

Technical Notes

Proof that a Material Particle Would Behave as Light at a Black Hole Surface

For a test particle moving radially around a black hole, the square of the coordinate speed is given by[1]

$$\left(\frac{dR}{dT}\right)^2 = \frac{(1 - 2M/R)^2}{E^2}\left[E^2 - (1 - 2M/R)\right] \qquad (1)$$

where E is the conserved energy per unit rest mass of the test particle. Also, for radial motion of the material particle, the spacetime metric around the black hole reduces to

$$ds^2 = (1 - 2M/R)dT^2 - \frac{dR^2}{1 - 2M/R} \qquad (2)$$

These two foregoing equations can be combined into a highly insightful form:

$$ds^2 = dT^2\,\frac{(1 - 2M/R)}{E^2} \qquad (3)$$

Since ds^2 is an invariant, Eq. (3) is valid in all coordinate systems including the Kruskal ones. Since for photons $E = \infty$, Eq. (3) confirms that photons have $ds^2 = 0$ everywhere, including at $R < 2M$. But for material particles having finite E, Eq. (3) shows that:

$$\text{Sign of } ds^2 = \text{Sign of } (1 - 2M/R) \tag{4}$$

But the worldline of the material particle must always remain time-like, i.e., $ds^2 > 0$, and thus the material particle *must never* arrive at the event horizon. And this is possible only when the corresponding comoving proper time τ_H (tau) $\rightarrow \infty$.

For a test particle starting its journey from $R = R_b$, the comoving proper time to reach the event horizon is

$$\tau_H = \frac{2}{3}\frac{\pi R_b^{3/2}}{\sqrt{2M}} - \pi M \tag{5}$$

and which can be infinite only if the mass of the black hole M=0[1]. Note, the result that $M_{BH} = 0$ has been obtained by using the Kruskal coordinates too.[1]

Note, equation (1) also shows that $dR = 0$ at $R = 2M$. This strongly suggests that the minimum of R occurs at $R = 2M$. But the minimum of R is $R = 0$, and which too suggests that mathematical BHs correspond to $M = 0$.

For collapse of massive stars too, we obtained an equation similar to (4):

$$\text{Sign of } ds^2 = \text{Sign of } (1 - 2M(r,t)\ /R)$$

And since the motion of stellar matter, must always be time-like, $ds^2 > 0$, no apparent horizon ($R = 2M$) or no trapped surface ($R < 2M$) is allowed by general relativity.

Notes and References

Chapter 1 Introduction

1. A. Einstein (1939), 'On a Stationary System with Spherical Symmetry Consisting of Many Gravitating Masses', *Annals of Mathematics*, 40 (4), p. 922.

2. J.R. Oppenheimer and H. Snyder (1939),'On Continued Gravitational Contraction', *Physical Review*, 56, p. 455.

3. Ibid., p. 456.

4. Ibid.

5. A.I. Janis, E.T. Newman and J. Winicour (1968), 'Reality of the Schwarzschild Singularity', *Physical Review Letters*, 20, p. 878.

6. L. Bel (1969), 'Schwarzschild Singularity', *Journal of Mathematical Physics*, 10 (8), p. 1051.

7. S. Weinberg (1972), *Gravitation and Cosmology: Principles and Applications of the General Theory of Relativity*, New York: John Wiley, p. 349.

8. Ibid., p. 299.

9. F. Hoyle (1994), *Home is Where the Wind Blows: Chapters from a Cosmologist's Life*, USA: University Science Books, pp. 406, 413.

10. J.V. Narlikar and T. Padmanbhan (1988), 'The Schwarzschild Solution: Some Conceptual Difficulties', *Foundations of Physics*, 18 (6), p. 659.

11. https://www.seeker.com/black-hole-ejects-great-balls-of-fire-1765585533.html

12. https://www.sciencedaily.com/releases/2014/06/140604133818.htm

Chapter 2 Astrophysics Tidbits

1. E.C. Stoner (1929), 'Limiting Density of White Dwarf Stars', *Philosophical Magazine*, 7 (41), p. 63.

2. W. Anderson (1929), 'Über die Grenzdichte der Materie und der Energie', *Zeitschriftfür Physik*, 56, p. 851.

3. S. Chandrasekhar (1931), 'The Maximum Mass of Ideal White Dwarfs', *The Astrophysical Journal*, 74, p. 81.

4. D.R. Wilkins, L.C. Gallo, D. Grupe, K. Bonson, S. Komossa and A.C. Fabian (2015), 'Flaring from the Supermassive Black Hole in Mrk 335 Studied with Swift and NuSTAR', *Monthly Notices of the Royal Astronomical Society*, 454 (4), p. 4440.

5. B.K. Harrison, K.S. Thorne, M. Wakano and J.A. Wheeler (1965), *Gravitation Theory and Gravitational Collapse*, Chicago: University of Chicago Press, p. 75.

6. Ya. B. Zeldovich and I.D. Novikov (1971), *Relativistic Astrophysics*, Vol. 1, Chicago: University of Chicago Press, p. 297.

Chapter 3 Stars Losing Mass-Energy during Contraction

1. A. Mitra (2006), 'Why Gravitational Contraction Must Be Accompanied by Emission of Radiation in Both Newtonian And Einstein Gravity', *Physical Review D*, 74, p. 024010.

Chapter 4 Black Holes Everywhere

1. M. Smith (1963), '3C 273: A Star-Like Object with Large Red-Shift', *Nature*, 197 (16 March), p. 1040.

2. Ibid.

3. F. Hoyle and W. Fowler (1963), 'Nature of Strong Radio Sources', *Nature*, 197 (9 Feb.), p. 533.

4. F. Hoyle and W. Fowler (1963), 'On the Nature of Strong Radio Sources', *Monthly Notices Royal Astronomical Society*, 125 (2), p. 169.

5. G.R. Burbidge (1959), 'Estimates of the Total Energy in Particles and Magnetic Field in the Non-Thermal Radio Sources', *The Astrophysical Journal*, 129, p. 849.

6. V. L. Ginzburg (1964), 'The Magnetic Fields of Collapsing Masses and the Nature of Superstars', *Soviet Physics*, 9, p. 329.

7. E.E. Salpeter (1964), 'Accretion of Interstellar Matter by Massive Objects', *The Astrophysical Journal*, 140, p. 796; Ya. B. Zel'dovich (1964), 'The Fate of a Star and the Evolution of Gravitational Energy upon Accretion', *Doklady Akademii Nauk*, 155, p. 67, English translation (1964): *Soviet Physics–Doklady*, 9, p. 195; D. Lynden-Bell (1969), 'Galactic Nuclei as Collapsed Old Quasars', *Nature*, 223, p. 690.

8. The Event Horizon Collaboration (2019), 'First M87 Event Horizon Telescope Results. II. Array and Instrumentation', *The Astrophysical Journal Letters*, 875, p. 1.

9. K.S. Virbhadra and G.F.R. Ellis (2000), 'Schwarzschild Black Hole Lensing', *Physical Review D*, 62 (8), p. 084003.

10. Ibid.

Chapter 6 Black Holes: General Relativistic Solutions

1. K. Schwarzschild (1916),'On the Gravitational Field of a Mass Point according to Einstein's Theory', *Sitzungsber.Preuss.Akad. Wiss. Berlin*, p. 89. English translation was made only recently by

S. Antoci and A. Loinger:arXiv:physics/9905030. Also republished in *General Relativity and Gravitation* (2003), 35, p. 951.

2. J. Droste (1917), 'The Field of a Single Center in Einstein's Theory of Gravitation, and the Motion of a Particle in that Field', Proceedings of Royal Netherlands Academy of Arts and Sciences, 19 (I), p. 197. Available atwww.dwc.knaw.nl/DL/publications/PU00012325.pdf, see pp. 200–15.

3. D. Hilbert (1917), 'Die Grundlagen der Physik: zweite Mitteilung', *Nachr. Ges.Wiss. Göttingen, Math. Phys. Kl.*, 55, p. 201.

Chapter 7 Critique and Consolidation of the Black Hole Paradigm

1. M. Brillouin (1923), 'The Singular Points of Einstein's Universe', *Journal Physics Radium*, 23, p. 43. See English translation: arxiv.org/abs/physics/0002009

2. L. Bel (2007), 'Uber das Gravitationsfeld eines Massepunktes nach der Einstenschen Theorie', arXiv:0709.2257.

3. Ibid.

4. Y. Hagihara (1920), 'Theory of the Relativistic Trajectories in a Gravitational Field of Schwarzschild', *Japanese Journal of Astronomy and Geophysics*, 8, p. 67.

5. A. Eddington (1924), 'A Comparison of Whitehead's and Einstein's Formulae', *Nature*, 2832.

6. G. Lemaitre (1929), 'L'universen expansion', *Publication du Laboratoire d'Astronomie et de Géodésie de l'Université de Louvain*, 9, p. 205.

7. J.R. Oppenheimer and H. Snyder (1939), 'On Continued Gravitational Contraction', *Physical Review*, 56, p. 455

8. A. Einstein (1939), 'On a Stationary System with Spherical Symmetry Consisting of Many Gravitating Masses', *Annals of Mathematics*, 40 (4), p. 922.

9. M. Kruskal (1960), 'Maximal Extension of Schwarzschild Metric', *Physical Review*, 119, p. 1743.

Chapter 8 Yet More Critique of the Black Hole Paradigm

1. P.A.M. Dirac (1962), 'Particles of Finite Size in the Gravitational Field', *Proc. R. Soc. Lond. A*, 270, p. 354.

2. W.H. McCrea (1964), 'The Interpretation of the Schwarzschild Metric and the Release of Gravitational Energy', *Astrophisica Norvegica*, 9, p. 89.

3. Elizabeth Hilton (1965), 'The Singularity in the Schwarzschild Space-Time', *Proc. R. Soc. Lond. A*, 283, p. 491.

4. A.I. Janis, E.T. Newman and J. Winicour (1968), 'Reality of the Schwarzschild Singularity', *Physical Review Letters*, 20, p. 878.

5. L. Bel (1969), 'Schwarzschild Singularity', *Journal of Mathematical Physics*, 10 (8), p. 1051.

6. N. Rosen (1970), 'The Complete Schwarzschild Solution', *Annals of Physics*, 63 (1), p. 127.

7. N. Rosen (1985), 'Some Schwarzschild Solutions and Their Singularities', *Foundations of Physics*, 15 (4), p. 517.

8. F.I. Cooperstock and G.J.G. Junevicus (1973), 'Perspectives on the Schwarzschild Singularity', *Nuov Cim B*, 16, p. 387.

9. Ibid., p. 391.

10. D.H. Menzel (1976), 'Superstars and the Black Hole Myth', D.H. Menzel, *Memoires Societe Royale des Sciences de Liege*, 6 (1976), p. 343.

11. Ibid., p. 352

12. E.J. Opik (1977), 'Black Holes—A Myth?', *Irish Astronomical Journal*, 13, p. 125.

13. V. De Sabbata V. and T.K. Shah (1978), 'Is There Any Gravitational Field Outside a Black Hole?' *Nuovo Cimento*, 23, p. 409.

14. R. Gautreau (1980), 'On Kruskal-Novikov Co-ordinate Systems', Nuovo Cimento, 56B, p. 49; R. Gautreau (1999), 'The Incompleteness of Kruskal-Szekeres Space-Time', *International Journal of Modern Physics A*, 14 (16), p. 2593.

15. L. S. Abrams (1979), 'Alternative Space-Time for the Point Mass', *Physical Review D*, 20, p. 2474; L.S. Abrams (1996), 'Black Holes: The Legacy of Hilbert's Error', *Canadian Journal of Physics*, 74, 701, arXiv:gr-qc/0102055.

16. S. Antoci (2004), 'David Hilbert and the Origin of the "Schwarzschild Solution"', arXiv: physics/0310104, (2004); S. Antoci and D.-E. Liebscher (2005), 'The Topology of Schwarzschild's Solution and the Kruskal Metric', arXiv:gr-qc/0308005.

17. W.B. Bonnor (1992), 'Physical Interpretation of Vacuum Solutions of Einstein's Equations. Part I, Time-Independent Solutions', *General Relativity & Gravitation*, 24, p. 551.

18. Ibid., p. 557

19. Ibid., p. 556

20. T.M. Karade (1975), 'The Nature of the Singularity in the Gravitational Field of a Charged Particle', *Acta Physica Academiae Scientiarum Hungaricae*, 39, p. 227; M.S. Borkar and T. Karade (2003), 'On Singularity of Spherically Symmetric Space Times', *Indian Journal of Pure & Applied Mathematics*, 34, p. 1219.

21. S.I. Chermysnin (1992), 'A New Type of Solution of the Schwarzschild Problem for a Point-Source', *Astrophysics & Space Science*, 197, p. 233.

22. N.N. Fimin, V.M. Chechetkin (2009), 'The Collapse of Matter and the Formation of Black Holes: Conceptual Aspects', *Astronomy Reports*, 53, 824.

23. Ibid.

24. Ibid.

25. A.A. Logunov, M.A. Mestverishvili and V.V. Kiselev (2006), 'Black Holes: A Prediction of Theory or Phantasy?', *Phys. Part. Nuclear*, 37, p. 317, arXiv: gr-qc/0412058 (2004),

26. A.A. Logunov and M.A. Mestvirishvili (2012), 'Hilbert's Causality Principle and Equations of General Relativity Exclude

the Possibility of Black Hole Formation, *Theoretical & Mathematical Physics*, 170, p. 413.

27. R. Burghardt (2015), 'Collapsing Schwarzschild Interior Solution', *Journal of Modern Physics*, 6, p. 1895.

28. J.V. Narlikar and T. Padmanabhan (1988), 'The Schwarzschild Solution: Some Conceptual Difficulties', *Foundations of Physics*, 18 (6), p. 659.

29. Ibid.

Chapter 9 Ocean of Confusion in 'Black Hole Interior'

1. F. Salzman and G. Salzman (1969), 'Acceleration of Material Particles to the Speed of Light in General Relativity', *Lettere Nuovo Cimento*, 1 (17), 11.

2. A.I. Janis (1973), 'Note on Motion in the Schwarzschild Field', *Physical Review D*, 8, p. 2360.

3. G. Cavalleri and G. Spinelli (1977), 'Note on Motion in the Schwarzschild Field', *Physical Review D*, 15, p. 3065.

4. P. Crawford and I. Tereno (2002), 'Generalized Observers and Velocity Measurements in General Relativity', *General Relativity & Gravitation*, 34, p. 2075.

5. V. Sabbata, M. Pavsic and E. Eecami (1977), 'Black Holes and Tachyons', *Lett. Nuovo Cimento*, 19, p. 441; R. Goldoni, (1975), 'Black-and-White-Holes. II. Faster-than-Light Phenomena and Their Connection with the Complete Schwarzschild Manifold', *Acta Phys. Austriaca*, 41, p. 133; J.V. Narlikar (1978), 'Cosmic Tachyons: An Astrophysical Approach', *American Scientist*, 66, p. 587; K.D. Krori and B.B. Paul (1977), 'Light-Like Motions of Particles in Gravitational Fields', *Journal of Physics A*, 10, p. 1887 (1977); A. Das, N. Tariq and T. Biech (1995), 'Analytical Solutions of Spherically Symmetric Collapse of an Anisotropic Fluid Body into a Black Hole', *Journal of Mathematical Physics*, 36 (I), p. 340.

6. A.J.S. Hamilton and Jason P. Lisle (2008), 'The River Model of Black Holes', *American Journal of Physics*, 76, p. 519.

Chapter 10 Time Reversal Symmetry Forbids Black Holes

1. M. Francis (2016), 'Where Nature Hides the Darkest Mystery of All There's No Boundary Quite Like a Black Hole Boundary', www.nautil.us/issue/35/boundaries/where-nature-hides-the-darkest-mystery-of-all

2. J. Preskill, (2013), 'What's Inside a Black Hole', https://quantumfrontiers.com/2013/08/29/whats-inside-a-black-hole

3. 'Advanced Civilizations may live inside Supermassive Black Holes',www.dailygalaxy.com/my_weblog/2013/01/from-the-x-files-advanced-civilizations-may-live-inside-supermassive-black-holes.html

4. V.I. Dokuchaev (2011),'Is There Life Inside Black Holes?', *Classical & Quantum Gravity*, 28, p. 235015.

Chapter 11 No Real Theoretical Evidence for Black Hole Formation

1. J.R. Oppenheimer and H. Snyder (1939),'On Continued Gravitational Contraction', *Physical Review*, 56, p. 456.

2. Ibid.

3. Ibid.

4. A. Mitra (2011),'The Fallacy of Oppenheimer Snyder Collapse: No General Relativistic Collapse at All, No Black Hole, No Physical Singularity', *Astrophysics & Space Science (Letter)*, 332, p. 43; A. Mitra (2012),'Kruskal Coordinates and Mass of the Schwarzschild Black Hole: No Finite Mass Black Hole', *International Journal of Astronomy and Astrophysics*, 2, p. 236; A. Mitra and K.K. Singh

(2013), 'The Mass of the Oppenheimer Snyder Black Hole: Only Finite Mass Quasi-Black Holes', *International Journal of Modern Physics* (D), 22, p. 1350054.

5. A. Mitra (2010),'Does Pressure Increase or Decrease Active Gravitational Mass Density', *Physics Letters B*, 685, p. 8; A. Mitra (2013),'Does Pressure Accentuate General Relativistic Gravitational Collapse Formation of Trapped Surfaces?', *International Journal of Modern Physics D*, 22, p. 1350021.

6. A. Mitra (2006), 'Why Gravitational Contraction Must Be Accompanied by Emission of Radiation in Both Newtonian And Einstein Gravity', *Physical Review D*, 74, p. 024010.

7. A. Mitra (2012), 'Revisiting the Old Problem of General-Relativistic Adiabatic Collapse of a Uniform-Density Self-Gravitating Sphere', *Gravitation & Cosmology*, 18, p. 17.

8. S.S. Bayin (1979), 'Radiating Fluid Spheres in General Relativity', *Physical Review D*, 19, p. 2838.

9. B.C. Tewari (1988), 'Radiating Fluid Spheres in General Relativity', *Astrophysics and Space Science*, 149, p. 233.

10. B.C. Tewari and Kali Charan (2014), 'Radiating Star, Shear-Free Gravitational Collapse without Horizon', *Astrophysics and Space Science*, 351, p. 613; B.C. Tewari and K. Charan (2015), 'Horizon free eternally collapsing anisotropic radiating star', *Astrophysics and Space Science*, 357, id.107.

11. K.S. Newton and N. Pant (2015), 'Modeling quasar central engine as a relativistic radiating star', *Astrophysics and Space Science*, 355, p. 171.

Chapter 12 Pillars of the Black Hole Paradigm Crumbled

1. N.A. Doughty (1981), 'Acceleration of a Static Observer Near the Event Horizon of a Static Isolated Black Hole', *American Journal of Physics*, 49, p. 412.

2. A. Karlhede, U. Lindstrom, J.E. Aman (1982), 'A note on a local effect at the Schwarzschild sphere', *General Relativity and Gravitation*, 14, 569.

3. R.G. Gass, F.P. Esposito, L.C.R. Wijewardhana, and L. Witten (1998), 'Detecting Event Horizons and Stationary Surfaces', arXiv:gr-qc/9808055.

4. S.K. Chakrabarti and A.R. Prasanna (1990), 'The Newtonian Forces in the Kerr Geometry', *Journal of Astrophysics and Astronomy*, 11, p. 29.

5. T. Padmanabhan (1988), 'Phase Volume Occupied by a Test Particle around an Incipient Black Hole', *Physics Letters A*, 136, p. 203.

Chapter 13 Non-Occurrence of True Black Holes

1. C.W. Misner, K.S. Thorne and J.A. Wheeler (1973), *Gravitation*, New York: W.H. Freeman.

2. S. Weinberg (1972), *Gravitation and Cosmology: Principles and Applications of the General Theory of Relativity*, New York: John Wiley, p. 349

3. Ibid.

4. M. Kriele (1995),'On the Collapse of a Spherically Symmetric Star', *Journal Mathematical Physics*, 36, p. 3676.

5. A. Mitra (1998a), 'Final State of Spherical Gravitational Collapse and Likely Source of Gamma Ray Bursts',eprint:arXiv: astro-ph/9803014; A. Mitra (1998b), 'Towards the Final State of Spherical Gravitational Collapse and Likely Source of Gamma Ray Bursts', eprint:arXiv: astro-ph/9803013; Mitra (1998a), 'Final State of Spherical Gravitational Collapse'.

6. Ue-Li Pen, A. Loeb and N. Turok (1998), 'Gamma-Ray Bursts from Baryon Decay in Neutron Stars', *Astrophysical Journal*, 509, p. 537; F. Halzen and D. Hooper (2002), 'High-Energy

Neutrino Astronomy: The Cosmic Ray Connection', *Reports on Progress in Physics*, 65, p. 1025.

7. A. Mitra (2000), 'Non-occurrence of Trapped Surfaces and Black Holes in Spherical Gravitational Collapse: An Abridged Version', *Foundations of Physics Letters*, 13, p. 543.

8. A. Mitra (2002), 'On the Final State of Spherical Gravitational Collapse', *Foundations of Physics Letters*, 15, p. 439.

9. R.W. Lindquist, R.A. Schwartz and C.W. Misner (1965), 'Vaidya's Radiating Schwarzschild Metric', *Physical Review*, 137, p. 1364.

10. A. Mitra (2004),'A New Proof for Non-occurrence of Trapped Surfaces and Information Paradox', eprint:arXiv:astro-ph/0408323; A. Mitra (2005),'Comments on "Derivation of the Raychaudhuri Equation" by Dadhich', eprint:arXiv:gr-qc/0512006.

11. D.J. Leiter and S. Robertson (2003), 'Does the Principle of Equivalence Prohibit Trapped Surfaces from Forming in the General Relativistic Collapse Process?', *Foundations of Physics Letters*, 16(2), p. 143.

12. A. Mitra (2009), 'Quantum Information Paradox: Real or Fictitious?', *Pramana*, 73, p. 615, arXiv:0911.3518.

13. A. Raychaudhuri (1955), 'Relativistic Cosmology. I', *Physical Review*, 98, p. 1123.

14. A. Raychaudhuri (1957), 'Relativistic and Newtonian Cosmology', *Zeitschrift für Astrophysik*, 43, p.161.

15. C.G. Tsagas (2006), 'Magnetic tension and gravitational collapse', *Classical and Quantum Gravity*, 23, p. 4323 .

Chapter 14 Static Black Hole Alternatives

1. P.O. Mazur and E. Mottola (2004),'Gravitational Vacuum Condensate Stars', *Proceedings National Academy of Science*, 101, p. 9545;

2. G. Chapline (2005), 'Dark Energy Stars', arXiv:astro-ph/0503200.

3. A. Mitra (2005), 'Comments on the Proposal of Dark Energy Stars by Chapline', arXiv:astro-ph/0504384.

4. S. Mathur (2005), 'The Fuzzball Proposal for Black Holes: An Elementary Review', *Fortsch. Phys.*, 53, p. 793.

5. R.H. Hoffman & other contributors (1997), 'What Exactly Is a Wormhole? Have Wormholes Been Proven to Exist or Are They Still Theoretical?', *Scientific American*, 15 September, https://www.scientificamerican.com/article/follow-up-what-exactly-is/; 'Could Wormholes Really Work? Probably Not', *Space*, 1 February2017, https://www.space.com/35522-stop-talking-about-wormholes.html

Chapter 15 Why Eternally Collapsing Objects (ECOs)

1. A. Mitra (2004), 'A New Proof for Non-occurrence of Trapped Surfaces and Information Paradox', eprint:arXiv:astro-ph/0408323; A. Mitra (2005), 'Comments on "Derivation of the Raychaudhuri Equation" by Dadhich', eprint:arXiv:gr-qc/0512006; A. Mitra (2009), 'Quantum Information Paradox: Real or Fictitious?', *Pramana*, 73, p. 615, arXiv:0911.3518.

2. A. Mitra (2006), 'A Generic Relationship between Baryonic and Radiative Energy Densities of Stars', *Monthly Notices Royal Astronomical Society (Lett.)*, 367, p. L66

3. A. Mitra (2006), 'Radiation Pressure Supported Stars in Einstein Gravity: Eternally Collapsing Objects', *Monthly Notices Royal Astronomical Society*, 369, p. 492; A. Mitra (2006), 'Sources of Stellar Energy, Einstein–Eddington Timescale of Gravitational Contraction and Eternally Collapsing Objects', *New Astronomy*, 12(2), p. 146; A. Mitra and N.K. Glendenning (2010), 'Likely

Formation of General Relativistic Radiation Pressure Supported Stars or Eternally Collapsing Objects', *Monthly Notices Royal Astronomical Society*(Lett.), 404, pp. L50–L54.

4. A. Mitra (2006),'Radiation Pressure Supported Stars'; Mitra (2006),'Sources of Stellar Energy'; A. Mitra and N.K. Glendenning (2010), 'General Relativistic Radiation Pressure Supported Stars'; A. Mitra (2006), 'Black Holes or Eternally Collapsing Objects: A Review of 90 Years of Misconception', in *Focus on Black Hole Research*, Paul V. Kreitler (ed.), New York: Nova, pp. 1–94; A. Mitra (2014), 'Einsteinian Revolution's Misinterpretation: No True Black Holes, No Information Paradox: Just Quasi-static Balls of Quark Gluon Plasma', in *New Results and Actual Problems in Particle & Astroparticle Physics and Cosmology*, edited by R. Ryutin, V. Petrov, and V. Kiselev, ebook, World Scientific, pp. 153–63.

Chapter 16 Why Magnetospheric Eternally Collapsing Objects (MECOs)

1. V.L. Ginzburg (1964), 'The Magnetic Fields of Collapsing Masses and the Nature of Superstars', *Soviet Physics*, 9, p. 329.

2. S.L. Robertson and D.J. Leiter (2002), 'Evidence for Intrinsic Magnetic Moments in Black Hole Candidates', *Astrophysical Journal*, 565, p. 447.

3. S.L. Robertson and D.J. Leiter (2002), 'On Intrinsic Magnetic Moments in Black Hole Candidates', *Astrophysical Journal*, 596, p. L203; S.L. Robertson and D.J. Leiter (2004), 'On the Origin of the Universal Radio-X-ray Luminosity Correlation in Black Hole Candidates', *Monthly Notices Royal Astronomical Society*, 350, p. 1391; S.L. Robertson and D.J. Leiter (2006), 'The Magnetospheric Eternally Collapsing Object (MECO) Model of Galactic Black Hole Candidates and Active Galactic Nuclei', in *New Developments in Black Hole Research*, Paul V. Kreitler (ed.), New York: Nova Science Publishers, Inc., p.1.

4. R.E. Schild, D.J. Leiter and S.L. Robertson (2006), 'Observations Supporting the Existence of an Intrinsic Magnetic Moment inside the Central Compact Object within the Quasar Q0957+561', *Astronomical Journal*, 132, p. 420.

5. R.E. Schild, D.J. Leiter and S.L. Robertson (2008), 'Direct Microlensing-Reverberation Observations of the Intrinsic Magnetic Structure of Active Galactic Nuclei in Different Spectral States: A Tale of Two Quasars', *Astronomical Journal*, 135, p. 947.

6. J. Lovegrove, R.E. Schild and D.J. Leiter (2011), 'Discovery of Universal Outflow Structures above and below the Accretion Disc Plane in Radio-Quiet Quasars', *Monthly Notices Royal Astronomical Society*, 412, p. 2631; R.E. Schild and D.J. Leiter (2010), 'Black Hole or Meco: Decided by a thin Luminous Ring Structure Deep Within Quasar Q0957+561', *Journal of Cosmology*, 6, p. 1400.

7. S.L. Robertson and D.J. Leiter (2010), 'Does Sgr A* Have an Event Horizon or a Magnetic Moment?', *Journal of Cosmology*, 6, p. 1438.

Chapter 17 Have True Black Holes Been Detected?

1. K.S. Virbhadra and G.F.R. Ellis (2000), 'Schwarzschild Black Hole Lensing', *Physical Review D*, 62 (8), p. 084003.

2. V. Cardoso, F. Edgardo and P. Pani (2016), 'Is the Gravitational-Wave Ringdown a Probe of the Event Horizon?', *Physical Review Letters*, 116, p. 171101.

3. R. Narayan (2003), 'Evidence for the Black Hole Event Horizon', *Astronomy & Geophysics*, 44(6), p. 6.22.

4. A. Mitra (2006), 'On the Non-occurrence of Type I X-ray Bursts from the Black Hole Candidates', *Advances in Space Research*, 38, p. 2917.

5. A. Mitra (2005), 'Why the Observed Black Hole Candidates Do Not Show Spin Pulsation', arXiv: astro-ph/0510205.

6. M.A. Abramowicz, W. Kluzniak and J.P. Lasota (2002), 'No Observational Proof of the Black-Hole Event-Horizon', *Astronomy & Astrophysics*, 396, p. L31.

Chapter 18 Fall of the Black Hole Paradigm

1. N.A. Doughty (1981), 'Acceleration of a Static Observer Near the Event Horizon of a Static Isolated Black Hole', *American Journal of Physics*, 49, p. 412.

2. A. Karlhede, U. Lindstrom and J.E. Aman (1982),'A Note on a Local Effect at the Schwarzschild Sphere', *General Relativity & Gravitation*,14, p. 569.

3. J.R. Oppenheimer and H. Snyder (1939),'On Continued Gravitational Contraction', *Physical Review*, 56, p. 455.

4. A. Mitra (2011), 'The Fallacy of Oppenheimer Snyder Collapse: No General Relativistic Collapse at All, No Black Hole, No Physical Singularity', *Astrophysics & Space Science (Letter)*, 332, p. 43; A. Mitra and K.K. Singh (2013),'The Mass of the Oppenheimer Snyder Black Hole: Only Finite Mass Quasi-Black Holes', *International Journal Modern Physics (D)*, 22, p. 1350054.

5. A. Mitra (2017), 'Mass of Schwarzschild Black Holes Is Indeed Zero And Black Hole Candidates Are Quasi Black Holes', arXiv:1708.07404.

6. D.J. Leiter and S. Robertson (2003),'Does the Principle of Equivalence Prohibit Trapped Surfaces from Forming in the General Relativistic Collapse Process?', *Foundations of Physics Letters*, 16(2), p. 143; A. Mitra (2009), 'Quantum Information Paradox: Real or Fictitious?', *Pramana*, 73, p. 615, arXiv:0911.3518

7. A. Mitra (2005),'Comments on "Derivation of the Raychaudhuri Equation" by Dadhich', eprint: arXiv:gr-qc/0512006; Leiter and Robertson (2003), 'Principle of

Equivalence'; Mitra (2009), 'Quantum Information Paradox'; P.O. Mazur and E. Mottola (2004), 'Gravitational Vacuum Condensate Stars', *Proceedings National Academy of Science*, 101, p. 9545.

8. R. Arnowitt, S. Deser and C.W. Misner (1960), 'Finite Self-Energy of Classical Point Particles', *Physical Review Letters*, 4, p. 375.

9. A.I. Janis, E.T. Newman and J. Winicour (1968), 'Reality of the Schwarzschild Singularity', *Physical Review Letters*, 20, p. 878.

10. Ibid.

11. L. Bel (1969), 'Schwarzschild Singularity', *Journal of Mathematical Physics*, 10 (8), p. 1051.

Chapter 19 Basic Failure of Black Hole Astrophysics

1. N.I. Shakura and R.A. Sunyaev (1973), 'Black Holes in Binary Systems, Observational Appearance', *Astronomy & Astrophysics*, 24, p. 337.

2. R.D. Blandford and R.L. Znajek (1977), 'Electromagnetic Extraction of Energy from Kerr Black Holes', *Monthly Notices Royal Astronomical Society*, 179, p. 433.

3. Ibid.

4. I. Contopoulos (2015),'A Cosmic Battery around Black Holes', in *The Formation and Disruption of Black Hole Jets*, I. Contopoulos, D. Gabuzda and N. Kylafis (eds), Astrophysics and Space Science Library, Volume 414, Switzerland: Springer International Publishing, p. 227.

5. D.A. Macdonald, R.H. Price, W.M. Suen and K.S. Thorne (1986), 'Black Holes: the membrane paradigm', in *Black Holes: The Membrane Paradigm*, K.S. Thorne, R.H. Price and D.A. Macdonald (eds), New Haven, London: Yale University Press.

6. Ibid., p. 46.

7. S.E. Woosley (1993), 'Gamma-Ray Bursts from Stellar Mass Accretion Disks around Black Holes', *Astrophysical Journal*, 405, p.

273; S.E. Woosley and A. Heger,'Long Gamma-Ray Transients from Collapsars', *Astrophysical Journal*, 752, p. 32.

8. *GRBs as Hypernovae:* B. Paczynski, arXiv: astro-ph/9706232, (1997).

9. N.I. Shakura and R.A. Sunyaev (1973), 'Black Holes in Binary Systems', *Astronomy and Astrophysics*, 24, p.337.

10. B. Paczynski (1997), 'GRBs as Hypernovae', arXiv: astro-ph/9706232.

Chapter 20 Tentative Evidence against True Black Holes

1. http://www.newsweek.com/black-holes-burp-implications-physics-782041

2. http://www.skyandtelescope.com/astronomy-news/black-hole-shoots-bullets/

3. D.R. Wilkins, L.C. Gallo, D. Grupe, K. Bonson, S. Komossa and A.C. Fabian (2015), 'Flaring from the Supermassive Black Hole in Mrk 335 Studied with Swift and NuSTAR',*Monthly Notices Royal Astronomical Society*, 454, p. 4440.

4. https://mysteriousearth.net/2017/03/18/nasa-observes-object-coming-out-of-a-blackhole-for-the-first-time-ever/

Chapter 21 Direct Evidence against True Black Holes

1. N.I. Shakura and R.A. Sunyaev (1973), 'Black Holes in Binary Systems, Observational Appearance', *Astronomy & Astrophysics*, 24, p. 337.

2. Ibid.

3. Yu.N. Gnedin, N.V. Borisov, T.M. Natsvlishvili, M.Yu. Piotrovich and N.A. Silant'ev (2003), 'Magnetic and Electric Fields around the Black Hole in Cyg X-1', arXiv:astro-ph/0304158.

4. Ibid.

5. M.D. Johnson et al. (2015), 'Resolved Magnetic-Field Structure and Variability Near the Event Horizon of Sagittarius A*', *Science*, 350(6265), p. 1242.

6. I. Marti-Vidal et al. (2015), 'A Strong Magnetic Field in the Jet Base of a Supermassive Black Hole', *Science*, 348(6232), p. 311.

7. M. Zamaninasab, E. Clausen-Brown, T. Savolainen and A. Tchekhovskoy (2014), 'Dynamically Important Magnetic Fields Near Accreting Supermassive Black Holes', *Nature*, 510(7503), p. 126.

8. https://www.thenakedscientists.com/articles/science-news/are-black-holes-magnetic

9. http://www.skyandtelescope.com/astronomy-news/our-magnetic-black-hole-0312201523/

10. N.I. Shakura and R. Sunyaev (1973), 'Black Holes in Binary Systems', p. 337.

11. R. Narayan, I.V. Igumenshchev and M.A. Abramowicz (2003), 'Magnetically Arrested Disk: An Energetically Efficient Accretion Flow', *Publications Astronomical Society of Japan*, 55, p. L69.

12. Qiu-He Peng, Jing-Jing Liu and Chih-Kang Chou (2016), 'A Possible Influence on Standard Model of Quasars and Active Galactic Nuclei in Strong Magnetic Field', *Astrophysics & Space Science*, 361, p. 388.

Chapter 22 Scientific Developments Post Research

1. http://edition.cnn.com/2002/TECH/space/01/22/gravastars/index.html

2. http://www.nature.com/news/2004/040715/full/news040712-12.html

3. http://news.bbc.co.uk/2/hi/science/nature/3913145.stm

4. http://www.nature.com/news/2005/050328/full/news050328-8.html

5. http://www.scienceagogo.com/news/black_hole_observations.shtml

6. https://www.newscientist.com/article/dn9620-mysterious-quasar-casts-doubt-on-black-holes/

7. https://www.universetoday.com/383/a-new-view-of-quasars/

8. https://www.newscientist.com/article/dn12089-do-black-holes-really-exist/

9. http://www.sciencemag.org/news/2007/06/no-more-black-holes

10. http://www.nature.com/news/stephen-hawking-there-are-no-black-holes-1.14583

11. www.npr.org/sections/13.7/2014/02/05/272004778/do-black-holes-exist

12. https://www.universetoday.com/114802/there-are-no-such-things-as-black-holes/

13. www.dailygalaxy.com/my_weblog/2014/11/black-holes-are-actually-eternally-collapsing-objects-indian-physicist-refutes-hawking.html

14. www.discovermagazine.com/2015/april/20-no-such-thing-as-a-black-hole

15. www.naturalphilosophy.org/site/harryricker/2015/05/13/supermassive-black-holes-more-fiction-than-scientific-fact

16. https://listverse.com/2015/10/26/10-strange-theoretical-stars/

17. https://www.pbs.org/wgbh/nova/article/are-black-holes-real/

18. http://www.techtimes.com/articles/111865/20151130/black-holes-are-ultra-hot-balls-of-fire-like-our-sun-scientist.htm

19. https://www.npl.washington.edu/av/altvw192.html

20. https://www.express.co.uk/news/science/974091/black-hole-worm-hole-space-news-gravitational-waves

21. https://www.skyandtelescope.com/astronomy-news/physicist-proposes-new-black-hole-alternative/

22. https://www.techquila.co.in/5-stunning-alternatives-to-black-holes-in-case-they-dont-exist/

23. https://www.scientificamerican.com/article/black-hole-pretenders-could-really-be-bizarre-quantum-stars/

24. https://phys.org/news/2018-07-black-holes-ever-growing-balls.html

25. M. Visser, C. Barcelo, S. Liberati and S. Sonego (2009), 'Small, Dark, and Heavy: But Is It a Black Hole?, arXiv: 0902.0346; S. Kalyana Rama (2014), 'Massive Compact Objects in a Quantum Theory of Gravity', arXiv:1409.3462; B. Holdom and J. Ren (2017), 'Not Quite a Black Hole', *Physical Review D*, 95, p. 084034; A. Davood 'Do Horizons Exist?', arXiv:160701286.

26. C. Corda and H.J. Mosquera Cuesta (2010), 'Removing Black Hole Singularities with Nonlinear Electrodynamics', *Modern Physics Letters A*, 25, p. 2423; C. Corda, D. Leiter, H. Mosquera Cuesta, S. Robertson and R. Schild (2011), 'Farewell to Black Hole Horizons and Singularities', *Journal of Cosmology*, 17, p. 13.

27. R. Goswami and P.S. Joshi (2005), 'A Resolution of Space-Time Singularity and Black Hole Paradoxes through Avoidance of Trapped Surface Formation in Einstein Gravity', arXiv:gr-qc/0504019; P.S. Joshi and R. Goswami (2007), 'On Trapped Surface Formation in Gravitational Collapse', *Classical & Quantum Gravity*, 24, p. 2917; R. Goswami, P.S. Joshi and P. Singh (2006), 'Quantum Evaporation of a Naked Singularity', *Physical Review Letters*, 96, p. 031302.

28. F. Fayos and R. Torres (2008), 'A Class of Interiors for Vaidya's Radiating Metric: Singularity-Free Gravitational Collapse', *Classical & Quantum Gravity*, 25, p. 175009; F. Fayos

and R. Torres (2010), 'Local Behaviour of Evaporating Stars and Black Holes around the Total Evaporation Event', *Classical & Quantum Gravity*, 27, p. 125011; R. Torres and F. Fayos (2015), 'On the Quantum Corrected Gravitational Collapse', *Physics Letters B*, 747, p. 245.

29. T. Vachaspati, D. Stojkovic and L.M. Krauss (2007), 'Observation of Incipient Black Holes and the Information Loss Problem', *Physical Review D*, 76, p. 024005; Z. Chang, Cheng-Bo Guan, Chao-Guang Huang and Xin Li (2008), 'Gravitational Collapse without a Remnant', *International Journal of Theoretical Physics*, 47, p. 2479; C. Barceló, S. Liberati, S. Sonego and M. Visser (2008), 'Fate of Gravitational Collapse in Semi classical Gravity', *Physical Review D*, 7, p. 044032; L. Mersini-Houghton (2014), 'Backreaction of Hawking Radiation on a Gravitationally Collapsing Star I: Black Holes?', *Physics Letters B*, 738, p. 61; Pei-Ming Ho (2016), 'The Absence of Horizon in Black-Hole Formation', *Nuclear Physics B*, 909, p. 394; V. Baccetti, R.B. Mason and D.R. Terno (2017), 'Do Event Horizons Exist?', *International Journal Modern Physics*, 26, p. 743008.

30. Baccetti et al. (2017), 'Do Event Horizons Exist?', p. 743008

31. V. Baccaetti, R.B. Mann and D.R. Terno (2017),'Horizon Avoidance in Spherically-Symmetric Collapse', arXiv:1703.09369; V. Baccetti, R.B. Mann and D.R. Terno (2018), 'Role of Evaporation in Gravitational Collapse', *Classical and Quantum Gravity*, 35, p. 185005.

32. Pei-Ming Ho (2017), 'Asymptotic Black Hole', *Classical & Quantum Gravity*, 34, p. 085006.

33. R.B. Mann, I. Nagle and D.R. Terno (2018), 'Transition to Light-Like Trajectories in Thin Shell Dynamics', *Nuclear Physics B*, 936, p. 19.

34. Kalyana Rama (2014), 'Massive Compact Objects'; Corda and Mosquera Cuesta (2010), 'Removing Black Hole Singularities'; Corda et al. (2011), 'Farewell to Black Hole Horizons'.

Chapter 23 Why the Black Hole Paradigm is a Mirage

1. A.I. Janis, E.T. Newman and J. Winicour (1968), 'Reality of the Schwarzschild Singularity', *Physical Review Letters*, 20, p. 878.

2. L. Bel (1969), 'Schwarzschild Singularity', *Journal of Mathematical Physics*, 10 (8), p. 1051.

3. A.G. Agnese and M. La Camera (1985), 'Gravitation without black holes', *Physical Review D*, 31, p. 1280

4. J.V. Narlikar and T. Padmanbhan (1988), 'The Schwarzschild Solution: Some Conceptual Difficulties', *Foundations of Physics*, 18 (6), p. 659.

5. Ibid.

6. Ibid.

Chapter 24 Towards an Alternative Paradigm

1. 'Scientific Controversies No. 15: Black Holes',26 July 2018, https://pioneerworks.org/programs/scientific-controversies-no-15-black-holes/

2. Camille M. Carlisle (2016), 'What's Inside a Black Hole?'28 December 2016, http://www.skyandtelescope.com/astronomy-resources/whats-inside-a-black-hole/

3. R. Doran, F.S.N. Lobo and P. Crawford (2008), 'Interior of a Schwarzschild Black hole Revisited', *Foundations of Physics*, 38, p. 160.

4. J. Abedi, H. Dykaar and N. Afshordibedi (2017), 'Echoes from the Abyss: Evidence for Planck-Scale Structure at Black Hole Horizons', *Physical Review D*, 96, p. 082004.

5. J. Abedi and N. Afshordi (2019), 'Echoes from the Abyss: A Highly Spinning Black Hole Remnant for the Binary Neutron Star Merger GW170817',*Journal of Cosmology & Astrophysics*, 1911 (11), p. 010.

6. J. Abedi, H. Dykaar, N. Afshordi (2017), 'Echoes from the Abyss: Evidence for Planck-scale structure at black hole horizons' *Physical Review* D, 96, 082004.

7. Z. Mark, A. Zimmerman, S.M. Du and Y. Chen (2017), 'A Recipe for Echoes from Exotic Compact Objects', *Physical Review* D, 96, p. 084002; Q. Wang and N. Afshordi (2018), 'Black Hole Echology: The Observer's Manual', arXiv:1803.02845; V. Cardoso and P. Pani (2017), 'Tests for the Existence of Horizons through Gravitational Wave Echoes', *Nature Astronomy*, 1, p. 586; V. Cardoso and P. Pani (2019), 'Testing the Nature of Dark Compact Objects: A Status Report', http://thegravityroom.blogspot.in/2017/03/can-exotic-compact-objects-exist.html

8. V. Cardoso and P. Pani (2017), 'Tests for the Existence of Horizons'.

9. B. Arderucio-Costa and W. G. Unruh (2018),'Model for Quantum Effects in Stellar Collapse', *Physical Review D*, 9, p. 1024005.

10. W.G. Unruh, Chih-Hung Wu and Dong-Han Yeom (2018), 'Pre-Hawking Radiation Cannot Prevent the Formation of Apparent Horizon', *Physical Review D*, 97, p. 064045.

11. Paolo Pani (2017), 'Can Exotic Compact Objects Exist?', blog, 3 March 2017.

12. A. Mitra and K.D. Krori (2011),'Why No Energy Can Be Extracted From Rotating Kerr Black Holes', *Journal of Cosmology*, 17, p. 7064; A. Mitra (2011),'General Relativistic Radiation Pressure Supported Stars as Quasar Central Engines in a Universe which is Recycling Matter', *Journal of Cosmology*, 17, p. 7376.

13. V. Cardoso, F. Edgardo and P. Pani (2016), 'Is the Gravitational-Wave Ringdown a Probe of the Event Horizon?', *Physical Review Letters*, 116, p. 171101.

14. Cardoso and Pani (2017), 'Tests for the Existence of Horizons'.

15. Cardoso and Pani (2019), 'Testing the Nature of Dark Compact Objects'.

16. A. Lobanov (2007), 'The VLBI Space Observatory ProgrammeVSOP-2', https://www.mpifr-bonn.mpg.de/1041012/lobanov-vsop2.pdf

17. A. Lobanov (2009), '*Fundamental Physics with Radio Observations*', https://physikseminar.desy.de/sites2009/site_physikseminar/content/e212/e68319/e94631/e96282/Lobanov-desy-col.pdf

18. A. Lobanov(2017), 'Beyond the Event Horizon or Altogether Without It?', *Nature Astronomy*, 1, p. 0069.

19. Ibid.

20. A.A. Logunov, M.A. Mestverishvili and V.V. Kiselev (2004), 'Black Holes: A Prediction of Theory or Phantasy?', *Phys. Part. Nuclear*, 37, p. 317, arXiv: gr-qc/0412058.

21. V.V. Kiselev (2005), 'Radial Geodesics as a Microscopic Origin of Black Hole Entropy', *Physical Review D*, 72, p. 124011.

22. J.V. Narlikar and T. Padmanabhan (1988), 'The Schwarzschild Solution: Some Conceptual Difficulties', *Foundations of Physics*, 18 (6), p. 659.

23. A. Mitra, C. Corda and H.J. Mosquera Cuesta (2020), 'How to distinguish an actual astrophysical magnetized black hole mimicker from a true (theoretical) black hole', *Astrophysics & Space Science* (submitted)

24. A. Mitra (2020), 'Rebuttal of "A revisit of the problems of Abhas Mitra's Eternally Collapsing Object"' (arXiv/submit/3462013), https://www.academia.edu/44522543/Rebuttal_of_A_revisit_of_the_problems_of_Abhas_Mitras_Eternally_Collapsing_Object

25. S. Chandrasekhar (1931), 'The Maximum Mass of Ideal White Dwarfs', *The Astrophysical Journal*, 74, p. 81.

26. D. Terno (2019), 'Self-Consistent Description of a Spherically-Symmetric Gravitational Collapse', arXiv:1903.04744.

27. V. Baccetti, R.B. Mason and D.R. Terno (2017), 'Do Event Horizons Exist?', *International Journal Modern Physics*, 26, p. 1743008.

28. A.E. Broderick and A. Loeb (2013), 'Portrait of a Black Hole', *Scientific American*, 21 May, https://www.scientificamerican.com/article/portrait-of-a-black-hole-extreme-physics-special/

29. 'Off The Wall: Black Hole of Proof', 12 January 2018, http://mikerowe.com/2018/01/otw-black-hole-of-proof/

30. 'Black Holes Might Not Exist: Here Are 5 Weirder Alternatives', *Curiosity*, 25 June 2018, https://curiosity.com/topics/black-holes-might-not-exist-so-here-are-5-weirder-alternatives-curiosity/

Epilogue

1. R. Arnowitt, S. Deser, and C.W. Misner (1960), 'Finite Self-Energy of Classical Point Particles', *Physical Review Letters*, 4, 375.

2. J.R. Oppenheimer and H. Snyder (1939), 'On Continued Gravitational Contraction', *Physical Review*, 56, 455. See P. 546.

3. R. Penrose (1965), *Gravitational* 'Collapse and Space-Time Singularities', *Physical Review Letters*, 5, 57.

4. C. Misner, K.S. Thorne and J.A. Wheeler (1973), 'Gravitation', W.H. Freeman and Co., San Fransisco, 1973, p. 967.

5. S. Weinberg (1972), 'Gravitation and Cosmology: Principles and Applications of the General Theory of Relativity', John Wiley, New York.

6. A. Mitra (2010), 'Does Pressure Increase or Decrease Active Gravitational Mass Density', *Physics Letters B* 685, 8.

7. A. Mitra (2013), 'Does Pressure Accentuate General Relativistic Gravitational Collapse and Formation of Trapped Surfaces', *International Journal of Modern Physics D* 22, id. 1350021.

8. M. Kriele (1995), 'On the collapse of a spherically symmetric star', *Journal of Mathematical Physics*,36, 3676.

9. A. Mitra (2011), 'The Fallacy of Oppenheimer Snyder Collapse: no general relativistic collapse at all, no black hole, no physical singularity', *Astrophysics & Space Science (Letter)*, 332, 43.

10. A. Mitra and K.K. Singh (2013), 'The Mass of the Oppenheimer Snyder Black Hole: Only Finite Mass Quasi-Black Holes' *International Journal of Modern Physics* (D), 22, 1350054.

11. A. Mitra (2004), `A new proof for non-occurrence of trapped surfaces and information paradox, eprint arXiv:astro-ph/0408323.

12. A. Mitra (2009), `Quantum information paradox: Real or fictitious?', *Pramana*, 73, 615.

13. J.R. Oppenheimer and H. Snyder (1939), `On Continued Gravitational Contraction', *Physical Review*, 56, 455. See p. 456.

Technical Notes

1. A. Mitra (2012), 'Kruskal Coordinates and Mass of the Schwarzschild Black Hole: No Finite Mass Black Hole', *International Journal of Astronomy and Astrophysics*, 2, p. 236; A. Mitra (2000), 'Non-occurrence of Trapped Surfaces and Black Holes in Spherical Gravitational Collapse: An Abridged Version', *Foundations of Physics Letters*, 13, p. 543; A. Mitra (2002), 'On the Final State of Spherical Gravitational Collapse', *Foundations of Physics Letters*, 15, p. 439.

Research Publications behind the MECO Paradigm

1. 'Towards the Final State of Spherical Gravitational Collapse and Likely Source of Gamma Ray Bursts', A. Mitra, arXiv: astro-ph/9803013 (1998).
2. 'Final State of Spherical Gravitational Collapse and Likely Source of Gamma Ray Bursts', A. Mitra, arXiv: astro-ph/9803014 (1988).
3. 'On the Nature of the Compact Objects in the AGNs', A. Mitra, paper presented in 19th Texas Symposium on Relativistic Astrophysics, Paris, arXiv:astro-ph/9812135 (1998).
4. 'Is General Theory of Relativity Actually Free of Singularities', A. Mitra, abstracts of the 19th Texas Symposium on Relativistic Astrophysics and Cosmology, held in Paris, France, 14–18 December (1998).
5. 'Why General Theory of Relativity Allows the Existence of Only External Black Holes', A. Mitra, arXiv:hep-th/9905182 (1999).

6. 'Final Comments on "Another View on the Velocity at the Schwarzschild Horizon" by Tereno', A. Mitra, arXiv:astro-ph/9905329 (1999).
7. 'Non-occurrence of Trapped Surfaces and Black Holes in Spherical Gravitational Collapse: An Abridged Version', A. Mitra, *Foundations of Physics Letters*, 13(6), 543 (2000).
8. 'On the Question of Trapped Surfaces and Black Holes', A. Mitra, invited talk given in a workshop on black holes, Calcutta, organized by Centre for Space Physics, arXiv:astro-ph/0105532 (2001).
9. 'On the Final State of Spherical Gravitational Collapse', A. Mitra, Foundations of Physics Letters, 15(5), 439 (2002).
10. 'On the Nature of the Compact Condensations at the Centre of Galaxies', A. Mitra, *Bulletin of the Astronomical Society of India*, 30, 173, arXiv:astro-ph/0205261 (2002).
11. 'How Black Are Black Hole Candidates?', S.L. Robertson and D.J. Leiter, arXiv:astro-ph/0208333 (2002).
12. 'Evidence for Intrinsic Magnetic Moments in Black Hole Candidates', S.L. Robertson and D.J. Leiter, *Astrophysical Journal*, 565, 447 (2002).
13. 'Does the Principle of Equivalence Prohibit Trapped Surfaces from Forming in the General Relativistic Collapse Process?', D.J. Leiter and S. Robertson, *Foundations of Physics Letters*, 16(2), 143 (2003).
14. 'A New Proof for Non-occurrence of Trapped Surfaces and Information Paradox', A. Mitra, arXiv: astro-ph/0408323 (2004).
15. 'Why the Astrophysical Black Hole Candidates Are Not Rotating Black Holes', A. Mitra, arXiv:astro-ph/0407501 (2004).

15. 'On the Origin of the Universal Radio-X-ray Luminosity Correlation in Black Hole Candidates', S.L. Robertson and D.J. Leiter, *Monthly Notices Royal Astronomical Society*, 350, 1391 (2004).
16. 'Do Black Hole Candidates Exhibit Magnetic Moments Instead of Event Horizons?' D.J. Leiter and S.L. Robertson, paper presented in American Physical Society, April meeting, 1–4 May (2004).
17. 'Comments on the Proposal of Dark Energy Stars by Chapline', A. Mitra, arXiv: astro-ph/0504384 (2005).
18. 'Why the Observed Black Hole Candidates Do Not Show Spin Pulsation', A. Mitra, arXiv: astro-ph/0510205 (2005).
19. 'Comments on "Derivation of the Raychaudhuri Equation" by Dadhich', A. Mitra, arXiv: gr-qc/0512006 (2005).
20. 'On the Probable Nature of the "Dark Particle Accelerators" Discovered by HESS', A. Mitra, *Proceedings of the 29th International Cosmic Ray Conference*, 3–10 August 2005, Pune, India, Volume 4, p.187, arXiv:astro-ph/0507697 (2005).
21. 'Magnetospheric Eternally Collapsing Objects (MECOs): Likely New Class of Source of Cosmic Particle Acceleration', A. Mitra, *Proceedings of the 29th International Cosmic Ray Conference*, Volume 3, p.125, arXiv:physics/0506183 (2005).
22. 'On the Non-occurrence of Type I X-ray Bursts from the Black Hole Candidates', A. Mitra, *Advances in Space Research*, 38, 2917 (2006).
23. 'Does Sgr A* Have an Intrinsic Magnetic Moment Instead of an Event Horizon?', S.L. Robertson and D.J. Leier, arXiv:astro-ph/0603746 (2006).

24. 'Why Gravitational Contraction Must Be Accompanied by Emission of Radiation in Both Newtonian and Einstein Gravity', A. Mitra, *Physical Review D*, 74, 024010 (2006).
25. 'The Magnetospheric Eternally Collapsing Object (MECO) Model of Galactic Black Hole Candidates and Active Galactic Nuclei', S.L. Robertson and D.J. Leiter, in *New Developments in Black Hole Research*, ed. Paul V. Kreitler, Nova Science Publishers, Inc., New York, p. 1, (2006).
26. 'Black Holes or Eternally Collapsing Objects: A Review of 90 Years of Misconception', A. Mitra, in *Focus on Black Hole Research*, ed. Paul V. Kreitler, Nova Science Publishers, Inc., New York, pp. 1–94 (2006).
27. 'Observations Supporting the Existence of an Intrinsic Magnetic Moment inside the Central Compact Object within the Quasar Q0957+561', R.E. Schild, D.J. Leiter, S.L. Roberston, *Astronomical Journal*, 132, 420 (2006).
28. 'A Generic Relationship between Baryonic and Radiative Energy Densities of Stars', A. Mitra, *Monthly Notices Royal Astronomical Society: Letters*, 367, L66 (2006).
29. 'Radiation Pressure Supported Stars in Einstein Gravity: Eternally Collapsing Objects', A. Mitra, *Monthly Notices Royal Astronomical Society*, 369, 492 (2006).
30. 'Sources of Stellar Energy, Einstein -Eddington Timescale of Gravitational Contraction and Eternally Collapsing Objects', A. Mitra, *New Astronomy*, 12(2), 146 (2006) (One of the highlight publications of Max Planck Society, Germany, 2006).
31. 'Masses of Radiation Pressure Supported Stars in Extreme Relativistic Realm', A. Mitra, *Proceedings of*

IAU Symposium #238, 21–25 August 2006, Prague, pp. 409–10, arXiv:0712.2927.

32. 'A Secular Quark Gluon Plasma Phase Preceding Black Hole Formation', A. Mitra and N.K. Glendenning, Lawrence Berkeley National Lab, e-preprint,https://escholarship.org/uc/item/65418182#page-1(2006).
33. 'Black Holes or Eternally Collapsing Objects?', A. Mitra and N.K. Glendenning, *Proceedings of the MG11 Meeting on General Relativity*, 23–29 July 2006, Berlin, Germany, pp. 1526–28.
35. 'Quantum Information Paradox: Real or Fictitious?', A. Mitra, *Pramana*, 73, 615–22 (2009).
36. 'Does Pressure Increase or Decrease Active Gravitational Mass?' A. Mitra, *Physics Letters B*, 685(1), 8 (2010).
37. 'The Fallacy of Oppenheimer Snyder Collapse: No General Relativistic Collapse at All, No Black Hole, No Physical Singularity', A. Mitra, *Astrophysics & Space Science (Letter)*, 332, 43, (2011).
38. 'Kruskal Coordinates and Mass of the Schwarzschild Black Hole: No Finite Mass Black Hole', A. Mitra, *International Journal of Astronomy & Astrophysics*, 2, 236 (2012).
39. 'The Mass of the Oppenheimer Snyder Black Hole: Only Finite Mass Quasi-Black Holes', A. Mitra and K.K. Singh, *International Journal of Modern Physics (D)*, 22, 1350054 (2013).
40. 'Direct Microlensing-Reverberation Observations of the Intrinsic Magnetic Structure of Active Galactic Nuclei in Different Spectral States: A Tale of Two Quasars', R.E. Schild, D.J. Leiter and S.L. Robertson, *Astronomical Journal*, 135, 947 (2008).

41. 'Cosmological Properties of Eternally Collapsing Objects (ECOs)', A. Mitra, *Problems of Practical Cosmology, Proceedings of the International Conference*, 23–27 June 2008, St. Petersburg, pp. 304–13.
42. 'Likely Formation of General Relativistic Radiation Pressure Supported Stars or Eternally Collapsing Objects', A. Mitra and N.K. Glendenning, *Monthly Notices Royal Astronomical Society (Letters)*, 404, L50–L54 (2010).
43. 'Black Hole or Meco: Decided by a Thin Luminous Ring Structure Deep within Quasar Q0957+561', S.L. Robertson and D.J. Leiter, *Journal of Cosmology*, 6, 1400 (2010).
44. 'Does Sgr A* Have an Event Horizon or a Magnetic Moment?', S.L. Robertson and D.J. Leiter, *Journal of Cosmology*, 6, 1438 (2010).
45. 'Discovery of Universal Outflow Structures Above and Below the Accretion Disc Plane in Radio-Quiet Quasars', J. Lovegrove, R.E. Schild and D.J. Leiter, *Monthly Notices Royal Astronomical Society*, 412, 2631 (2011).
46. 'Why No Energy Can Be Extracted from Rotating Kerr Black Holes', A. Mitra and K.D. Krori, *Journal of Cosmology*, 17, 7064 (2011).
47. 'General Relativistic Radiation Pressure Supported Stars as Quasar Central Engines in an Universe which is Recycling Matter', A. Mitra, *Journal of Cosmology*, 17, 7376 (2011).
48. 'The Fallacy of Oppenheimer Snyder Collapse: No General Relativistic Collapse at All, No Black Hole, No Physical Singularity', A. Mitra, *Astrophysics & Space Science (Letter)*, 332, 43, (2011).

49. 'Kruskal Coordinates and Mass of the Schwarzschild Black Hole: No Finite Mass Black Hole', A. Mitra, *International Journal of Astronomy & Astrophysics*, 2, 236 (2012).
50. 'The Mass of the Oppenheimer Snyder Black Hole: Only Finite Mass Quasi-Black Holes', A. Mitra and K.K. Singh, *International Journal of Modern Physics* (D), 22, 1350054 (2013).
51. 'Does Pressure Accentuate General Relativistic Gravitational Collapse Formation of Trapped Surfaces?', A. Mitra, *International Journal of Modern Physics* D, 22, 1350021, (2013).
52. 'Einsteinian Revolution's Misinterpretation: No True Black Holes, No Information Paradox: Just Quasi-static Balls of Quark Gluon Plasma', A. Mitra, plenary talk,in *New Results and Actual Problems in Particle & Astroparticle Physics and Cosmology*, ebook, World Scientific, pp. 153–63 (2014).
53. 'Exploring Magnetospheric Origin of Jets for Both Neutron Star and "Black Hole" Systems', A. Mitra, plenary talk at the international workshop 'Jet Triggering Mechanisms in Black Hole Sources', Tata Institute of Fundamental Research, Mumbai, 20–23 January 2016,http://www.tifr.res.in/~tifrjet/presentations/MitraJetWorkshopTIFR.pdf
54. 'Mass of Schwarzschild Black Holes Is Indeed Zero and Black Hole Candidates Are Quasi Black Holes', A. Mitra, arXiv:1708.07404 (2017).

As discussed in this book, there are innumerable research papers that directly or indirectly suggest that

'Schwarzschild singularity' is a physical singularity, which implies that mathematical black holes have zero gravitational mass (M=0). Three such papers are:

55. 'Finite Self-Energy of Classical Point Particles', R. Arnowitt, S. Deser and C.W. Misner, *Physical Review Letters*, 4, 375 (1960).
56. 'The Schwarzschild Solution: Some Conceptual Difficulties', J.V. Narlikar and T. Padmanbhan, *Foundations of Physics*, 18, 659 (1988).
57. 'Reality of the Schwarzschild Singularity', A.I. Janis, E.T. Newman and J. Winicour, *Physical Review Letters*, 20, 878 (1968).

Finally the following paper explicitly showed that mathematical black holes indeed have M=0, *whose implication is that the so-called black holes are only black hole mimickers:*

58. 'Schwarzschild Singularity', L. Bel, *Journal of Mathematical Physics*, 10, 1051 (1969).

There are many other papers by other authors that too lend support to the MECO paradigm by showing that realistic collapse may lead to a horizon-less radiating fluid sphere, something like ECOs. Few are mentioned below:

59. 'Radiating Fluid Spheres in General Relativity', S. Bayin, *Physical Review D*, 19, 2838 (1979).
60. 'Evolution of Radiating Fluid Spheres in General Relativity', L. Herrera, J. Jimenez and G.J. Ruggeri, *Physical Review D*, 22, 2305 (1980).
61. 'Radiating Fluid Spheres in General Relativity', B.C. Tewari, *Astrophysics & Space Science*, 149, 233 (1988).

62. 'Some Analytical Models of Radiating Collapsing Spheres', L. Herrera, A. di Prisco and J. Ospino, *Physical Review D*, 74, 044001 (2006).
63. 'Horizon-Free Radiating Star, Shear-Free Gravitational Collapse without Horizon', B.C. Tewari and Kali Charan, *Astrophysics & Space Science*, 351, 613 (2014).
64. 'Horizon Free Eternally Collapsing Anisotropic Radiating Star', B.C. Tewari and K. Charan, *Astrophysics & Space Science*, 357, id.107 (2015).
65. 'Modeling Quasar Central Engine as a Relativistic Radiating Star', K. S. Newton and N. Pant, *Astrophysics & Space Science*, 355, 171 (2015).
66. 'Not Quite a Black Hole', B. Holdom and J. Ren, *Physical Review D*, 95, 084034 (2017).
67. 'Do Horizons Exist?', A. Davood, arXiv:160701286.
68. 'Self-Consistent Description of a Spherically-Symmetric Gravitational Collapse', D. Terno, arXiv:1903.04744(2019).
69. 'Do Event Horizons Exist?', V. Baccetti, R.B. Mason and D.R. Terno, *International Journal of Modern Physics*, 26, 1743008 (2017).
70. A. Mitra, C. Corda and H.J. Mosquera Cuesta (2020), 'How to distinguish an actual astrophysical magnetized black hole mimicker from a true (theoretical) black hole', *Astrophysics & Space Science* (submitted).
71. A. G. Agnese and M. La Camera (1985), 'Gravitation without black holes', *Physical Review D*, 31, p. 1280.

Glossary of Terms

Acceleration: Rate of change of velocity.

Acceleration due to gravity: Acceleration of a particle caused by gravitational pull. On the surface of the Earth, it is 981 cm/s^2. On the surface of a black hole, this becomes infinitely large, which is the physical reason why nothing can escape a black hole. But this suggests that in real world, there should not be any exact black hole because in real life, everything is finite, howsoever large.

Accretion: Massive astrophysical objects accumulate surrounding matter by pulling it towards themselves by their gravitational attraction.

Accretion disk: Planets move in orbits as they possess angular momentum. Similarly, the matter pulled by massive astrophysical objects possesses angular momentum and, accordingly, forms disks around such objects. In the disk, accreted matter swirls like what happens in the rings of Saturn.

Angular momentum: The quantity that is a sort of measure of the rotation and heaviness (mass) of an object.

Anti-particle: A particle with opposite quantum properties. Since an electron has negative charge –e, its anti-particle positron has plus +e charge.

Ampere's law: The magnetic field around a current-carrying wire is proportional to the current but decreases with the distance from the wire.

Black hole: An object that is so compact and whose gravitation is so strong that nothing, not even light, can escape from it. Consequently, it is fundamentally impossible to directly detect 'black holes'. Thus often astronomers refer to the so-called black holes as black hole candidates.

Black hole mimickers: Objects that have sizes practically the same as that of theoretical black holes of the same mass. Unlike the case of exact black holes, light can escape black hole mimickers, albeit with extreme difficulty because they do not possess any 'event horizon'. They are also known as quasi-black holes or horizon-less compact objects.

Chandrasekhar limit: The maximum mass of a star supported by only the cold quantum pressure of electrons. However, this limit gets invalidated for ultra-hot stars where radiation pressure plays a major role.

Conductor: Materials like metal and ionized gases (plasma) that have intrinsic free electrons. On application of electric field, these free electrons can move and give rise to current as well as a magnetic field. Momentary current can pass through the vacuum between two electrodes. Yet, vacuum is not a conductor because the electrons moving in it belong to the electrodes. Materials having no or negligible free electrons are insulators. Thus vacuum is actually an insulator. In the same vein, vacuum black holes are insulators rather than conductors.

Coordinate distance: The distance measured by a straight scale by ignoring gravitational effect, ignoring the likely curvature of space due to gravity (crow flight distance)

Coordinate time interval: As if the time interval measured by a timescale that is straight and ignores the change or bending of time due to gravity. Far away from a massive body, there is no gravity and coordinate time is the actual or physical time interval.

Corona: A region containing very hot ionized gas (plasma) of very low density.

Coronal mass ejection: Massive outburst of charged particles and fire (energy) from the Sun or other stars.

Curved space-time: In the presence of gravity, locally measured physical spatial and temporal intervals are different from their respective values in the absence of gravity. Essentially, proper intervals become different from 'coordinate intervals'. For illustration, this appears as warping or curving of space-time. However, this does not at all mean that space-time is a physical membrane, which warps or sags because of weight!

Degeneracy pressure: Elementary particles having half-integer spins huddled together resist being together, and this creates a pressure.

Eddington luminosity: The outward radiation from an extremely bright/luminous star exerts outward pressure either on the star material itself or external matter falling towards the star due to its gravitational attraction. If the star radiates at its Eddington luminosity, the outward radiation pressure on the surrounding matter = inward gravitational pull on the same. Hypothetically, the Sun will have to be 0.1 million times more luminous to attain its Eddington luminosity.

Event horizon: The imaginary spherical boundary of (Hilbert) black holes. Nothing, not even light can escape either from the event horizon or from its interior.

Eternally collapsing object (ECO): An ultra-compact ball of plasma/fire that is so hot that its outward radiation pressure just balances the inward pull of gravitation. It is, however, always contracting and radiating at a negligible rate in order to asymptotically attain the mathematical black hole state having zero gravitational mass.

Fermions: Elementary particles like half integer particles such as electrons, protons and neutrons.

Kelvin: Temperature measured from the lowest possible temperature called absolute zero. It is approximately higher than the ordinary Celsius scale temperature: K = C + 273.

Gamma rays: Electromagnetic radiation having energy million times or more than that of visible light.

Gamma-ray bursts (GRBs): Intense bursts of cosmic gamma rays lasting around 0.1–10 s.

Gravitation: Universal property by which all bodies try to attract each other.

Gravitational collapse: Contraction of a massive star due to its own weight or gravity.

General theory of relativity: Einstein's theory of gravitation, which is 'general', i.e., even accelerating observers are allowed.

Gluon:Particles whose exchanges keep sub-structures (quarks) of protons and neutrons together.

Infinity (∞): A number that is larger than the largest finite number one may conceive, trillion trillion and so on. One can mathematically obtain infinity by diving any finite number by 0: $4/0=\infty$. No physical quantity should ever be ∞, and the occurrence of ∞ somewhere suggests that either the theory is breaking down or such a region should not actually occur. On a black hole, surface acceleration becomes infinite, which suggests there should not be any exact black hole.

Jets: Conical or beamed outflows often found around astrophysical compact objects.

Kelvin–Helmholtz process: As a star contracts, its negative gravitational binding energy becomes even more negative. Then in order to conserve energy, some positive energy is generated. Part of this new positive energy adds up to the existing heat energy and the rest is radiated out.

Magnetic pressure: Magnetic field (B) embedded in a gas generates an isotropic pressure $B^2/8\pi$ in addition to the kinetic or gas pressure.

Magnetospheric eternally collapsing object (MECO): An ultra-magnetic ECO. Stellar mass MECOs may have magnetic fields that are thousands of trillions of gauss, more than magnetars. The MECO magnetic fields, however, drop dramatically away from the surface, and they may even behave like old neutron stars with very low magnetic fields ~ a hundred of million gauss.

Nebula: Something that looks cloudy or nebular in the cosmos.

Neutron star: An ultra-compact star with lots of free neutrons inside whose cold quantum pressure supports it against its own gravity. While the mass of a neutron star could be comparable to that of the Sun, its radius could be only 10 km.

Photon: Light also behaves like particles that are called photons. A photon is a packet (quantum) of light.

Plasma: Normal matter comprises neutral atoms and molecules. But if such a matter gets extremely hot, the electrons may be partly stripped off from the atoms to render them as positively charged ions. This process is known as ionization. A highly ionized matter is called plasma.

Photon sphere: While light gets trapped within a black hole event horizon at R= 2M, the virtual trapping of light starts even for an object whose size is less than R=3M. This spherical surface at R=3M defines the boundary of the photon sphere. The global effect of gravity is already so strong at R=3M that light can move in closed circular orbits there.

Proper distance: The distance measured locally by respecting the effect of gravity, as if distance is being measured by a curved tape instead of a straight scale. In special relativity, where there is no gravity, proper distance is the distance measured by an observer who is at rest with respect to the event.

Proper time interval: In special relativity, proper time interval means the interval measured by a clock that is at rest with the event. In general relativity, due to the presence of gravity, physical time intervals change even in the absence of any relative motion. One may imagine time interval being measured by a time scale that is like a flexible curved tape rather than a rigid straight scale.

Proper speed: Speed defined in terms of locally measured proper (physical) distance and proper time intervals.

Quantum mechanics: Rather strange physics of elementary particles reflecting wave-like behaviour, and most of the physical attributes appear in packets or quanta, like charge or angular momentum.

Quark: Both protons and neutrons have a substructure; each of them is made of three different types of quark having fractional charges.

Quark gluon plasma: At extremely high temperature, neutrons and protons melt into their constituents: a soup of quarks and gluons.

Raychaudhuri equation: A mathematical identity which shows that, locally, the trajectories of self-gravitating matter tend to get closer reaffirming the attractive nature of gravity. And if one would ignore all effects which resist gravity, such as rotation, buoyancy forces, heat flow, radiation flow, magnetic field etc., then despite non-uniformity and asymmetry, a big bang type or black hole singularity could be present. However, the Raychaudhuri equation cannot say anything about the formation or non-formation of event horizons.

Redshift: A given spectral line has a given (electromagnetic) wavelength at the source of its origin, which could be a star in a galaxy. But a telescope away from the source may measure a larger wavelength for the same line. Then the spectrum appears more reddish, and hence such a shift is called redshift.

Gravitational redshift: Redshift occurring as light/radiation/photon leaves a region of strong gravity.

Cosmological redshift: Redshift occurring as light/radiation/photon moves over cosmological (extremely large) distances.

Scalar: In general relativity, a scalar is a quantity whose value appears to be the same for all observers, and consequently, its value remains unchanged (invariant) under all coordinate transformations. If the value of a physically significant scalar would appear to be 0 or infinite (limitless) at a given region, it is likely that this region is a physical singularity, and it must not be realized.

Semi-classical gravity: Matter described by special relativistic quantum field theory but gravity still described by classical general relativity.

Signature of space-time: Collection of signs of space and time components of the space-time interval. The simplest space-time interval = $+dt^2 - dx^2$ and signature = (+, -). For 3-D cases, signature = (+, -, -, -). The important thing here is that the space and time components bear opposite signs. But this cardinal rule may get violated in a black hole interior.

Singularity: A situation where physically meaningful quantities become infinite or limitless. For instance, there is a singularity at the centre of a spherical black hole. In the real world, singularities cannot occur. But they can appear in models using wrong physics or wrong assumptions.

Singularity theorems: A set of theorems which argue that as per general relativity, a space-time should develop big bang or black hole like singularities even in the absence of uniformity or spherical symmetry of the matter distribution, provided that the matter obeys some reasonable conditions like positivity of the total mass-energy density, and an unusual strong condition, namely, existence of trapped surfaces in the space-time. Note, the interior of black holes contain trapped surfaces, and thus singularity theorems begin by *assuming that the interior of the stars or the fluids must become like interiors of black holes!* But there are research publications which claim that even for spherical symmetry, trapped surface formation is not allowed to ensure that stellar matter continues to move like 'matter' and not like 'light'. And if trapped surfaces cannot form for spherically symmetric matter, they should not form for asymmetric matter distribution where resistive effects like centrifugal repulsion may be present.

Space-time: In non-relativistic physics, time and space intervals appear the same to all observers. But in relativity, only a certain combination of time and spatial intervals appear the same to all observers. This gave rise to an abstract mathematical concept that three spatial coordinates (say, x,y,x) and time (t) together form a 4-D continuum: 'space-time'. However, for any given observer, there are always three distinct space coordinates and one-time coordinate. There is no such real or physical membrane for either space or time or space-time.

Space-time Interval: The square of the space-time interval for two nearby events. If the spatial and temporal intervals for the two events are dx and dt, in special relativity, the mixed-up distance between the two events $ds^2 = c^2dt^2 - dx^2$. In general relativity, the metric coefficients are more complicated than c^2 and (-1).

Special theory of relativity: Relativity theory in which speed of light appears to be for all observers moving (specially) with fixed relative speed (no acceleration).

Spin: Elementary particles rotate like micro-tops, and 'spin' denotes the associated internal angular momentum.

Supernova: Extremely powerful explosions in cosmos, which make the site of the explosion suddenly visible as a 'new' bright star; before slowly fading from sight over several weeks or months.

Tachyon: A hypothetical elementary particle that moves faster than light. This idea is unphysical because the rest mass of a tachyon is imaginary, which makes hardly any sense. It would require infinite energy to slow a tachyon down to light speed.

Time-like trajectory: A trajectory in space-time (x, t) for which the time part is larger than the space part. Physically this means that the local proper speed of the particle is less than the speed of light.

Trapped surface: Something like the spherical surfaces within a black hole ($R < 2M$) where even light cannot move outwards. Trapped surfaces are assumed to form within the collapsing matter of massive stars. The outermost trapped surface is called an apparent horizon ($R=2M$). For a static black hole, the event horizon and apparent horizon are synonymous.

Vacuum: A region free of any matter and usually free of any net mass–energy too. However, a vacuum can contain a field-like gravitational field .

Worm hole: As if a black hole and its inverse, a white hole, are joined together at the event horizon, which is called its neck. However, there is no point singularity in the interior of a worm hole.

White dwarf: A compact star whose mass could be comparable to that of the Sun but radius could be only 1 per cent of the Sun. It is supported against gravity by the cold quantum of electrons.

White hole: A theoretical time-reversed version of a black hole where matter and energy are supposed to gush out of nothingness (which might be a singularity). There is no evidence for any white hole, and now even black hole believers think that there should not be any white hole. This is an admission that even a nice 'exact solution' could be physically meaningless.

Worldline: Graph of motion of a particle in x (space) and t (time).

X-rays: Electromagnetic radiation with energy that is several thousand times that of visible light.

Acknowledgements

In 1998, I sent my first manuscript to Professor Prahalad Chunnilal Vaidya, one of the most noted general relativists in India. To my surprise, I got his response within a week, and without his comment that my research was on the right track, my relevant research may not have progressed. I am grateful to this great researcher and human being.

The same year, I submitted a much longer version of this manuscript, claiming the non-occurrence of exact black holes from various independent angles to *Foundations of Physics*. While I waited for a response, I sent an email to the famous particle physicist Professor Gerard 't Hooft who was one of the editorial board members of the journal. It was only after a nudge by him to the editor that the paper eventually got published in December 2000. I am thankful to Prof 't Hooft for this great professional help. It is a great coincidence that Prof 't Hooft co-won the Nobel Prize in Physics the following year, and I felt very happy about it.

Between 1997 and 2001, when I was carrying out my research in the Theoretical Physics Division of the Bhabha

Atomic Research Centre (BARC), Mumbai, I had to go through many rough times. But fortunately, some of my BARC friends, namely, Dr Arun Pati (who now is an internationally famous physicist with expertise in the foundations of quantum mechanics), Dr Harish Parab, Dr Zafar Ahmed and Dr G. Ganeshan offered me an oasis of relaxation in the scorching heat. I am thankful to all these friends.

My preprints on the non-occurrence of exact black holes were on the web for a long time. The first physicist to congratulate me and later help me in various ways was Dr Sabbir Ahmad, a PhD in theoretical particle physics from the Massachusetts Institute of Technology. I am immensely thankful to him.

Following the publication of my paper in *Foundations of Physics Letters* in 2000, several physicists congratulated me, and I am thankful to all of them. In particular, Dr Stanley Robertson and Dr Darryl Leiter evinced keen interest in my work and virtually became my co-workers. We exchanged long emails regularly for the next six to seven years and less regularly later. Such animated discussions helped me a lot, even though we did not fully agree on all the finer points. Thus they are like invisible co-authors in my papers, and I too am an invisible co-author in some of their papers, which showed that the so-called 'black hole candidates' might have strong intrinsic magnetic fields. The implication of such evidence is that these so-called black holes are likely to be MECOs, rather than true mathematical black holes that have no fire or magnetic field. Later, I had many discussions on such issues with two more American astrophysicists, namely, Dr Rudolph Schild (Center for Astrophysics, Harvard University) and Dr Norman Glendenning (University of

California at Berkeley). I immensely benefitted from the intense scientific exchanges with them. It is sad that cancer snatched Darryl away in 2011.

I was fortunate to be in touch with an unsung hero of general relativity research from India, Professor K.D. Krori. He happens to be the seniormost living general relativist in India, and he established general relativity as a research topic in the north-east of India. Originally, he was the head of the Department of Physics of the famed Cotton College, Guwahati, and later became the principal of the college, which now is a deemed university. The fact that he was convinced about my research and also arranged for a felicitation ceremony for me at Guwahati University in 2014 greatly boosted my spirits. Let me express my regards for this unsung hero.

The maiden editor of *Nature India*, a magazine that focuses on Indian science and is affiliated to Nature Publishing Group, was Dr K.S. Jayaraman. He is a PhD in nuclear physics from the University of Maryland and has covered news about Indian science for *Nature* (London) for a long time. I was fortunate that he interviewed me in 2001, and also a couple of times later, on my research related to black holes and cosmology. My research got disseminated to Indian researchers by the lucid and insightful science news released by him. I am indeed grateful to him.

I am thankful to my friend Dr Vinod Wadhawan, a noted scholar and researcher in material science, for going through a preliminary draft of this book and offering me useful suggestions. Similarly, I am thankful to Professor Fred Cooperstock of the University of Victoria, a noted researcher on the physical aspects of general relativity.

He played the devil's advocate by quizzing me over some crucial astrophysical contents of the book. I am sure that I could convince him. I really feel sorry that he passed away in 2018 before seeing this book published.

Facebook has an amazing astrophysics page called 'The Secrets of the Universe'. This page has around three lakh followers and was founded by a bright young astrophysics aficionado and great astrophysics blogger Rishabh Naakra, who is presently studying for an MSc in physics. I am thankful to him that having gone through the draft of this book, he commented, 'A gem for someone who has passed high school and has ambitions of becoming a professional astrophysicist.'

The person who spurred me into writing such a book is Sandya Iyer, former managing director of Jaico Publishing House, and I am grateful to this wise and visionary lady. Next, I am grateful to Dr Prasun Chatterjee, editorial director of Pan Macmillan India, for suggesting a thorough overhaul of the original manuscript to make it much more readable.

I must thank my distant friend in New York, Chitranjan Sharma, for constantly boosting my morale for this research. Dr Christian Corda, a researcher on various aspects of general relativity and gravity, too has helped my research through various discussions, and lots of thanks to him.

I do not have words to express my gratitude to the NASA Astrophysical Data Service, which is virtually my online library.

And of course, I am indebted to my wife Bandana and several other family members for having stood by me through very difficult times.

